INTERGOVERNMENTAL RELATIONS IN THE UNITED STATES

Research Monograph Number 10

INTERGOVERNMENTAL RELATIONS IN REVIEW

by

WILLIAM ANDERSON
University of Minnesota

GREENWOOD PRESS, PUBLISHERS
WESTPORT, CONNECTICUT

Library of Congress Cataloging in Publication Data

Anderson, William, 1888-
Intergovernmental relations in review.

Reprint of the ed. published by the University of Minnesota Press, Minneapolis, which was issued as Intergovernmental relations in the United States; research monograph, no. 10.
Bibliography: p.
1. Federal government--United States.
2. Minnesota--Politics and government--1951-
I. Title. II. Series: Intergovernmental relations in the United States; research monograph, no. 10.
[JK6117.A8 1974] 353.9'292 73-16639

Library of Congress Cataloging in Publication Data
ISBN 0-8371-7208-X

Originally published in 1960 by the University of Minnesota Press, Minneapolis

Reprinted with the permission of the University of Minnesota Press

Reprinted in 1973 by Greenwood Press, a division of Williamhouse-Regency Inc.

Library of Congress Catalogue Card Number 73-16639

ISBN 0-8371-7208-X

Printed in the United States of America

INTERGOVERNMENTAL RELATIONS IN THE UNITED STATES

(as Observed in Minnesota)

A Series of Monographs
Edited by William Anderson and Edward W. Weidner

1. INTERGOVERNMENTAL RELATIONS AND THE COURTS
by Forrest Talbott

2. INTERGOVERNMENTAL RELATIONS IN HIGHWAYS
by R. A. Gomez

3. INTERGOVERNMENTAL RELATIONS IN EDUCATION
by Robert L. Morlan

4. INTERGOVERNMENTAL RELATIONS IN PUBLIC HEALTH
by Laurence Wyatt

5. INTERGOVERNMENTAL RELATIONS IN SOCIAL WELFARE
by Ruth Raup

6. INTERGOVERNMENTAL RELATIONS IN EMPLOYMENT SECURITY
by Francis E. Rourke

7. INTERGOVERNMENTAL RELATIONS AT THE GRASS ROOTS
by Paul N. Ylvisaker

8. INTERGOVERNMENTAL FISCAL RELATIONS
by William Anderson

9. INTERGOVERNMENTAL RELATIONS AS SEEN BY PUBLIC OFFICIALS
by Edward W. Weidner

10. INTERGOVERNMENTAL RELATIONS IN REVIEW
by William Anderson

Foreword

It is a fortunate circumstance when a need and a unique opportunity can be matched by a person who has the interest and the ability to serve that need and opportunity in a distinguished manner. Such a circumstance occurred in 1946 when the author of this volume received a grant from the Rockefeller Foundation to finance a study of intergovernmental relations in Minnesota. Both the opportunity and the man are clearly but modestly described by the author in his Preface.

The decision of the Foundation to support the study deprived our department of the administrative services of its able and beloved chairman. This was a sacrifice which his colleagues and the university were reluctant but willing to make. Looking back upon the intervening years, it is obvious that the actions of the Foundation, the university, and the department have paid large dividends, not only in the extensive research which has been accomplished and the publications which have resulted therefrom, but in the contributions which the director of the study has made to the subject on a national scale. He served as a member of the Committee on Federal-State Relations of the first Hoover Commission in 1947-48 and of the Commission on Intergovernmental Relations in 1953-55. In the course of his work on the latter commission, he prepared a volume aptly titled The Nation and the States, Rivals or Partners? Within the department, he developed a graduate seminar on federalism and intergovernmental relations and through it, as well as through his guidance and direction of graduate research assistants in the preparation of the studies in this series, he has stimulated a goodly number of young scholars to make noteworthy contributions to this significant field of American government, politics, and administration.

The federal system of government, involving as it does a constitutional division of power between a central or national government and state or provincial governments, has been a subject of discussion in the United States since the foundations of our nation were laid by the constitutional convention in 1787. "States rights" versus "national power" has been a never-ending subject of debate and political controversy in Congress and state legislatures, in party campaigns, on the public platform, and in collegiate forensic combat. The Supreme Court, in exercising the power of judicial review, frequently has been called upon to decide where the line between national and state power is drawn by the Constitution. This continuing interest and concern in the federal system, however, has taken on a new dimension during the twentieth century as government in the United States has faced an ever-increasing demand for new or expanded and improved governmental functions and services. The "issue" of federalism tends to become more and more a question of what level or unit of government can best perform and finance a function rather than what level of government has the constitutional power to perform that function.

This does not mean the abandonment of the question of constitutional power, but rather an increasing disposition to accommodate constitutional arrangements to the urgencies of effective governmental action. The crisis of war and economic depression, and the consequences of such developments as industrial and commercial centralization, urbanization, and automotive and air transportation, have hastened if not made inevitable this tendency. It is perhaps not too much to say that, with all the centralizing tendencies of the modern age, the very future of the federal system is dependent upon our ability to accommodate it to the practical requirements of governance in our time. A nostalgia for "returning power to the states," however understandable and in some circles politically popular, will not suffice.

In the face of these and other developments, it becomes imperative that we examine thoroughly and objectively the manner in which specific functions of government are being performed and the degree to which all levels of government are participating in the discharge of these functions. Such a study is an essential preliminary to any future planning and decision-making with reference to the respective roles of our various units of government.

To such a task Professors Anderson and Weidner set themselves, with a corps of graduate research assistants, in 1946. The state of Minnesota was their laboratory. The interrelations of governments, national-state, interstate, state-local, and national-local, were the objects of special concern. The ten monographs in the series, of which this is the final and summary one, reveal clearly how well the task has been performed. Scholars and statesmen in this country and around the world will be challenged by the findings of the research that has been done, and by the thoughtful, temperate observations made by the writer of this concluding volume. To one who knows and admires him as friend and colleague, it is not surprising that his answer to the query posed in the title of his earlier book—whether the nation and the states in our federal system are rivals or partners—is a clear and convincing case for partnership.

August 1959

Lloyd M. Short, Chairman
Department of Political Science
University of Minnesota

Preface

Dr. Weidner and I and the other members of our research group probably regret more than anyone else the delays in completion of this series of monographs. Circumstances at least partly beyond our control, various calls to other duties, the practical exhaustion of our research funds by 1951, the dispersion of our original staff of workers, and our inability to employ others, have resulted in stretching out an effort which, begun late in 1946, should have been completed with final publication by 1953 instead of 1960. Our apologies for the delay go the the Rockefeller Foundation, which provided the bulk of our funds; to the University of Minnesota Press; and to friends, students, teachers, and administrators everywhere who were led to expect earlier publication.

It is probable that there have been some benefits from the delay. Dr. Weidner and I have had a longer time to digest the large quantities of data that our staff and co-workers collected and an opportunity to consult other materials, thus enabling us to acquire a more mature view of intergovernmental relations, not only in Minnesota but throughout the United States. Valuable materials from many sources have come to hand, as other studies, particularly those made for and by the Commission on Intergovernmental Relations (1953-55) have been completed and published.

Whatever the scientific and utilitarian values of our studies may, in the long run, prove to be, the experience of initiating and carrying through this research project has been most rewarding and satisfying to me. I have seen a number of young understudies, challenged to do their best work in a joint research enterprise, rise to the opportunity, becoming capable and productive scholars in a few short years. All of them did this work while pursuing heavy programs of graduate studies. A number of them were working on doctoral theses while also preparing monographs or contributing to the gathering of data for the project. The first six monographs in the series were written by such students. At the end of this volume I again list their names along with those of all others who gave important services to the project. To each of them, and particularly to my associate director on the project, Dr. Edward W. Weidner, I extend my sincere thanks and my continuing best wishes.

My thanks go also to the Rockefeller Foundation and its staff in the Social Science Division not only for the funds granted for the project but also for their patience through several years of delay; to the University of Minnesota Press and its staff, in particular to Jeanne Sinnen of the editorial staff, for friendly and effective service and cooperation; to the University of Minnesota for space, facilities, and some adjustment for several years in my teaching schedule; to the University of Minnesota Library and other divisions of the university for many services rendered; to my colleagues in political science; to Myrtle Eklund, librarian of the Public Administration Center and custodian of the Political Science Seminar collections; and to all and sundry others who helped us on our way. Many, many thanks!

Before beginning in this final monograph a more or less formal consideration of data, conclusions, and suggestions concerning intergovernmental relations, I feel it may be of some interest and value to review my own "education" in this field. The personal experiences of one who has been associated with the study of intergovernmental relations for a good part of his professional life may throw some light on the growth of interest in such study, on the directions it has taken over the years, and on some of the problems it has encountered. At the least, this statement of my training and experience will provide a record of my qualifications as a student of intergovernmental relations—and perhaps, implicitly, of my limitations and prejudices as well!

In high school (North High, Minneapolis, 1903-7) I had no course in "civics," and very little study in American history, but I recall a genuine interest in ancient history, based on the reading of a book by Wolfson. Outside of school I did relatively little reading, and I read practically nothing on government. Going to college in 1909 (College of Science, Literature, and the Arts, University of Minnesota) after several post-high-school years of private employment, I had vague ideas of becoming a lawyer. In college I had some outstanding teachers, notably Cephas D. Allin and William A. Schaper in political science, A. B. White and Wallace Notestein in English history, William Stearns Davis in medieval history, and Frank Maloy Anderson in American history, and equally able ones in English, sociology, zoology, mathematics, German, French, and economics.

Under Cephas Allin I did my first serious reading in works on American government and politics—for example, in Charles A. Beard, parts of James Bryce, extracts from The Federalist, some documents and a few Supreme Court decisions—which all dealt to some extent with the federal system. This reading came, I believe, in my junior year, along with courses by William Schaper on municipal government and on jurisprudence (mainly T. E. Holland and some elementary law). In my senior year I studied comparative government (England, France, and Germany, especially) under Cephas Allin, and also took his more advanced course in comparative federal government, based on the constitutions of Canada, Australia, Germany, Switzerland, and the United States. As a Canadian by birth, and a specialized student of British, Australian, and Canadian as well as American government, Allin was especially well qualified to present the problems of federal government, and he was a brilliant, stimulating teacher. It was with him, and to some extent with Frank Maloy Anderson in American history, that I got my start in the study of federal systems of government and in what I came later to call intergovernmental relations.

In my graduate studies at Harvard, 1913-16, I assisted Professor William Bennett Munro in "Gov. 1," where American government was the main theme, and The Federalist essays, Supreme Court decisions, and so on, again came in for study. But I also assisted him in his course on municipal government ("Gov. 17"), and saw some of the connections between the local units of government and the state and national "levels." I shall ever regret, however, that my program of studies did not permit me to take Professor Arthur Holcombe's excellent course on state government. I came to know him, of course, and from other graduate students I learned something about what he was doing in the course; and later I profited greatly from the study of his book on State Government in the United States. Thus my studies spanned or at least sampled the three levels, national, state, and local, at which government and politics are carried on in the United States, and I came to see something of the complexities in the interrelations of the levels.

Incidentally, as a part-time tutor in government under the leadership of Arthur Holcombe, I assigned to some of my "tutees" various readings on problems of federal government, read their reports thereon, and engaged in relevant discussions with them. This was my first teaching in the specific problems of intergovernmental relations. My Ph.D. thesis on "The Regulation of Gas and Electric Utilities in Massachusetts" (a rather poor thesis, I have always thought) had some state-local intergovernmental implications but not many.

Back at Minnesota as an instructor in political science in 1916, I taught various courses including American government, and in 1917 I added the municipal government course. This led to some studies on state-local legal relations in Minnesota, and the publication of articles in the Minnesota Law Review on "Special Legislation" and "Municipal Home Rule in Minnesota,"[1] and separate volumes on a History of the Constitution of Minnesota,[2] which raised a few interesting points in national-state relations, and City Charter Making in Minnesota,[3] which did something similar for state-local relations.

I do not recall that it ever occurred to me in those days to make intergovernmental relations as such a distinctive field of study. Each study that I made was undertaken for some specific reason, if nothing more than to fill some gap in the literature or to provide a useful handbook. It is clear to hindsight, however, that the themes of distinct units of government operating in close proximity to each other and having interrelations in law and practice are recurrent in these writings. This was certainly true of articles on "The Extraterritorial Powers of Cities";[4] on the taxability of municipal bonds under the United States income tax;[5] on the "Reorganization of Local Government in Minnesota";[6] and on legislative encroachments on the powers of cities in Minnesota.[7] My 1925 textbook on American City Government had chapters on state-local relations, and some suggestions on national-local relations as well.[8] A few years later I collaborated with Professor O. B. Jesness and Rafael Zon in a study of Land Utilization in Minnesota,[9] in which national, state, local, and private relations in land use and ownership were involved.

Between 1931 and 1934 I was engaged in an attempt to define, identify, enumerate, classify, and test for functional adequacy all the "units of government" in the United States. The first edition of the resulting report was published under the title The Units of Goverment in the United States.[10] About the same time I was also engaged in writing Local Government and Finance in Minnesota.[11] It dealt rather fully with the theme of state-local relations in Minnesota and gave more attention than earlier works had done to state-local financial relations in the fields of taxation, borrowing, expenditures, and state aids to local units. With these publications, my concept of the scope and contents of intergovernmental relations as a field of study became clearer than before, and my interest in the field increased.

---

[1]Minnesota Law Review, 7:133-51, 187-207, 306-31 (1923).

[2]Minneapolis: University of Minnesota, March 1921; vii + 323 pp.

[3]Minneapolis: University of Minnesota, April 1922; ix + 198 pp.

[4]Minnesota Law Review, 10:475-97, 564-83 (1926).

[5]Minnesota Law Review, 8:273-94 (1924).

[6]Minnesota Municipalities, 18:37-48, 99-111 (1933); also reprinted as a separate pamphlet.

[7]Minnesota Municipalities, 26:9-20 (1941).

[8]New York: Henry Holt and Co.; see pp. 36-79. On national-local relations, see also my article, "The Federal Government and the Cities," National Municipal Review, 13:288-93 (May 1924).

[9]Minneapolis: University of Minnesota Press, 1934.

[10]Chicago: Public Administration Service, 1934; vi + 37 pp. Later editions appeared in 1936, 1942, and 1949. The United States Bureau of the Census issued its first enumeration of governments in the United States in 1942; its most recent one in 1957.

[11]Minneapolis: University of Minnesota Press, 1935; xii + 355 pp.

In the meantime, in 1933, I had become a member of the Social Science Research Council as a representative of political science, and in 1934 I was appointed to the council's Committee on Public Administration under the chairmanship of Louis Brownlow, then director of the Public Administration Clearing House in Chicago.

The fight against the Great Depression was at this time well begun, and the New Deal was in progress in Washington and throughout the land. New federal agencies were being created in considerable numbers and new national programs in such fields as welfare, agriculture, conservation, public works, the regulation and promotion of industry, and the protection of labor were being started or at least planned. It appeared, however, that the national government was not sufficiently prepared for the rapid expansion of central government activities that took place. Along with other citizens, state and local authorities became confused by the multiplicity and the overlapping of national agencies; and the occasional conflicts and contradictions that developed among the federal agencies themselves only added to the confusion at the "grass roots," where all the programs and activities impinged upon the people. The consequences of all this confusing activity for the effectiveness of the national government itself, for the state and local governments, and for the federal system as a whole, were not easy to forecast, but there was considerable shaking of heads and a feeling of great uncertainty. There were predictions that the state governments were about to be liquidated and that the national government was going to centralize all governmental powers and functions in Washington.

Such considerations as these occupied the thoughts of the Committee on Public Administration and provided subjects for its discussions at a number of early meetings. Indeed the themes of federalism and intergovernmental relations—how to administer national programs effectively without inter-program conflicts and without damage to the positions of state and local governments in the federal system, and, indeed, how best to develop the energies and the inventiveness of state and local officials in connection with the new national activities—constituted a large part of the committee's program to the end of its work.

In the committee meetings I brought up the need to get a "grass roots" view of the impacts of the new federal "action" programs, while other members emphasized the desirability of having a new series of Federalist papers suited to modern constitutional arrangements and the experiences with federal systems in connection with plans for supra-national organization in Europe and elsewhere, and the need to "capture and record" the experiences of the major new federal agencies and programs such as those in social welfare, labor relations, public works, and TVA, all of which had important intergovernmental aspects.

Several specific projects were undertaken. At the request of the committee a number of scholars prepared memorandums on the problems of federal government in the twentieth century. These proved to be stimulating reading for committee members, which was the primary use for which they were intended. Two studies on grants-in-aid were made for the committee, and promptly published, one by Dr. V. O. Key, Jr., on The Administration of Federal Grants to States,[12] and one by Luella Gettys (Mrs. V. O. Key) on The Administration of Canadian Conditional Grants: A Study in Dominion-Provincial Relationships.[13] (In the same year that the latter volume was published, 1938, I brought out the first edition of my general text on American Government, in which I devoted a number of chapters to the formal aspects of intergovernmental relations.[14])

[12]Chicago: Public Administration Service, 1937; xviii + 388 pp.

[13]Chicago: Public Administration Service, 1938; xiii + 193 pp.

[14]New York: Henry Holt and Co., 1938; vii + 1080 pp. See especially Chapters 12-15.

Of a more general nature than the projects on grants-in-aid was a proposal in the committee for a handbook and guide to help promote studies of federal governmental systems and intergovernmental relations. Two scholars, Drs. Herman Finer and George Graham, made preliminary contributions to this project but because of a lack of time were unable to bring the task to completion. As the committee's work neared its end, I undertook to finish the handbook and did so with considerable editorial help from Mrs. Key.[15]

While the Committee on Public Administration was thus trying to stimulate and to assist in studies in the field of intergovernmental relations, other scholars were at work on related problems. At the same time national and state officials were showing an increasing concern over the practical developments that were taking place in the relations between the national and the state and local governments. An experienced and observant former official of the national government, Guy Moffett, made an extensive tour through the states to note developments and to sound out opinion. His findings and comments, reported orally and at length to Harold D. Smith, then director of the United States Budget Office, and to several other heads of important federal agencies, led these men to take a step that Smith had already been contemplating. They proceeded in 1940 to organize a Council on Intergovernmental Relations, consisting of Harold Smith as chairman, several other heads of important federal agencies that had a considerable involvement in intergovernmental relations (Paul V. McNutt, administrator of the then Federal Security Agency, M. L. Wilson, director of the Extension Service of the United States Department of Agriculture, Phillip B. Fleming, administrator of the then Federal Works Agency), and four other persons, namely, Luther H. Gulick, director of the Institute of Public Administration in New York, Earl D. Mallery, executive director of the American Municipal Association, Frank Bane, executive director of the Council of State Governments, and myself. National, state, local, and academic viewpoints were all represented on this council.

The general objective agreed upon was not to carry out an extensive survey of intergovernmental relations that would result in a substantial scholarly publication, but to conduct several local experimental projects with local talent in different parts of the country, with a view to encouraging the coordination of national, state, and local public services in selected counties.[16] First three and later two more such local projects were set up, each in a different state. To do this with the proper "grass roots" approach, first a Council on Intergovernmental Relations at the state level was established with official aid and approval in each state, and then with the assistance of this state council a county was selected and a council at the county level was organized to carry on the local project.

The funds for the entire program were provided by the Spelman Fund. A staff of two men with administrative experience, plus secretarial help, was set up in Washington, D.C., and each of the county councils was supplied with sufficient funds for a local staff and operations. Each local council, composed of leaders in local government and business, was given a brief orientation on the problem of and the need for coordinating national, state, and local services, and on the sort of staff and procedure it might need. Thereafter it was entirely on its own responsibility. The state councils in general became relatively inactive and had little to do with the county projects.

---

[15] Federalism and Intergovernmental Relations: A Budget of Suggestions for Research (Chicago: Public Administration Service, 1946; x + 192 pp.).

[16] For more detailed accounts of the objectives and the work of this organization, see Grass Roots: A Report and an Evaluation (Washington, D.C.: Council on Intergovernmental Relations, September 1947); and pp. 3-8 in Monograph 7 in the present series, Intergovernmental Relations at the Grass Roots, by Paul N. Ylvisaker (Minneapolis: University of Minnesota Press, 1956).

The five county projects had distinctly different programs and results. In no case was the project as such an outstanding success, and in several places the results were very meager indeed. I kept in touch with the various projects primarily through membership on the national council and through visits with the central office staff in Washington and Minneapolis. I also had a certain amount of contact with the Blue Earth County project in Minnesota, because of my acquaintanceship with its director, R. M. McCurdy, and its principal researcher, Paul N. Ylvisaker, but I conformed to central office policy of encouraging local responsibility and inventiveness. I volunteered no advice or suggestions, and made no trips to Blue Earth County while the project there was going forward, from 1943 to 1945.

The Blue Earth County project was the most successful of the original three without any question, and yet it ended in a sort of frustration. The most important contribution to come out of any of the five projects was certainly the manuscript by Paul Ylvisaker on "government locally" in Blue Earth County. This became his doctoral thesis in government at Harvard, and was later recast for publication as Monograph 7 in the present series, under the title Intergovernmental Relations at the Grass Roots.

At the request of the Spelman Fund, I joined with Dr. Rowland Egger of the University of Virginia in preparing a final summary and appraisal of the whole project under the national Council on Intergovernmental Relations. The report was not laudatory. It was not published.

While the projects under the Council on Intergovernmental Relations were pursuing their several courses, I was engaged for a considerable part of my time in completing the budget of suggestions for research published under the title Federalism and Intergovernmental Relations as mentioned above. My academic conscience would not permit me to be wholly satisfied with the results, however, or to be content merely to make suggestions for research that other persons might undertake. I felt a challenge to continue my studies in the field. What could I do as a professor of political science at the University of Minnesota, in the field that I had now more clearly outlined?

It occurred to me that it would be exceedingly useful to make a comprehensive survey of intergovernmental relations—national-state-local, interstate, and interlocal—on the basis of experiences in the state of Minnesota from its earliest days to the present, with special reference to recent and current relations. This would call for a many-pronged attack, with some forces concentrating on the intergovernmental relations involved in handling particular functions like highways, welfare, health, and the conservation of resources, and others on aspects that cut across many functions, as in legislation, finance, personnel relations, constitutional powers, and general cooperativeness between the officials of different units of government. Such a study would require a great deal of interviewing and field work, and at best it could not cover every kind of governmental activity or problem.

Since the Rockefeller Foundation had shown, through substantial financial support, its interest in the field of public administration and in the studies of federal and intergovernmental problems undertaken by the Committee on Public Administration, I formulated and presented my plan to the Foundation, through the directors of its Social Science Division, Dr. Joseph H. Willits and Roger F. Evans, and in due time received their approval of it. The sum of $72,000 was made available for it by the Foundation on a five-year basis, 1946 to 1951, and arrangements were made for the University of Minnesota to receive and administer the fund, to provide space for work, and to reduce my teaching and administrative load for the duration of the study. This project gave me my most protracted and intimate contacts with intergovernmental relations and permitted my greatest concentration upon them. Appendix 3 to Dr. Weidner's monograph, Number 9 in the series, gives a sufficient account of the project so that no details need be repeated here.

While I was completing my work for the Committee on Public Administration on the Federalism and Intergovernmental Relations volume, and initiating the Minnesota study, a number of groups and organizations besides the Council on Intergovernmental Relations were undertaking investigations bearing on the subject. To some extent I was drawn into several of the major efforts of this kind.

The Council of State Governments, whose members are the governments of the fifty states, plus the Commonwealth of Puerto Rico, and whose secretariats in Chicago, Washington, and regional offices serve the Governors' Conference and other interstate organizations as well, had important studies going forward in the 1940s. One of these, for which I did a small amount of consulting, resulted in the publication in 1946 of a volume on State-Local Relations.[17] Another, with which I had a little more to do, was published in 1949 under the title Federal Grants-in-Aid.[18] Both studies were actually made by council staff members with the aid of selected persons from the faculties of the University of Chicago and other nearby institutions. Each study was supervised by Frank Bane and a committee of state officials acting on behalf of the Council of State Governments.

The widely felt need for some reorganization of the executive branch of the national government following the abnormal developments of World War II led Congress to establish in 1947 a Commission on the Organization of the Executive Branch of the Government to study and report upon the problems involved. This body came to be called the Hoover Commission, from the name of its chairman, former President Herbert Hoover. (Because there was a later commission for this purpose also headed by Mr. Hoover, the original one came to be known later as the first Hoover Commission.) As chairman Mr. Hoover proceeded promptly to designate the several areas of studies to be undertaken, to set up special study committees and "task forces" for the different fields, and also to contract for the research to be done.

One of the areas the commission decided to investigate was that of federal-state relations, and I was appointed to the study committee on this subject. The committee served under the chairmanship of Thomas Jefferson Coolidge of Boston, then chairman of the board of the United Fruit Company, and a fairly close friend of Mr. Hoover's. The other committee members were John E. Burton, budget director of the State of New York under Governor Thomas E. Dewey; Senator Harry F. Byrd of Virginia; Senator Frank Carlson, former governor of Kansas; William L. Chenery, editor of Collier's Magazine; John W. Davis, attorney, Democratic candidate for President in 1924; Charles A. Edison, former governor of New Jersey; Professor William I. Myers of Cornell University; and Sinclair Weeks, former senator from Massachusetts and later Secretary of Commerce.[19] The basis for the selection of this committee I do not know, but in a sense the list speaks for itself. In no way does it reflect the fact that Mr. Truman was President at the time with a program similar to that of his predecessor, Mr. Roosevelt.

Mr. Hoover contracted with the Council of State Governments to do the research for the study of federal-state relations. Frank Bane was designated director of the

---

[17]Chicago: Committee on State-Local Relations, Council of State Governments, 1946; vii + 8 + 288 pp.

[18]Chicago: Council of State Governments, 1949; viii + 322 pp.

[19]Commission on Organization of the Executive Branch of the Federal Government, "Report on Federal-State Relations"; printed in a pamphlet containing reports on Overseas Administration, Federal-State Relations, and Federal Research (Washington, D.C.: Government Printing Office, March 1949).

research task force; he reported directly to Mr. Hoover and the commission, not to the Committee on Federal-State Relations. Mr. Bane recruited a small staff of able persons, including some of the faculty of the University of Chicago, and the study went forward in Chicago along lines proposed by Mr. Bane and approved by Mr. Hoover and the commission. The research involved essentially an investigation of the national executive agencies (and their field offices) that have relations with state and local officials through grant-in-aid programs and other cooperative or cost-sharing devices.

Two questions may be raised here. Why had the Council of State Governments been chosen as the agent for a supposedly objective study of federal-state relations, when the council represented only the states and had already gone on record for certain important changes in those relations? And, had the program of research really gone to the heart of "federal-state relations"? I cannot answer the first. As to the second, it is true that the main task of the Hoover Commission had to do with problems of how to do things within the national executive organization. But the basic questions in the area of federal-state relations are questions of policy, questions of what to do, of whether or not to do them at all, and of who is to foot the bill, not questions of how to do them. The commission itself indicated some misgivings on this issue in its closed sessions.

Since the study committee was separated from the research task force (although Mr. Bane gave generous assistance to the committee when possible and made available to it sections of the task force report) and had no staff of its own, it decided to limit its discussions and recommendations mainly to a major issue of policy, namely the "division of duties and responsibilities between state and national governments." The discussions brought out some interesting differences of opinion and theory as to the nature of the American federal system, and the respective advantages of the national and state governments in the financing and performance of various functions.

The course and fate of the final report of the committee are somewhat confused. A report drafted by the committee chairman, which disregarded the research findings that the committee had discussed, was apparently the one presented to the commission by Mr. Hoover, although Mr. Burton, Mr. Chenery, and I had suggested a number of changes in it and Mr. Chenery had drafted a revised report which we had understood was to be the committee report. At any rate, because of the controversy over the recommendations of Mr. Coolidge's report that was stirred up both within the commission and in other quarters (which I have no desire to rehash here), it decided to drop all that had been done by both the committee and the task force. The commission did, however, include in its own report a recommendation for a continuing national agency to deal with problems of federal-state relations.

The commission itself did not publish Mr. Coolidge's report, the revised committee report, or the study made by the research task force. At the instigation of others, the latter two were later published in a Senate document, although neither the title nor the table of contents of this document indicated that anything more than the research report was included. The title was Federal-State Relations, by the Council of State Governments, with the subtitle Report of the Commission on Organization of the Executive Branch of the Government. Pursuant to Public Law 162, 80th Congress.[20] (In addition this publication includes a detailed appendix on federal-state relations in eighteen functional fields, and two memorandums prepared under the committee's auspices, one on state-federal overlapping taxes and one on the development of governmental powers in the United States.) Thus the work done by the committee was pretty well buried, but since the revised report had had to be done hurriedly and represented a tissue of compromises, I for one was not sorry.

---

[20]See Senate Document No. 81, 81st Congress, 1st Session (Washington, D.C., 1949); 231 pp.

This episode in my education in intergovernmental relations was not a particularly rewarding one. But the next national committee with which I was associated had a different fate.

I have already published an article on the work of the Commission on Intergovernmental Relations, so that it will not be necessary to repeat the substance of that article here.[21] Suffice it to say that in 1953, on the recommendation of President Eisenhower, Congress established by law a Commission on Intergovernmental Relations, for which there had long been agitation. I became a member of that commission by appointment of the President. Among his fifteen appointees were six governors and ex-governors, a mayor, several high-ranking national officials, and several university administrators—I being the only member of the group who was strictly a university professor. There were also five senators appointed by the vice president and five representatives appointed by the speaker of the House. Thus there were twenty-five members in all.

This commission undertook a thorough survey and appraisal of the federal system and especially of the relations between the national government and the states. The grant-in-aid system and other fiscal relations received especially close attention.

Unlike the Committee on Federal-State Relations under the first Hoover Commission, this commission had its own funds, its own staff, and its own research program. It reported directly to Congress and the President. After a rather slow start and some reorganization, the commission proceeded diligently with its task. Its findings and recommendations were published in 1955 in a one-volume report which was widely distributed.[22] Also published at the same time were fifteen special studies prepared by members of the research staff and by special study committees.[23]

As a result of some writing that I did in the early days of this commission's work, I produced and had published at this time a semipopular book of my own covering some parts of the field. This work is entitled *The Nation and the States, Rivals or Partners?*[24]

At the present writing, the work of the commission is being followed up by Congress and the executive branch of the national government and by the Governors' Conference. The Senate Committee on Government Operations has issued, among other things, an exhaustive *Index to the Reports of the Commission on Intergovernmental Relations.*[25] The House Committee on Government Operations has put out a series of reports prepared by its own staff, one summarizing the recommendations of the commission and showing how they might be implemented;[26] others give the results of questionnaires sent to

---

[21]*Journal of Politics*, 18:211-31 (1956).

[22]Commission on Intergovernmental Relations, *A Report to the President for Transmittal to Congress* (Washington, D.C.: Government Printing Office, June 1955; xi + 311 pp.).

[23]For a list of these, see *ibid*., p. 295.

[24]Minneapolis: University of Minnesota Press, 1955; xvi + 263 pp.

[25]Senate Document No. 111, 84th Congress, 2nd Session (Washington, D.C.: Government Printing Office, 1956).

[26]*Recommendations and Major Statements of the Commission on Intergovernmental Relations, Annotated to Show Method of Implementation and Federal Agency and Program Affected* (Washington, D.C.: Government Printing Office, August 1956).

national, state, and local officials[27] and provide a Selected Bibliography on Intergovernmental Relations in the United States.[28] On the executive side President Eisenhower designated Howard Pyle, former governor of Arizona, of the White House staff, as his deputy assistant for intergovernmental relations. In following through on the recommendations of the commission he has been assisted by Meyer Kestnbaum, also of the White House staff and former chairman of the commission, and by Robert E. Merriam, assistant director of the Bureau of the Budget.

At the 49th annual meeting of the Governors' Conference, at Williamsburg, Virginia, June 23-27, 1957, President Eisenhower urged the governors to join with his administration in a combined effort to adjust the functional and financial relations and arrangements between the national government and the states so as to make for more effective and responsive government, and help the states to "regain and preserve their traditional responsibilities and rights."[29] The Governors' Conference responded to this proposal by resolving "to appoint a special committee to work with appropriate federal officials appointed by the President from the executive branch to develop ways and means of attaining a sound relationship of functions and finances between the federal government and the states and to formulate definite proposals to these ends."[30] A "joint task force" was set up consisting of three heads of federal departments, three presidential assistants, and the director of the budget, and ten governors representing the states.[31]

Thus the study of the intergovernmental relations goes forward in official as well as academic circles. My direct participation in official studies at the national level ended with the termination of the Commission on Intergovernmental Relations in June 1955. Later I served briefly with the Task Force on State Functions and Intergovernmental Relations of the Minnesota Self-Survey under Governor Orville L. Freeman and Commissioner of Administration Arthur Naftalin. For this committee I prepared a short report on intergovernmental relations based in large part on information from Minnesota officials concerning Minnesota problems.[32]

In the meantime I had been periodically engaged in editing our Minnesota monographs and writing Number 8 in the series, Intergovernmental Fiscal Relations, and the present review volume.

---

[27]See, for example, House Report No. 575 (Union Calendar No. 200), 85th Congress, 1st Session, Sixth Report by the Committee on Government Operations, giving "Replies from State and Local Governments to Questionnaire on Intergovernmental Relation" (Washington, D.C.: Government Printing Office, xvi + 542 pp.).

[28]84th Congress, 2nd Session, House of Representatives Committee Print, Committee on Government Operations (Washington, D.C.: Government Printing Office, November 1956).

[29]See State Government: The Magazine of State Affairs, 30:168-70, 192 (August 1957), at p. 192.

[30]Ibid., p. 192.

[31]See Changing Patterns of American Federalism: From the Viewpoint of the Executive Branch, a paper prepared by Robert E. Merriam, assistant director, Bureau of the Budget, for the annual meeting of the American Political Science Association (Washington, D.C.: Executive Office of the President, Bureau of the Budget, Press Release of September 5, 1957), especially pp. 6-10.

[32]See The Minnesota Self-Survey: Reports of the Functional Task Forces and Summary Review [St. Paul, 1957], pp. 147-64.

With the publication of this, the tenth and final monograph, I put aside for the time being my specific studies in federal government and intergovernmental relations. I do this in order to devote my energies more fully for the next few years to another project—a history of the study of politics—which has already occupied much of my time for three years. The problems of federal government remain high on my list of research priorities, however, as they do on those of many other students of politics, here and abroad. If anything that my colleagues and I have done proves to be of help and stimulation to others, we shall feel amply rewarded for our efforts.

William Anderson

August 1959

Table of Contents

CHAPTER 1

Definitions and Objectives

Interest in the subject of federal government has shown a considerable revival in the past twenty years both in the United States and in other parts of the free world. Many persons who favor some form of international organization have renewed Tennyson's grand vision of "the Parliament of Man, the Federation of the world." The truly grandiose scheme of Mr. Ely Culbertson, better known for his mastery of contract bridge, envisioned a federation of all mankind based upon regional federations in various parts of the globe, these in turn composed of lesser federations. Atlantic union and the federation of western Europe are concepts expressing the more limited aspirations of others who seek some federal form of supra-national organization to promote international security and peace. Newly independent or reorganized nations like India and West Germany (the Federal Republic of Germany) have found federal types of organization suited to their needs, while on a smaller scale various parts of the British Commonwealth in Africa and the West Indies have also been organized under somewhat federalized forms.

The revival of interest in the federal system of the United States stems from quite different considerations. The American people had lived and grown wealthy and powerful under a federal system of government, had survived a great civil war, preserved their Union, and become not a little complacent about their institutions when, suddenly, the severe depression in the early 1930s shocked many of their leaders into grave doubts about the government, the economic system, and the future of the United States. The first reaction of a number of leaders of public opinion was that national action was needed to restore the American economy to its former condition of prosperity and high-level employment, but that under the United States Constitution the national government lacked the necessary powers to act with sufficient vigor. When the Supreme Court rejected as unconstitutional several major pieces of recovery legislation passed by Congress, the gloom of these leaders was deepened. Either the Constitution or the Supreme Court or both would have to be changed to ensure to the national government the necessary powers of action. A few extremists even questioned whether the states should not be wiped out and the government changed into a unitary system.

This mood soon changed. Congress went right on passing recovery and reform legislation, and the Supreme Court presently fell into line by reversing some of its earlier decisions and by upholding acts that a few years earlier would probably have been held unconstitutional. This change of attitude by the Supreme Court, beginning in 1936-37, opened the door to even more acts of Congress to strengthen the national government's control over the economy.

Those who earlier had voiced great concern over the restrictions on national powers now began to subside, but another group of critics with entirely different views rose to a certain leadership in public opinion. They clamored that the national government had gone too far, that it was invading and arrogating to itself the powers of the states and in effect destroying the federal system. As the specters of depression faded and the economy began to pulse with life again (aided by large expenditures for defense in 1940 and later years) the protests against centralization coupled with the demands for a return to "states' rights" increased in volume and in stridency.

Many governors of the states, members of Congress, lay leaders, and organizations, took up the cry. National measures that had once seemed necessary for economic salvation, including various grants-in-aid, labor laws, and TVA, came under strong condemnation.

Since the end of World War II this new line of attack upon the federal system as it is today has had wide currency, and not only in the Governors' Conference but also in various organizations of dissatisfied citizens. The issue of "returning powers to the states" has entered national party platforms and has even influenced Congress at times. It is, in fact, the frequent reiteration of the charge that centralization in Washington is threatening destruction of states' rights that has led to the first official national studies of the federal system and of the relations of the national government to the states. Of such studies the most important has been that by the Commission on Intergovernmental Relations established by Congress in 1953.

Why are so many people in different parts of the free world so interested in, and in fact so enamored of, federal systems of government? They are talking of something they call "federalism" as they would of "socialism" or any other ism, as if it were some essence, or some system of belief and action, that is possessed of magical power to achieve peace, security, good government. Would not a fairly broad but detailed study of a federal system as it operates in fact from day to day be a useful corrective to many hopes and beliefs that seem to be rather too rosy and exaggerated? I believed it would.

The federal system that I had been studying most intensively was, of course, that of the United States. It happens that this system, when established under the Constitution in 1788, was the first modern example of a federal system. During the nineteenth century it became the model, in a sense, for other attempts to establish federal systems—in Latin America, in Canada, in Australia. Germany and Switzerland also provided examples, although they were not so widely copied. But had people abroad really looked into the workings of the American federal system? How many people even at home, in the United States, had paid enough attention to it in detail to know how the system was operated and what its problems were?

I realized that a complete study of the United States federal system from all major points of view was more than any one person or a small group of researchers could accomplish. The older approaches were mainly through constitutional history, constitutional law, the theory of sovereignty, general history, and public finance. Without rejecting any of these approaches, I decided to try to supplement them by a study of the "working relations" of the national and state governments in their daily operations. This meant concentrating upon how the officials of the different governments interact with each other when they come into official contact in the performance of their duties, because it is largely through such official interactions that the relations of the governments themselves are adjusted.

This is what I call the intergovernmental relations approach to the study of the federal system. It involves all three branches of government, legislative, executive, and judicial, although for reasons that will appear the executive and administrative officials get more attention than those in the other two branches.

It involves also not only the national and state governments but local governments as well, since they too have such relations between officials. These relations are interconnected to a high degree. Vertically the official relations run both up and down, from local to state to national and from national to state to local, and horizontally they run across from state to state, and from local unit to local unit, in bewildering complexity. Therefore, although our principal objective was to study the federal system through the data on national-state relations, it seemed important to deal with all intergovernmental relations, up and down and crosswise, in order to see what are usually thought of as the "federal relations," namely, the national-state and interstate relations, realistically in this total relational context.

To elucidate some of the problems in our study as a whole, to provide a somewhat more general background for it, and to make its findings, if possible, a little more applicable to the study of federal government abroad as well as in the United States, I shall try to define here the principal concepts with which the study deals.

Intergovernmental relations, as used in our series of studies, is, I believe, a term indigenous to the United States, of relatively recent origin, and still not widely used or understood. I do not find it as a separate entry in Webster's New International Dictionary of the English Language of 1934, or in the latest issue of that work (1957). It does not appear in the text or in the Addenda and Corrigenda of the 1955 reprint of the third edition of the Oxford Universal Dictionary on Historical Principles or in the college edition of Webster's New World Dictionary of the American Language (copyrighted 1951, 1952, 1953). It is not a major entry or even an item in the index of the Encyclopaedia of the Social Sciences (1935). The article on "Loans, Intergovernmental" in that work refers to public loans by one nation to another as distinguished from private loans.

On the other hand, the American Academy of Political and Social Science named an entire number of the Annals, for January 1940, "Intergovernmental Relations in the United States" (edited by W. Brooke Graves). Before this the term had appeared in textbooks on American government (e.g., in my American Government, 1938) and in articles in such journals as State Government. Parallel terms like intergovernmental tax immunities also began to appear in print. In the 1940s various state Commissions on Interstate Cooperation sponsored by the Council of State Governments began to designate themselves as Commissions on Intergovernmental Cooperation. In 1942 the Council on Intergovernmental Relations was set up by certain national officials in Washington, and this council in turn sponsored various state and local councils with similar titles. Congress put its seal of approval on the term intergovernmental in 1953 when it established the Commission on Intergovernmental Relations.

The article on "Loans, Intergovernmental" in the Encyclopaedia of the Social Sciences referred to above reveals how easily intergovernmental and international can be confused. To avoid this difficulty some persons use the longer term national-state-local relations instead of intergovernmental relations.

Enough has been said to indicate that in the United States, at least, the phrase intergovernmental relations has become accepted as a term to designate an important body of activities or interactions occurring between governmental units of all types and levels within the federal system. It is essentially a class name that brackets together and embraces in one concept a series of classes of relations or interactions that may be designated by the names of the units concerned, "national-state," "interstate," "state-local," "interlocal," "national-local," "city-county," etc., or classified by the nature or content of the functions, interests, and powers involved, such as constitutional, legal, financial, functional, political, legislative, administrative, or judicial relations between all types of governmental units that operate within the American federal system.

Underlying the concept of intergovernmental relations is the fact that the nation as a whole, each one of the states, and every county, town, city, village, school district, and other special district or local unit is a territorial and corporate or quasi-corporate entity that has a legal existence, rights, functions, powers, and duties within its territory, distinct from those of every other such unit. This is true even though the smaller units are generally embraced geographically within the larger ones. Being all separate legal entities, they are all capable of legal and other relations with each other.

No two governmental units can actually meet or sit down together to work out common problems. As in the case of international relations everything has to be done through representatives who are in most cases officials. In short, as indicated above, intergovernmental relations are carried out through the actions of public governing bodies and governmental officials. The final written agreements reached in important matters are binding on the governmental units themselves, but there are countless informal agreements that are known only to the officials. Thus, it is people in more or less official capacities who are the real actors in intergovernmental relations, whether they are relations of conflict or of cooperation. It is human beings clothed with office who are the real determiners of what the relations between units of government will be. Consequently the concept of intergovernmental relations necessarily has to be formulated largely in terms of human relations and human behavior under the conditions that prevail when different people represent the interests of different units and different functions of government. All the monographs in our series throw some light on this fact, but Dr. Ylvisaker in Number 7 and Dr. Weidner in Number 9 bring it out most clearly.

It is in federal systems of government, with their three "layers" or "levels" of units—national, state, and local—that intergovernmental relations appear to be most important and the interactions of governmental units are most numerous. Federal government is, then, the next concept to be discussed, and along with it the idea of federalism.

The root word from which federal stems is the Latin noun foedus, meaning a league, treaty, or compact, or its verb form foederare, which means to form a league, treaty, or compact. Because of the meaning of this Latin root, various writers have tended to think of a federal form of state or government as necessarily resulting always from the voluntary joining together of a number of previously independent states into a new and larger political system that has a central government but that also leaves a considerable measure of autonomy to the member states of the federal system. This approach tends to put the emphasis not so much on the type of polity or government that results as on the process of attaining the result, whatever it is. Those who follow this line encounter a major difficulty in trying to fit the actual historical steps that lead up to a federal system into a preconceived mold of what is believed to be necessary. In my judgment this approach also puts too much stress upon a mere word, federal, and the meaning of its Latin root, and not enough upon the type of political system that today carries the designation of federal. Two of the best known federal systems, those of Canada and Australia, were established by acts of the British Parliament for groups of semiautonomous colonies and not by treaties between sovereign independent states. The federation act for Canada actually created two new major provinces, Ontario and Quebec, in the process of setting up the federation.

I will not comment upon the origins of the federal-type systems of Switzerland, the Federal Republic of Germany, or India, except to say that they do not clearly follow the pattern of a treaty between sovereign states. As to the United States, the thirteen British colonies that were united under British rule and administration declared their independence in unison and never acted separately as sovereignties. The Articles of Confederation, to which they reluctantly agreed, were soon after overthrown by a peaceful revolution engineered in the name of the people of the United States and were wholly superseded by the Constitution of the United States, which established what men chose to call a federal government without its being so named in the document.

The unfortunate obsession with the idea that a federal system is based upon a voluntary treaty or compact between previously independent sovereign states creates a sort of optical illusion and prevents a clear view of the governmental system that has been established. The fact of the system's having arisen or not arisen from such a treaty has no necessary bearing on the result. Numerous such treaties have resulted in nothing more than alliances or loose confederations among states that remain essentially independent and may soon fall apart. On the other hand it is entirely thinkable that under conditions of special stress and danger, a number of states might consent by treaty to being consolidated into a single unitary state with no trace of a federal system in its makeup.

Looking into the constitutions and governments of various nations, and into various writings about them, I have found four rather long established constitutions that are generally recognized as being of the federal type and that are the basis for actual governments generally conceded to be federal, those of the United States, Switzerland, Canada, and Australia. Outstanding among the more recent ones of this type are the governmental systems of India and the Federal Republic of Germany. No two of these are identical by any means; in fact, each one is unique in more than one respect. What are the common characteristics that justify a person in classifying them all as federal? They may be listed as follows:

Each has a single supreme written constitution that establishes a central government for the whole country; recognizes and to some extent regulates the affairs of a series of state, provincial, or regional governments, whose combined areas make up practically the whole country; divides the powers and functions of government between the central or national government and the regional governments; authorizes both levels of government, acting autonomously, to legislate for, to tax, and to operate directly upon the people; and provides for or recognizes one or more means, including a supreme court, to resolve disputes between the central and the regional governments over their respective rights and powers. All these constitutions also assert more or less clearly the supremacy of the national government's powers, laws, and treaties over the actions of the state or regional governments. Perhaps I should add that all are essentially republican in form, and subject to popular control through elections, although traces of the monarchical form linger on in Canada and Australia.

These are, I believe, the common features that characterize federal systems, whatever the variations in detail may be—and they are many! If I were asked to point out the key provisions I would mention <u>the constitutional division of the powers and functions of government between two autonomous and constitutionally recognized levels of government, the central and the regional</u>. No strictly unitary system of government like that of Great Britain, France, Spain, Italy, or Sweden has any such arrangement. Borderline types, between federal and unitary, are found in the Union of South Africa, in several Latin American countries, and in a few other places.

Earlier analyses of the nature of federal states turned upon such questions as the inalienability and indivisibility of sovereignty. John C. Calhoun in the United States and various writers in Great Britain and Germany, for example, discussed the problem of national versus state sovereignty in federal systems as if this were the central issue. More recently an able British Commonwealth authority has offered a different approach to the central principle of federal government. In his widely used book, <u>Federal Government</u>, Professor K. C. Wheare of Oxford University says: "By the federal principle I mean the method of dividing powers so that the general and regional governments are each, within a sphere, coordinate and independent."

It seems to me that the words <u>coordinate</u> and <u>independent</u> are by nature incapable of qualification. In other words they are absolutes. Two things cannot be more or less coordinate, or more or less independent. They either are coordinate or not, independent or not independent. The notion that powers can be divided into separate spheres lies near the center of Professor Wheare's analysis. I do not think such a division is possible. When two autonomous levels of government legislate for the same people, there is hardly anything that one level can do without affecting the powers and functions of the other. In an all-out war, for example, or even in a period of great international tensions, the power of defense simply must invade and override all other powers. At a less critical level, the power to regulate commerce must inevitably collide with the powers to regulate industry or agriculture. But if absolutely separate spheres of power are impossible, so is coordinateness and so is independence. The only practicable arrangement is to provide for the supremacy of one level over the other, and that in practice has to mean national supremacy over the states, the right of the nation to override the laws of the states and to regulate their functions in the national interest. This in effect is what the American federal system does. It does not make the states either coordinate with or independent of the nation. And as Professor Wheare says in another passage, "The modern idea of what federal government is has been determined by the United States of America."

Without further analysis of ideas about federal government, I would stand by the descriptive definition given above in the form of a list of common features of federal systems. A little needs to be said, however, about another term that is being widely used today.

Federalism adds the suffix -ism to the root word federal. This suffix has various uses and meanings in modern English and American, such as (i) an action or its result (hypnotism, baptism); (ii) a condition or state of being (barbarism, despotism); (iii) a doctrine, theory, belief, or practice (stoicism, platonism, liberalism, conservatism, communism); and (iv) a peculiarity of speech (a localism, or an Americanism), usually preceded, as here, by the indefinite article a (*Webster's New International Dictionary*).

In the word federalism I believe the suffix is used in its third sense, that is, to indicate a doctrine, theory, or belief. It is the widespread belief or faith in federation among political units as a cure for the ills of war and insecurity that has led to global schemes for federating all the nations, and to some of the large regional schemes like those proposed for western Europe. It is a similar faith, but on a more limited scale and with a more practicable and immediate objective, that has led to plans for federating the British West Indies and various groups of former colonies in Africa.

Unfortunately for clear thinking, the word federalism is not always confined to the political or governmental field of human activity, but is also used to designate schemes of social pluralism, much as federation is used in the names of large-scale church, labor, and other social and economic organizations. Although it is an abstract noun, federalism is also beginning to be used to designate concrete examples of federal governmental organization. Thus Canada or the United States is referred to as "a federalism," and all countries operating under federal forms are being designated as "federalisms." We see in this example how the meanings of words can undergo unexpected changes. Our studies did not go off into these other applications of the federal idea, nor did we use the term federalism in any but its governmental sense, and that only very rarely.

In this, the final monograph of our series, I try to adhere to the original objective of contributing something to knowledge about the United States federal system primarily from the viewpoint of intergovernmental relations. This does not involve simply summarizing and interpreting the earlier studies in our project. I feel the need to bring into this review some small fruits from other studies that I have made over the years and to pose some of the questions that have arisen in my mind as I have pondered federal government in general. I present, therefore, a composite sort of volume, one that summarizes the work we did on the project, and reveals its shortcomings, and one that adds some thoughts and questions that open new vistas for future studies in the field. The latter will come partly in the body of my study and partly in its last two chapters.

I have taken the liberty, also, of making this, the final volume, a somewhat more personal pronouncement than the other studies stemming from our project have been. When I use the term we it is not an editorial we, but a reference to the group who worked together on the project from 1946 to 1951; and when I wish to take personal responsibility for a statement no one will misunderstand if I say I.

My first four chapters present some background materials on federal government and intergovernmental relations in the United States; one of these bears directly on the national government in Minnesota. The next four chapters concern intergovernmental relations directly. The last two present some general hypotheses, conclusions, and questions arising out of all the materials covered.

CHAPTER 2

The Changing Scene and the American Federal System

It is trite to say, but not unimportant to recall, that place, time, and circumstances condition all the thoughts, works, and institutions of men. Our studies of intergovernmental relations in the United States as we observed them in Minnesota, and the human institutions, activities, and attitudes that provided the data for our observations, were what they were, we believe, in large part because of the many factors that conditioned the life of the American people in recent decades; and these factors in turn were influenced in part by more remote events going back to the discovery of America and beyond. Had we lived centuries ago and tried to make similar studies in the ancient Near East or in medieval Europe we probably would, indeed, have found intergovernmental relations (in some sense of that term) to attract our attention, but they would undoubtedly have been rather different types of relations.

As it was we studied intergovernmental relations in Minnesota and the United States of America in the years just following World War II. The conditions then prevailing there were the place-time-circumstance factors that need to be kept in mind and to be understood if our work is to have any significance. In short we recognize that, in the modern manner of speaking, our studies were decidedly "culture-bound." We wonder, however, whether we may not have hit upon at least a few examples of fairly general types of human behavior, some common propensities or tendencies in human interactions, which might also be found among other peoples, at other times and places.

In making the foregoing generalizations (which are by no means original) about the interdependence of things, I am stating a belief on the basis of which we proceeded in our studies. It is a belief not that a human society is organic in the biological sense but simply that all the important activities of men in a society interact with each other so that changes in relations and attitudes are brought about in the society, and that these changes cannot be understood at all in isolation from each other or from the human activities that seemed to produce them. We cannot say with positive assurance that industrialization, urban growth and rural decline, the development and integration of the whole country into one economic system, the spread of education, and the rise of nationwide media of rapid communication and transportation, for example, were the specific causes of increased emphasis upon national as against state governmental action and other changes in intergovernmental relations. Neither can we measure with anything like precision, if indeed we can measure at all, the influence and effects of various operative factors in a highly complicated, fluid, and changing system of human activities and organizations upon any one or more other variables in the total situation. We can say, however, that such and such things happened concurrently or in certain time sequences among the people of the United States. In other words we can show a certain association among various developments and surmise that they were interdependent developments with more or less effect on each other.

To sketch in a meaningful background for our studies would seem to require an outline of the entire culture of the American people for the many years leading up to and through World War II, but such is not possible in reasonable compass. What I will try to do instead is to call attention to certain factors and events that I believe almost intuitively to have had considerable importance in determining the shape and the thrust of the intergovernmental relations that we were studying. These factors will include the constitutional rules and framework (which I mention here but reserve mainly for the following chapter), the political and governmental institutions and practices, and to some extent the economic, social, and technological conditions and developments of the times. All the selected factors will be considered historically, so that there will be some depth to the picture presented. (For the benefit of any foreign readers who do not know the United States as well as Americans do, I have included some data that may seem unnecessary to the well-informed American reader.)

My reasons for the choice of the factors to be mentioned will in most cases be fairly obvious. In what I say as well as in what I omit I will be guided to a considerable extent by what the authors of the earlier monographs in the series said and did. We the authors of the several monographs are well aware of certain limitations on what we did, and have tried to indicate some of them here and there throughout our publications. The reader's attention is called especially to Appendix 3 in Monograph 9 where we describe our research methods. In the last chapter of the present monograph, also, I outline some "unfinished business." The thoughtful reader will undoubtedly find other grounds for criticism of what we did as well as more examples of things we should have done but failed to do. We hope, however, to have "left a trail" so that others who make studies of intergovernmental relations will be assisted in drawing up better models and plans for research in this field.

The place that we studied and in which we made our studies was of course the United States, with specific emphasis on the state of Minnesota. The latter has 80,000 square miles of land area and is located in the northern tier of American states, at the western end of the Great Lakes, and at the headwaters of the Mississippi River. Canada bounds it on the north, the two Dakotas on the west, Iowa on the south, and Wisconsin and Lake Superior on the east.

The time in which we made our most intensive studies was from the middle of 1946 to the middle of 1951; however, the period we actually studied cannot be defined that precisely. Most of our interviewing was done and our current data were gathered within the five-year period, but every author of a monograph necessarily went back farther than that (and no two equally far back) in order to get at the beginnings of the function or problem he was investigating. On the constitutional questions of national-state relations, for example, our reach goes back to the colonial period of United States history and the founding of the republic; but for most purposes we needed to trace developments only since the founding of Minnesota, first as a territory (1849) and then as a state in the Union (1858). We could not forget that all human arrangements are developments in time, some of them over a long period, but we tried to keep the historical accounts to a minimum. In addition, Dr. Weidner and I stayed with the project more or less in the years after 1951 when most of the staff had disbanded, and kept on adding data and insights right down to the writing of our final monographs, this one in 1958 and 1959.

The people whose intergovernmental relations we studied numbered, during the period of our most intensive investigations, about 150 million in the United States as a whole (151 million in the 1950 census), with about 3 million of these in Minnesota. By 1958, the Census Bureau estimated the nation's population to be over 172 million, while that of Minnesota had gone up to about 3 1/3 million. Of course our studies were directed mainly not to the entire population of either nation or state but to the units of government, national, state, and local, and the public officials we reached directly, by interview and questionnaire—some hundreds of national government officials both in Washington and in the Upper Midwest region, and some thousands of state and local officials in Minnesota and the adjoining states. We were conscious, however, of the fact that behind the officials who represented and served them stood millions of people. Their needs, attitudes, and aspirations in such matters as popular control of local government, local self-government, civil liberties, public service, and public finance were, we recognized, important background factors, but we could not make an independent study of them. It may be noted that these general attitudes are rather well reflected not only in public laws and policies, national, state, and local, but also in the attitudes of officials; Dr. Weidner in Monograph 9 considers certain attitudes of officials in some detail.

According to the censuses of 1940 and 1950, 99 per cent of the people in Minnesota were white, and about one third were foreign-born or born in Minnesota of foreign-born parents. The foreign-born for several generations had come largely from Sweden, Norway, Germany, and other north European countries including the British Isles, and from Canada, but there were significant numbers also from other countries. Minnesota had, indeed, been a melting pot of peoples with Finns, Poles, Icelanders, Danes, Hollanders, French, Italians, Greeks, Nisei, and other groups adding their characteristics to the whole. The native-born of native parents came largely from the New England and other northeastern states.

Despite intensive urbanization in the Minneapolis-St. Paul metropolitan area and some urbanization at Duluth and in other centers, the state still had at the time of our studies proportionately more rural population, 45 per cent, than the nation as a whole, 36 per cent, and a population density lower by a fourth than the national average (37 per square mile as against 50).

Within the present state boundaries the transition from the truly frontier conditions of the 1840s and 1850s to almost complete occupation of the state's area and considerable urbanization took place in about two generations, say by 1890 or 1900. This period was punctuated by crop failures and depressions as well as periods of almost boom prosperity, by great changes in agriculture, the rapid rise and the beginnings of decline in lumbering, the growth of iron mining and Great Lakes shipping, the rise of industries, commerce, finance, transportation and communications, public services, and education—with resultant high levels of literacy and well-being. Minnesota's development paralleled that of the nation as a whole. Great technological advances in industry, commerce, and communications accompanied the rapid industrialization and urbanization of nearly the whole country, and made possible further advances. Standards of living rose everywhere as the nation's great wealth of resources was exploited.

Along with these changes came a subtle but significant shift in public thinking—from acceptance of the ideals of laissez faire, of complete individual or family responsibility for subsistence and support, to belief in a certain degree of public responsibility for the economic welfare of the individual. Rather incongruously, many of those who had espoused a policy of laissez faire toward the individual had approved the idea of government aids to industry in such forms as tariffs, land grants to railroads, and profitable contracts for urban public works and buildings to contractors who did not have to submit to open competition or bidding. As the increasing complexity of the industrial structure made the individual ever more economically dependent on it, and ever more helpless in the face of the great depressions that marred the nation's prosperity in the 1870s, the early 1890s, and the 1930s, the more rigid and uncompromising principles of laissez faire were almost inevitably modified or abandoned. To look down upon the shiftless person for being "on the town" when employment was available was one thing, but to look down upon the millions of unemployed caught in a depression over which no one had any control, and for which no one would assume any responsibility, was something very different. It was an attitude that could not long be defended.

This shift in public thinking manifested itself fairly early in Minnesota's history in the form of agrarian movements demanding government action to curb monopolies, and to protect the shipper of farm products against excessive railroad rates and against buyers of farm produce who, under one pretext or another, gave less than the current market price for the produce they received from the farmers. Laborers and skilled workers wanted laws to assure prompt payment of all wages in cash, to ensure safe working conditions, to provide compensation for the injured worker, and so on. Demands for governmental protection of different classes increased and spread, finally including such ideas as guaranteed minimum wages and unemployment compensation for workers, government-insured "parity prices" for farmers and other producers of raw materials, and various kinds of concessions for small businessmen.

Bit by bit state and national governments began to respond to the new demands, though not without many a bitter struggle in the election contests between political parties, in legislatures, and even in the courts. Minor parties, both rural and urban, arose to sponsor particular programs, major parties split and sometimes reunited in the battle over issues, and major party faced major party in the final legislative contests over important measures. On the national scene names like those of Theodore Roosevelt with his New Nationalism and progressivism, Woodrow Wilson with the New Freedom, Warren G. Harding, Calvin Coolidge, and Herbert Hoover with their various forms of conservatism, Franklin D. Roosevelt with the New Deal, and Harry S. Truman with his Fair Deal mark successive stages in the continuing struggle over the issues of increased governmental services and responsibility for human welfare. In the state of Minnesota the names of Governors Floyd B. Olson and Harold E. Stassen (to take but two) are correspondingly outstanding, though not equally on the side of increased public services.

While the role of government in general in America and in Minnesota has been expanding, a process which has produced almost revolutionary results, there has been a parallel and related trend away from an early local and essentially parochial view of the problems of government to an acceptance of state and national political action on an ever-widening front. It is in this development that we find the problems of intergovernmental relations brought into the foreground. Such small units as villages and rural townships are clearly unsuited even to administer and much less to make the policies for most of the great public service programs of modern times. The counties suffice, with state assistance, for the local administration of some programs, but in policy-making and in financing, as well as some phases of the administration of other programs, even the states have been found wanting in a number of respects. A shift toward greater national responsibiltiy in certain fields—banking, agricultural credit, and highway construction—came in the Wilson administration before World War I, but the greatest strides in this direction were taken during the Franklin Roosevelt administration as part of the New Deal measures to combat the Great Depression in the 1930s. The movement slackened somewhat but did not stop in the Truman and Eisenhower administrations.

Many proponents of the new nationalizing measures have praised them as steps toward the creation of a "public service state"; they hold that all levels and units of government in a democracy, and not just the local ones, have a duty to provide public services to advance the general welfare. The opponents of this idea believe that what they call the "welfare state" or "paternalism" poses an insidious threat to a free people, that "centralization of government" means "socialism" is just around the corner. A great many sincere persons are still worried about this danger, but a clear majority of the people and both major political parties seem to have accepted in practice national leadership and national standards in the construction of main highways, the administration of social security, public airport and airways development, agricultural stabilization, provisions for employment security, and the protection of the basic rights of labor. Along with this they have approved the idea of using the fiscal powers of government to stabilize the economic system, not just to support a minimum list of traditionally recognized governmental functions.

This great expansion of the role of the national government obviously requires that more money be put at the disposal of the public treasury and that there be fiscal controls to prevent runaway inflation. Much of the machinery for these purposes was made available in the first four years of the Wilson administration. In 1913 the Sixteenth or Income Tax Amendment became a part of the Constitution and made legally possible a nationwide progressive tax on personal incomes to supplement the corporate income tax which had already obtained congressional and judicial approval. Congress proceeded at once to employ the new taxing power, and soon the combined corporate and personal income taxes became the main support of the national treasury, in peace as well as in war. Indeed the revenue-producing powers of the income tax proved to be far beyond what had been expected. New expenditures became possible, including substantial grants to the states for specific purposes. The previous revenue system, based upon import duties and selective excises like those on tobacco and liquor, had not easily permitted any such large expenditures. The opponents of the "welfare state," therefore, consider the national income tax to be so important a support for federal expenditures, including grants-in-aid, that many of them make the outright repeal of the income tax a first objective, while others strive for a new constitutional amendment to limit the tax to not over 25 per cent of any income.

To watch over the national economy in order to provide a stable and adequate currency, and to help prevent the extremes of both inflation and deflation, Congress has established several important agencies. One is the Federal Reserve System of national banking, headed by a Board of Governors with broad powers of control over the currency and over credit conditions. This system was established in 1913; thirty-three years later Congress passed the Employment Act of 1946 which makes it an obligation of the national government to maintain employment, production, and purchasing power at high and stable levels. To advise the President on what to do under this act Congress created a Council of Economic Advisers, a body to study trends in the national economy and suggests ways and means for preventing both inflation and deflation.

The Employment Act of 1946 clearly set the national government on a new course of policy, one that in effect gives that government a residual or "backstopping" responsibility for the welfare of the nation's economy. When unemployment increases beyond an agreed point the national government is to step in with increased expenditures, tax reductions, and other suitable measures to restore a high level of employment and income.

The effect of this policy on intergovernmental relations is hard to exaggerate. In earlier recessions and depressions the national government practically stood aside and followed a "hands off" policy. This left it to state and local governments and to private business, families, churches, and other voluntary groups, and to individuals, to initiate and carry out remedial measures. State governments usually did very little, and local governments were limited to providing poor relief and such local public works as they could afford. The philosophy of this policy was, as Grover Cleveland is reported to have said, that it is the duty of the people to support the government and not that of the government to support the people.

Now the philosophy has greatly changed. A recession brings immediate demands from many organizations, including state and local governments, for remedial action from Washington. Even without waiting for such demands the authorities there are already considering what needs to be done and what they can do to meet the new situation without encouraging inflation. There is no longer any question about the national government's power and duty to act, but only about the appropriate means and amounts and the proper timing of the actions to be taken.

Imbued in general with similar public service motives, but feeling themselves to be, and actually being, more limited in their fiscal powers, since only the national government has control over currency and credit, inflation and deflation, and only it has powers of borrowing and of raising revenues that are practically unlimited, state governments have little choice but to call upon the national government for aid in emergencies; and what they have to do in dire emergencies the state and local officials become accustomed to doing in less critical situations. In varying degrees, and with some changes of views under different administrations, all states now expect the national government to do what is necessary to maintain high levels of employment. It is perfectly clear that if this is not done, the states in which serious unemployment develops are going to face increased expenditures for relief and reduced revenues for all state purposes.

The relations of the national and state governments are, therefore, greatly affected not only by the economic cycle but also by the new attitudes toward national responsibility that have developed and spread in recent decades. More and more the national government takes the lead and provides in large part the funds and the plans for meeting every nationwide emergency. Even in fairly localized disasters it is the national authorities that are expected to shoulder much of the burden.

The substantial reversal in American policy that is involved in the public acceptance of a positive role for government in the promotion of the people's economic welfare is not the only important change in national policy that has taken place in the present century. The full recognition and protection by national authority of the rights of labor to organize and to bargain collectively, and the enactment of an extensive code of national laws to regulate all important sectors of the fields of commerce and finance, are important examples. In the conservation of resources the old policy of rapid disposal of public lands has given way to a national program of reacquiring large areas of land and keeping them under control for a variety of public uses. The old open-door policy in immigration has given way to a rather strict quota system, but on the other hand the old policy of high protective tariffs has been superseded by a policy of much lower tariffs and reciprocal trade agreements. In colonial affairs the granting of Philippine independence gave notice that the temporary expedient of controlling distant peoples that followed the Spanish-American War had been abandoned in favor of a policy that encouraged the establishment of self-governing republics. In foreign policy the shift has been away from a confused sort of isolationism that was exemplified by the United States Senate's rejection of the League of Nations to full participation in foreign affairs not only through the United Nations but also through regional alliances like NATO and SEATO and the Organization of American States. In addition, since World War II there have been a series of national programs of substantial aid for the defense and economic development of free peoples throughout the world. These programs have greatly increased the financial problems of the nation.

It was in such a period of changing public policies that our studies of intergovernmental relations took place. The nation's leaders were rethinking many of its old policies and experimenting with new ones.

On several issues, however, there appeared a strengthening and in part a revival of old views. The developments that came in the wake of the Bolshevik Revolution in Russia involved the setting up of Communist dictatorships not only in that country but in a ring of surrounding satellites that were brought to heel by internal subversion and strong pressure from Russia. With the struggle of the Russian people to overcome their poverty many Americans had great sympathy; and the successive five-year plans of the U.S.S.R. seemed to offer a real hope of better times for a large section of mankind. But the ruthless hands of the dictators showed themselves in the "liquidation" of all internal opposition, the confiscation of private property, the repression of religion and the suppression of freedom in the Baltic states and other neighbors of the U.S.S.R. What emerged soon looked to most Americans like a new Russian imperialism masked behind the pretense of "building socialism" and establishing peace. The new regime seemed far more interested in building a powerful army and in suppressing the major human freedoms of speech, press, religion, and political opposition than in human welfare.

This example of a "dictatorship of the proletariat" convinced most of the nation's leaders in industry, labor, agriculture, education, and politics that Americans should make their own policies in their own ways, without any help from socialists or communists and their theories. In particular many stressed the great importance of maintaining the "free enterprise system" based on the right of private property that had been at the root of practically all American industrial progress and the improvement of living standards. Others emphasized the great importance of protecting civil liberties, including especially the freedoms of thought, expression, and religious belief, as the indispensable conditions of the "democratic way of life" and the insurance of the dignity of the individual.

In general the basic system and philosophy of American government have not been subject to radical change. A fairly common belief in the political equality of men, and an almost exuberant assertion of the right of the voters to elect their own officers, national, state, and local, and of the capacity of the common man to serve well in public positions, have characterized American politics for over a century. There have been some doubts and dissents, of course, but faith in "the American way" remains strong.

Intergovernmental relations under such conditions are not treated as technical problems, to be "solved" only by experts, but as practical human problems to be met by the people and their elected representatives and officials through a process of continuous discussion, compromise, and adjustment. Americans early learned that some of the main adjustments between the rival claims of governments can be achieved through financial arrangements, by grants-in-aid, tax sharing, intergovernmental loans, and similar devices. The federal land grant to the states was one of the earliest and most potent of such arrangements.

In this general approach to governmental problems the major political parties have served an interesting but hardly a dominant role. Both major parties have changed their actual positions from time to time, according to circumstances, on the issue of national power and responsibility versus states' rights; but both continue to use similar phrases in their platforms on the importance of preserving the powers of the states. These platform expressions seem to have little relevance to the concrete problems that arise, however. Whether Republican or Democrat, the party in power nationally tends to act nationally. Rival claims of constitutional power are generally relegated to a minor position when practical negotiations to adjust national and state relations are in progress.

Aside from the division of powers between the national government and the states, which is one of the main themes of the study of American intergovernmental relations, the United States system of government is characterized by the so-called separation of powers of the legislative, executive, and judicial branches at both the national and state levels. This means, of course, that the executive is not directly responsible to the legislative branch, that he is not able to speak for it or to say what it will do, and that the legislature has a power to act somewhat independently of the chief executive and even to pass laws over his veto. This it sometimes does, and especially so when he and the legislative majority are of different political parties. Indeed the governor's position in a number of states is such that he does not even control all the administrative departments of his state, some of which have important relations directly with the national government.

This splitting-up of the political authority of the states and of the national government has the effect that no one in the national government (not even the President) can promise the states what the national government will do for them if new legislation or appropriations are required; and no one in any state government can commit the state in advance to any agreement with the national government. The situation is considerably different in the federal systems of Australia and Canada, where both the central and the state governments have parliamentary or cabinet systems. There the prime ministers of the central and state governments can speak for their respective governments with reasonable assurance that the agreements they make will be carried out.

In the United States the national authorities can and to some extent do by-pass the chief executives of the states and negotiate directly with the agencies that correspond to their own (like highway departments) in the states. This is so because the state legislatures have wanted it to be so. They have not been noted for wanting to aggrandize the governor by having everything clear through his office. The cabinets and prime ministers of the Australian and Canadian states or provinces have put up a more effective resistance to the federal authorities than have the governments of the American states. There appear to be a number of reasons for this, but one certainly is the fact that the authority of each American state is split up and not united.

The dealings between national and state authorities in the United States, then, have developed more and more along functional lines, in such separate fields as highways, public health, social welfare, agricultural extension work, and employment security, to give some important examples. These points of contact have been increased and strengthened by the development and close collaboration of appropriate organizations of national and state officials in the corresponding functional fields.

It is true that the state governors have their own national organization, the Governors' Conference, whose annual meetings receive considerable publicity and toward which the Presidents regularly express cordial good feelings. But it would be hard to name any major issue on which the governors have materially influenced the general trends in intergovernmental relations. Even less influence has been exercised, apparently, by the associations of state attorneys general, secretaries of state, and other state constitutional officers. It is in the functional fields, where large amounts of money and specific important public services are involved, that the national associations of state officials are influential; but such associations seem to speak more for the functional or service interests and less for the corporate interests of the states as governmental units.

Thus the changed and changing conditions in recent decades in the United States seem to lead to an ever-increasing importance for Congress and the national administration in the meeting of state and local problems on a nationwide scale.

CHAPTER 3

The Constitutional System of National-State Relations

Among the conditions that help to determine intergovernmental relations in practice surely one of the more important, by general agreement, is the framework of principles and rules of constitutional law within which the national, state, and local governments are presumed to, and normally do, operate and contrary to which they may not legally act. Included in this category of "legal" rules are not only the words of the written constitutions, national and state, and particularly those of the national Constitution, but also the decisions on constitutional questions of the highest courts. These rules are called legal because they are recognized as law, and "supreme law," following the words of the supremacy clause of the United States Constitution, and are in principle enforceable by the executive with the aid of the judicial process. The merely "customary" rules of government, on the other hand, such as the practices of the leading political parties, while they may be highly important in the conduct of government and in intergovernmental relations, do not normally have such legal sanction. They will not be dealt with here.

In contributing this chapter to our studies of intergovernmental relations I have tried to do at least three things, all of which are, I think, important to our studies.

First, I wished to show how great are the changes that have come about in the federal constitutional rules governing the relations between the national government and the states, and thereby to get the reader to see that if such changes have been brought about in the past, more constitutional changes may be possible, and indeed should be expected, in the future. The doors to constitutional change have not been closed. The federal system is not cast in a rigid mold for all time.

Second, I aimed to present in brief outline the major principles of national-state relations under the Constitution as they crystallized in the ten years just before our studies began and in the years of our studies. The constitutional law of this period of approximately twenty years (1937-58) stands in sharp contrast to the law of the preceding years. The increasing liberality of the rules governing both national and state action in this period made room for an astounding expansion of governmental action at both the national and the state levels, with a resulting great increase in intergovernmental contacts and cooperation—for, after all, cooperation is constitutionally possible only when both parties to the cooperation are empowered to act.

Third, I had also the purpose of showing how, with the great changes in the views of the Supreme Court justices on both national and state powers, and the subsequent great increases of governmental action and intergovernmental cooperation, the constitutional issues have changed. At one time the discussion of the relations between the national and state governments was largely in terms of their respective constitutional powers to do this and to do that, and the limits imposed by the Constitution upon the actions of both with respect to each other. This subject has not disappeared from controversy, and it was still controversial and of considerable importance while our studies were being made; but it is no longer a major topic for discussion in national-state relations except where private rights and civil liberties are affected, e.g., in school segregation. Instead the issues between the national government and the states are today largely those of public policy: What is the best course for the national government to pursue with respect to the states, and vice versa? What should each one do separately, what should they do cooperatively, and how should their cooperative activities be organized and financed? These issues of policy also raise interesting questions about what each level of government, national, state, and local, is best qualified to do, and the answers to such questions carry the study of intergovernmental relations beyond the field of constitutional powers into public finance, administrative organization, and procedure, official attitudes and behavior, and popular political reactions. A wide range of new research is thus opened up, into which we in our studies made only preliminary and exploratory advances.

The constitutional questions that affected intergovernmental relations during the period of our studies, some of which are not fully settled, can mostly be gathered under one broad heading, "the division of governmental powers." Does the national government have the power to perform a certain function or do the states have it or both? And if both may legally act in a certain field, which has priority or supremacy? And what happens when both act on the same matter? The specific applications of these questions arise concerning a broad range of governmental powers, such as taxation, the expenditures of funds, grants-in-aid, regulations of commerce and industry, banking and insurance, agriculture, labor relations, general law enforcement, the protection of civil liberties, and the provision and control of highways, education, health, welfare, and other services. In general the right of either the national government or the states to "interfere" with the operation of the other level in anything it undertakes to do may be a subject for judicial decision. There are, of course, certain constitutional questions also in interstate relations, but these are relatively minor.

As I have indicated in Chapter 1, I do not think there is any one constitutional principle of the relations between the central government and the states that applies in all federal systems of government. The constitutional systems that prevail at any one time in Canada, Australia, the Federal Republic of Germany, and the United States, for example, are all unique, sui generis, even though they display certain general similarities. The reasons for these constitutional diversities need only be suggested to be understood. Each federal-type constitution was drawn up at a different time from every other one, under different circumstances, by different leaders, under the influence of different ideas, to serve the special as well as the general needs of a different people. But this is not all. Each one has continued to change and to be developed over the years to meet the diverse alterations in the needs, conditions, and prevalent ideas of the country concerned. This process of continuous modification and development goes on in every country separately. Thus the legal rules of the Constitution of the United States are not what they were when Minnesota entered the Union a hundred years ago, or even what they were twenty or ten years ago. That is a major reason why it is necessary to discuss the constitutional rules and principles of the American federal system in their historical development. The constitutional relations of the nation and the states are not fixed but ever changing.

To get an exact photographic picture of the vast maze of intergovernmental rules and relations that we call the federal system of the United States is obviously impossible. The "system" is not a concrete or physical thing on which one can lay one's hands, but is essentially a concept of the mind. As such it is not a matter of record, and neither is it a concept on which all men will agree. From the beginning of United States history under the Constitution there have been sharp disagreements among men not only as to details but even as to the fundamentals of the system—for example, on whether the Constitution emanates from the whole people as the political "sovereign" of the nation, or was established by separate corporate entities called states by a sort of compact among themselves; and whether the Constitution does or does not recognize the "sovereignty" of the several states and leave them free to "interpose" their "sovereignty" whenever they do not accept Supreme Court decisions or congressional legislation. In the formation of individual views much will depend on whether a person has made a thorough and comprehensive study or only a partial one, on where and when he made it and when his studies stopped, on how willing he is to accept the decisions of the Supreme Court as binding law, and on other considerations. There are many questions about the Constitution that have not yet been decided. Even the justices of the Supreme Court are seldom in perfect agreement on the implications to be drawn from words in the Constitution or from earlier decisions of the Court. In a democracy with a written Constitution like the United States, where every man is in a sense his own constitutional lawyer, a new decision by the Supreme Court on a constitutional issue is not so likely to close debate as to start it off in new directions. Men will even question, as they did with the Dred Scott case, the NRA and Steel Seizure cases, the public school-church relations cases, and most recently the school desegregation cases, whether the Supreme Court decision itself is constitutional.

In the light of the foregoing discussion it will be understood that when I attempt, in the following pages, to outline the constitutional principles of the American federal system as they were in the period of our studies and earlier I must be understood as giving my own interpretation even when I quote Supreme Court decisions or other official pronouncements; like anyone else, I could be wrong!

The Constitution as drafted in 1787 conferred upon the national authorities almost complete and unlimited powers in foreign affairs and defense, and in addition granted to Congress very broad powers in taxation, borrowing, the regulation of foreign and interstate commerce, monetary matters, bankruptcies, the conduct of the post office, the disposition of public lands, Indian affairs, the granting of patents, and a number of other fields. In addition the Constitution asserts that "This Constitution and the laws of the United States which shall be made in pursuance thereof; and all treaties made, or which shall be made, under the authority of the United States, shall be the supreme law of the land; and the judges in every state shall be bound thereby, any thing in the Constitution or laws of any state to the contrary notwithstanding" (Article VI, paragraph 2).

In addition, the judicial power of the United States was extended to all cases, in law and equity, "arising under this Constitution, the laws of the United States and treaties made, or which shall be made, under their authority" (Article III, section 2). As Congress proceeded to enact laws to carry out the powers and discharge the responsibilities imposed upon the national government by the Constitution, cases began to reach the Supreme Court to test whether Congress had the powers it was claiming to exercise. Similar cases arose to test whether certain powers being exercised by the states were indeed among the powers reserved to them by the Tenth Amendment to the Constitution, adopted in 1791. In several leading cases both national and state legislation was involved.

In its first great era of activity the Supreme Court, under Chief Justice John Marshall (1801-35), took a strongly nationalist position. It upheld the national commerce power against state attempts to interfere with it; asserted the freedom of federal "instrumentalities" like the Bank of the United States from state interference through taxation; insisted upon the right of the Supreme Court to review and if necessary to overrule state court decisions touching upon "federal questions" and state legislation contrary to the Constitution; upheld a broad national power in treaty-making and in control of the militia; asserted the power of Congress to legislate for the states as well as for individuals; and in general gave a liberal interpretation to the authority of the nation under the doctrine of "implied powers" and to the supremacy of the national government over the states. It must be noted, however, that during the same three decades Presidents like Jefferson and Madison were questioning or denying, in one way or another, the power of Congress to engage in such internal improvements as highways on the grounds that such functions were reserved to the states;

and the famous John C. Calhoun later espoused a rigid state sovereignty theory of the union. (In this period the first white settlers were appearing in "the Minnesota country.")

Chief Justice Roger B. Taney (1836-64) served during the period when Minnesota passed through the stage of being a territory (1849-58) and became a state in the Union. The Taney Court did not directly reverse any of the Marshall Court's decisions on the powers of the national government or on national-state relations, but it took a turn toward emphasizing states' rights and the interstate compact theory of the origin of the Constitution. Marshall had reasserted in 1833 what he had already made very explicit in a famous decision in 1819, that "The Constitution was ordained and established by the people of the United States for themselves . . ." In both decisions the Supreme Court was unanimous. Thus the Constitution and the national government were not established by or subordinate to the states as such. Marshall went on to say that "the great revolution which established the Constitution of the United States was not effected without great opposition." This theory of the national, popular, and revolutionary origin of the Constitution receded into the background and was little heard of in the period of the Taney Court. Instead the Court took to speaking of the Constitution as a "compact" between "sovereign states," with the result that a provision of the Constitution (Article IV, section 2, paragraph 2) requiring the return by one state to another of a fugitive from justice was held not to justify interpreting an act of Congress of 1793 as making it the legal duty of a state executive to return the person accused to the other state. The moral duty of the governor to make the return depended on "the compact entered into with the other states when it adopted the Constitution of the United States and became a member of the Union." If the governor of a state should refuse to perform his moral duty "there is no power delegated to the General Government, either through the Judicial Department or any other department, to use any coercive means to compel him." This decision, written by Taney, came just on the eve of the Civil War when President Lincoln was acting on the theory of the Marshall Court that the Constitution is not a mere compact between the states but a national act of the whole people of the United States, and that there is power in the national government to coerce states to remain in the Union, and to obey its laws. If whole states may be coerced by force of arms, as they were, then it seems to follow that state officials may also be coerced by national authority, and by actions short of war, to perform their duties under the Constitution. This has in fact become the law and the practice.

The North's victory in the Civil War (in which Minnesota played an important part) was followed by the adoption of three constitutional amendments, the Thirteenth, Fourteenth, and Fifteenth, which bound the states even more firmly into the Union, and imposed new restrictions upon them. Of these restrictions I will mention only that the Thirteenth and Fifteenth bound the states unequivocally in the matters of abolishing slavery and ensuring equal suffrage for Negroes, and that by the Fourteenth Amendment "No State shall make or enforce any law which shall abridge the privileges or immunities of citizens of the United States; nor shall any State deprive any person of life, liberty, or property, without due process of law; nor deny to any person within its jurisdiction the equal protection of the laws." These provisions have been the basis for numerous federal court decisions coercing state officials negatively by forbidding them to violate the rights of citizens and other persons, and even positively by requiring them to accord equal protection of the laws to all persons within their jurisdictions.

Notwithstanding the momentous constitutional decisions made during and just after the Civil War with respect to the relations and powers of the national and state governments, the Supreme Court justices continued for some time to use language reminiscent of that of Taney, Jefferson, and even Calhoun to describe the relationships between the national and state governments. The majority of the justices were unwilling to give full and literal effect to the Civil War amendments—this while Minnesota was just getting into its stride as a state in the Union. They did not, however, during or after the war, deprive the nation of the necessary powers to wage the war successfully or to reconstruct the Union after it had ended. The essential military powers inherent in the financial and war powers of Congress, including the power to levy a wartime income tax, were upheld. Thus the national powers expanded during wartime.

When the work of the Supreme Court is looked at for the entire seventy years from the end of the Civil War in 1865 to the middle of the Great Depression in 1935 (covering more than two thirds of the history of Minnesota as a state) there emerges a sense of confusion as to just what ideas of national powers the Supreme Court held. There were numerous crosscurrents of influence playing upon the Court, and there was no strong, clear line of direction in what it did. Perhaps the simplest way to put it is to say that the Court was largely dominated by the idea that has come to be called "dual federalism." In essence this is the notion that the powers granted by the Constitution to the national government are limited by the powers reserved to the states by the Tenth Amendment. That provision (dating from 1791) provides that "The powers not delegated to the United States by the Constitution, nor prohibited by it to the States, are reserved to the States respectively, or to the people."

In effect "dual federalism" is a "Yes, but" doctrine. Yes, Congress has the power to regulate commerce among the states, for example, but it cannot do so in such a way as to regulate child labor in making goods for interstate commerce, or so as to regulate manufacture or agriculture as such, because these things are not themselves commerce, and the regulation of such matters is reserved to the states. Thus the reserved powers of the states were in effect placed upon the same level as, if not above, those granted to the United States, and they were interpreted as if they stood as a legal wall to hem in the national government. This notion was contrary to the expressed views of James Madison, the principal author of the Constitution, and to those of Chief Justice Marshall, the most authoritative and influential early expounder of the Constitution. These men agreed that the existence of powers in the states was no bar to the exercise by Congress of the powers granted to it, and that when each acted within its powers, national laws prevailed over state acts.

In the years following the Civil War, while the seceding states were being restored to full participation in the federal system, the Supreme Court said in Texas v. White (1869) that "The Constitution, in all its provisions, looks to an indestructible union, composed of indestructible States." The full and exact meaning of this statement will probably never be made entirely clear. When the justices tried to describe the nature of this union and of the federal system they at times used confusing language. Thus in a dictum in a decision in 1872 the Supreme Court said: "There are within the territorial limits of each State two governments, restricted in their spheres of action, but independent of each other, and supreme within their respective spheres. . . . Neither government can intrude within the jurisdiction of the other, or authorize any interference . . . by its judicial officers with the action of the other. The two governments in each State stand in the same independent relation to each other, except in one particular, that they would if their authority embraced distinct territories. That particular consists in the supremacy of the authority of the United States when any conflict arises between the two governments."

This interpretation of the federal system was written after the three Civil War amendments had been placed in the Constitution. All three contained important restrictions upon state action, and each one conferred on Congress the power to enforce its provisions by appropriate legislation. How in the light of those amendments and even of earlier provisions of the Constitution and various Supreme Court decisions the

Court could speak of the state governments as "independent" of the national government, assert that the national government had no power to "authorize any interference . . . by its judicial officers" with those of states embracing distinct territories, like, say, France and Spain, raises problems in the meanings of words that I do not wish, or feel competent, to discuss. It is fairly clear, however, that the passage quoted, from Tarble's case, is compatible with the "dual federalism" doctrine, and that this doctrine had general acceptance in this era. It was a time of political relaxation, when both national and state governments were comparatively inactive in domestic matters, and the United States was also pursuing a policy of relative isolation from international affairs. There was no sense of urgency. In short there was so little need for strong and united national action in either internal or external affairs that a certain weakness in the position of the central government and a high degree of "independence" in the states were not generally considered to be dangerous.

Throughout the period under consideration, from 1865 to 1935, the Supreme Court justices continued to reiterate that the national government was "a government of enumerated powers." The Court did not deny that Congress had the implied power to select and establish the means necessary to implement the enumerated powers, but it used the doctrine of enumeration on several occasions to veto what it conceived to be attempts by Congress to extend its legislative powers over non-enumerated subjects. In support of this general position it frequently referred to the Tenth Amendment as a clincher for its reasoning. Thus in a famous case in 1907 wherein the national government tried to intervene in a suit between states over rights to the waters of an interstate navigable stream, in order to control the use of the water for irrigation, the Court said it found no power stated in the Constitution that authorized Congress to do anything about the reclamation of arid lands. Under the Court's doctrine of enumerated powers, therefore, Congress had no such power. "This natural construction of the original body of the Constitution," said the Court, "is made absolutely certain by the tenth amendment. This amendment, which was seemingly adopted with prescience of just such [a] contention as the present, disclosed the widespread fear that the national government might, under the pressure of a supposed general welfare, attempt to exercise powers which had not been granted. With equal determination the framers intended that no such assumption should ever find justification in the organic act, and that if, in the future, further powers seemed necessary, they should be granted by the people in the manner they had provided for amending that act. It reads: 'The powers not delegated to the United States by the Constitution, nor prohibited by it to the states, are reserved to the states respectively, or to the people.'"

The decision in the Kansas v. Colorado case was delivered during the second term of President Theodore Roosevelt, a chief executive who strongly urged that the Court and the public take a larger view of the powers of the national government in order to permit it to meet national needs that the states were unable or unwilling to satisfy. He spoke for the New Nationalism and was especially critical of the "no man's land" that had grown up between the states and the national government as a result of Supreme Court decisions like the one just quoted. This was an ill-defined twilight zone or no man's land in the regulation of business and the provision of public services concerning which Supreme Court decisions denied the power of the national government to act, and in which the states were also unable to act either separately or collectively. It was an area in which large corporations in particular were practically immune from any governmental control.

In the case of Kansas v. Colorado, the Attorney General under President Roosevelt argued, in effect, that there should be no such no man's land, no "zone of anarchy." All legislative power should belong either to the states or to the national government; the states should be held to strictly internal affairs within their own territories, while the national government should exercise all powers that required national action. The answer to this Rooseveltian theory of nationalism the Court found in the Tenth

Amendment. Said the Court through Justice Brewer: "The argument of counsel ignores the principal factor in this article, to wit, 'the people.' Its principal purpose was not the distribution of power between the United States and the states, but a reservation to the people of all powers not granted. The preamble of the Constitution declares who framed it,—'We, the people of the United States,' not the people of one state, but the people of all the states; and article 10 [sic] reserves to the people of all the states the powers not delegated to the United States. The powers affecting the internal affairs of the states not granted to the United States by the Constitution, nor prohibited by it to the states, are reserved to the states respectively, and all powers of a national character which are not delegated to the national government by the Constitution are reserved to the people of the United States."

This decision (and there was more of it) has certain peculiarities, yet it undoubtedly expressed fairly well the doctrines prevailing generally among lawyers and publicists of the time as to the respective powers of the national and state governments, and as to the restrictions placed upon both. It left the no man's land untouched and in fact justified its existence. It said in effect to President Theodore Roosevelt and all other citizens: If you wish to overcome the Court's doctrines on the division and extent of governmental powers in the United States, you must get an amendment to the Constitution. This was the feeling that prevailed for another generation. That it had its effects on intergovernmental relations, and especially on those between the national government and the states, can hardly be doubted although those effects cannot be easily described and certainly cannot be exactly measured.

The decisions themselves, like that in Kansas v. Colorado and the later two that invalidated the efforts of Congress to suppress child labor by legislation under its commerce power and its taxing power, obviously had some effect in discouraging other efforts in Congress to extend the scope of national regulations over industry, labor, and agriculture. Thus the Court's decisions and general attitude tended to deter the proponents of new measures, to keep legislation by Congress within the old and rather narrow channels, and to cause the increasing accumulation of unmet demands for congressional legislation.

One major form of legislation affecting the relations of the national and state governments more or less escaped judicial scrutiny, however, and examples multiplied. I refer to laws that provided federal grants-in-aid to the states for a variety of public purposes. Federal land grants to the states for public schools and internal improvements were early recognized as a temporary and generally desirable method of aiding the states. The Constitution expressly grants to Congress the power to dispose of national property, and the power to grant lands to the states on such conditions as the states will accept has never been denied by the Supreme Court. A corresponding power in the states to accept the conditions in federal land grants is also fully approved. There was, however, considerable opposition from the early days of the Constitution down to the Civil War and later to national grants of money to the states for state purposes. In offering such grants, the argument ran, the national government was in effect trying to undermine the sovereignty of the states, while any states foolish enough to accept the grants would be willing participants in the undermining of their own authority. Leaders of the prewar Democratic party in particular took a strong stand in opposition to such grants—although the same leaders took a wholly different position with reference to national grants of money to the territories to get them started toward statehood.

During the administration of President Lincoln and under the auspices of the Republican party then and later this attitude of opposition to grants-in-aid underwent a great change. The Morrill Act of 1862 made a grant of federal public lands or its equivalent in land scrip to every state in proportion to its representation in Congress to be used to establish a college to teach agriculture and mechanic arts along with military tactics. Twenty-five years later, in 1887, Congress authorized the first annual cash grants to the states—these to be for the support of agricultural experiment stations in all states. In 1890 Congress authorized annual cash grants to the states to pay for instruction in the land-grant colleges. From then on came other such grants, first one by one and in small amounts and later in larger numbers and amounts. Just before World War I federal grants were established for agricultural extension work, forest protection, and statewide highways, and later came many others, including the great public assistance programs of the 1930s. Federal grants-in-aid to the states and even to local governments, requiring state matching of funds in some proportion and accompanied by federal standards and audits, had thus become fully established. These grants were obviously a method of bringing federal support and influence to bear on the states so as to induce them to inaugurate and maintain at minimum standards certain state and local functions that Congress considered to be of national importance.

This new type of measure did not go wholly unchallenged in the courts, however. There were, for example, two suits in the 1920s, one by a taxpayer and one by a state, against a federal matching grant to the states for maternal and child welfare. But the plaintiffs were told in effect that, as against the congressional appropriation for this purpose, they had no case that the Court could adjudicate and hence no standing to raise their questions. Neither could show a sufficiently specific or direct interest in the appropriation to warrant their bringing the suits. Thus the Court did not have to consider their substantive arguments that Congress had exceeded its powers, that it had invaded the realm of state powers, and that it was taking money from taxpayers for unconstitutional purposes. This left unsettled the question of the constitutionality of federal grants-in-aid.

In 1933 when the new Democratic Congress, spurred by President Franklin D. Roosevelt, began to enact a considerable number of new laws to bring about a business recovery and the reform of the economic system, opponents of the new policies promptly brought suits to have the laws declared unconstitutional. When these suits reached the Supreme Court the sitting justices, mostly elderly men, met them with the currently accepted concepts restricting national action.

One important New Deal measure to fall before the Supreme Court in 1936 was the Agricultural Adjustment Act (AAA) of 1933. Under this measure Congress levied a tax on the processing of agricultural products and also provided for payments to farmers (presumably from the proceeds of the tax) to induce them to accept certain crop controls designed to prevent overproduction. The decision turned in large part on the doctrine of dual federalism and brought together in the context of national-state relations interesting questions about the powers of Congress to tax, to spend, and to regulate agricultural production by means of a scheme of expenditure.

The power of Congress to levy the tax on agricultural processing was not denied. Indeed the almost unlimited power of Congress to tax, except as restricted by express provisions of the Constitution, and by a vague implied prohibition against selecting out state and local governments for discriminatory and burdensome federal taxation, such as might tend to destroy their essential operations and hence their very existence, has for a long time been fully accepted. The Income Tax Amendment adopted in 1913 was needed primarily to overcome one of the few major Supreme Court decisions to put any serious limits on the taxing powers of the United States.

In the AAA case, however, the Supreme Court contrived to hold the processing tax unconstitutional by the following line of reasoning: The tax was but a part of a general plan whose purpose was not taxation for the general support of government but was instead the regulation and control of agricultural production, an invasion of the reserved rights of the states. Here the Court followed to some extent the general line of the second child labor decision in which it had invalidated an act of Congress that levied a special tax on the interstate shipment of goods made by child labor in an attempt to discourage the employment of children in manufacturing.

But the facts in the AAA case were distinctly different, since the processing tax was a general one, designed to put substantial amounts of money into the treasury, and the accompanying expenditure plan was not to penalize farmers who did not accept crop controls but to pay out money to reward those who did. However, this proposed expenditure of federal funds was attacked on the ground that it was not an expenditure for any function that was entrusted to Congress. The Constitution says nothing about Congress doing anything relating to agricultural production, in fact does not even mention agriculture. Congress may tax, and it may even spend for "the general welfare" of the United States; this much was conceded. The Constitution says expressly that Congress "shall have . . . power to lay and collect taxes, duties, imposts and excises, to pay the debts and provide for the common defence and general welfare of the United States . . ." (Article I, section 8, paragraph 1). But James Madison and other "strict constructionists" had contended that the general welfare for which Congress may spend federal funds includes only those functions like national defense and the regulation of foreign and interstate commerce which are explicitly entrusted to the national government by the Constitution. They held it would be an unconstitutional invasion of the proper functions of the states for Congress to try to define the general welfare and to spend for the general welfare in terms of the functions reserved to the states. An example of this distinction had appeared in the heated early controversy over the power of Congress to spend money for public roads within the states. Alexander Hamilton and his followers, on the other hand, held that it was for Congress itself to define the general welfare, and that it had power to spend for any welfare purpose whatsoever provided the welfare need was a geographically general one and not simply local.

The Supreme Court majority conceded in the AAA case that Hamilton's views as rephrased by Justice Joseph Story of the Marshall Court in his Commentaries on the Constitution was the correct one and that it had become accepted in practice and by the Supreme Court. This was an important admission for the Court to make in 1936, and it might well have led to the conclusion that the proposed expenditures under the AAA were constitutional. Such was not the outcome. The direct dealings of the national government with individual farmers in a plan to regulate agricultural production was too much for six of the justices to accept. Said this majority: "The act invades the reserved rights of the states. It is a statutory plan to regulate and control agricultural production, a matter beyond the powers delegated to the federal government. The tax, the appropriation of the funds raised, and the direction for their disbursement, are but parts of the plan. . . . They are but means to an unconstitutional end. . . . The Congress cannot invade state jurisdiction to compel individual action; no more can it purchase such action."

Here was, indeed, a reassertion of the doctrine of dual federalism, an insistence that the powers clearly and explicitly granted to Congress by the Constitution are limited by the powers vaguely and generally reserved to the states by the Tenth Amendment. In short the Tenth Amendment was made to prevail over not only the broad taxing and welfare spending powers stated in the first paragraph of Article I, section 8, but also over the national supremacy clause in Article VI and the blanket clause at the end of section 8 of Article I whereby Congress is given the power to make all laws necessary and proper to carry into execution the powers vested by the Constitution in the government of the United States.

This decision was in line with several decisions of the Court based on the commerce clause, in which the power of Congress to regulate commerce was held not to authorize the regulation of production for commerce, since the regulation of production is a power that belongs to the states. This, too, is but another form or application of the dual-federalism theory.

In some ways the confusing decision in the AAA case stands like an explorer at the topmost ridge of a great divide with one foot on the side up which he has just been climbing and one foot on the other side leading on to the new lands ahead. On the one side the decision rests on the old doctrine of dual federalism; on the other it finds footing on an unlimited power of Congress to spend for the general welfare. In a sense, too, the decision still holds to the idea that it is for the Court to decide for what general welfare purposes Congress may spend national funds. Like dual federalism, this doctrine was to be left behind in the forward journey in the years ahead.

The invalidation of the AAA and of NRA and other New Deal measures brought on a storm of demands for getting rid of the "nine old men" on the Supreme Court bench and for drastic reforms in the Court. Franklin Roosevelt, like the earlier Roosevelt, joined in the demand for court reform. During the heated controversy that followed the announcement of his plan for reform the Court itself began to see that the nation had entered upon a new stage of its development and to conform its decisions to the new demands. In a sense it was only going back to the liberal national ideas of Hamilton, Marshall, and Story concerning the powers of the national government, but in another sense it was going beyond them and developing a code of constitutional principles of its own.

Despite the early serious rebuffs from the Supreme Court, the Democratic Congress and the President, soon to be heartened by an overwhelming victory over the Republicans in the 1936 election, pressed forward with their program of legislative and administrative action to achieve economic recovery and reform. They enacted new statutes such as the National Labor Relations Act, the Fair Labor Standards Act (wage and hour act), the Social Security Act, a public housing act, and a new Municipal Bankruptcy Act to replace one declared invalid by the Court. Most of these acts brought the national government into new areas of national activity and some of them put it into fields in which at least some states already had legislation.

Litigation to test the new laws quickly arose, and thus, while the battle went furiously on in Congress and in the public press over President Roosevelt's plan to reorganize—or "pack" or "dominate"—the Supreme Court, the Court itself had several opportunities, which it promptly seized, to give up its old restrictive dual-federalism ideas and to accept a more liberal view of the powers of the national government. In a series of decisions beginning in the 1936 term, the Supreme Court found reasons to uphold one New Deal measure after another. At first the votes on the Court were fairly close, as only one or two justices changed over to a new position on the issues, but with the dropping out of one and then another of the older justices, and the appointment of more sympathetic new ones, the years brought larger and larger majorities of the Court to uphold the new legislation. No important New Deal legislation whatever was declared unconstitutional after 1936. In a number of decisions upholding new laws the justices specifically overturned previous decisions of the Court.

No attempt will be made here to review all the constitutional decisions of the decade 1937 to 1946, or even the major ones. Instead I will try to summarize in my own language with an occasional quotation what the new constitutional philosophy of the Supreme Court came to be.

The old mechanical idea that there are two wholly separate and exclusive "spheres" of power, one for the national government and the other for the states ("and never the twain shall meet," overlap, or intermingle) was presently discarded in favor of a more social and organic concept. Such is the interdependence and the commingling of all human activities, functions, and interests in any society that it is strange indeed that men should ever have thought it possible to parcel out powers and functions between two levels of government serving the same people without hampering the work of either level. The framers of the original Constitution evidently did not think in this way; the supremacy clause alone is sufficient evidence that they expected national and state laws to be in frequent contact and even collision. From 1937 on, therefore, the notion that because some public function or interest is presumably within the constitutional "sphere" or the "reserved powers" of the states it is more or less forbidden territory, into which the national government may not enter, was implicitly if not explicitly rejected by the Supreme Court, by other branches of the government, and by informed people generally. The adoption of the new view by the Supreme Court logically carried with it a rejection of the doctrine of dual federalism. The result was that in the leading constitutional decisions after 1936 the reserved powers of the states were not construed as limitations upon the powers granted to the United States government by the Constitution. This was probably the most significant and consequence-laden reversal of constitutional doctrine in the entire decade. Many strands soon fell into place to produce a new pattern in national-state relations.

In the leading decision upholding the national Fair Labor Standards Act one consequence was the demotion of the Tenth Amendment, which had provided the main support for the dual-federalism doctrine, to a position of unimportance. After upholding the constitutionality of regulation of the wages and hours of workers in a lumber mill engaged not directly in commerce but in the production of lumber for commerce, itself a major departure from earlier doctrines, the Court said: "Our conclusion is unaffected by the Tenth Amendment . . . The Amendment states but a truism that all is retained which has not been surrendered."

Now when cases are brought against acts of Congress on grounds that Congress has exceeded its powers and has passed an unconstitutional act, the Court no longer starts with a consideration of the existence of the states and of their possession of reserved powers that stand as supposed barriers to national action. Instead it starts where Marshall did, with a consideration of the words of the Constitution that grant powers to the national government. In so doing, also, the Court does not take a narrow and niggling view of the national powers, but a broad and generous one in conformity with the principle that Congress has not only the powers expressed in the Constitution but also implied and resultant powers. "Let the end be legitimate," as Marshall said, "let it be within the scope of the Constitution, and all means which are appropriate, which are plainly adapted to that end, which are not prohibited, but consist with the letter and spirit of the Constitution, are constitutional."

The reader will recall the view expressed by the Supreme Court in Kansas v. Colorado, that when an enumerated power sufficient to warrant national action cannot be found in the Constitution, the power must be denied to the national government until it becomes authorized by a new constitutional amendment. One surprising thing about "the constitutional revolution" that began late in 1936 was that it was achieved without the adoption of new amendments to authorize an extension of national legislation into new fields. It was found that all that was needed was for the Supreme Court justices to re-examine some of the Court's earlier doctrines and interpretations in the light of the needs of the times, and to see the written Constitution in this new light, or in the old-new light of the Marshall Court at the beginning of the nation's history. That view was, in general, that a constitution like that of the United States is not a mere code of laws, detailed, explicit, and confining. No, "we must never forget, that it is a constitution we are expounding" and that means "a constitution intended to endure for ages to come, and, consequently, to be adapted to the various crises of human affairs. To have prescribed the means by which government should, in all future times, execute its powers, would have been to change, entirely, the character of the instrument, and give it the properties of a legal code . . . To have declared that the best means shall not be used, but those alone without which the power given would be nugatory, would have been to deprive the legislature of the capacity to avail itself of experience, to exercise its reason, and to accommodate its legislation to circumstances."

If anyone wishes to argue that these quotations from John Marshall's great decision in McCulloch v. Maryland do not touch the point dealt with in Kansas v. Colorado, I would reply that technically this is true. Marshall seems to be dealing only with the means available to the national government, while Justice Brewer in Kansas v. Colorado seems to have been dealing with the ends or purposes for which the national government may act. In fact, however, this difference is far less important in my opinion than the complete difference in spirit and attitude between the two. The means-ends distinction is a somewhat unrealistic one. In human affairs, where year follows year and age succeeds age, the means of one time give rise to new ends, and old established ends call for new means. The great difference between Brewer and Marshall in these two decisions, over ninety years apart, was that Brewer wanted to tie the national government down to the powers expressly stated in the Constitution; he interpreted any deviation therefrom as an attempt to enlarge the ends or purposes for which the national government was created. On the other hand, Marshall, with his liberal views of the national government's powers, was willing to consider the creation of a national bank not as a new end or purpose but as a mere choice of means for carrying out its admittedly already extensive powers under the Constitution. The one breathed a spirit of fear, caution, restrictiveness, and negativeness respecting the national powers; the other a spirit of confidence, boldness, and liberality.

It was the liberal, bold, and positive attitude of Marshall that returned to dominate the new Court majority as it emerged in the 1936 term, and this spirit and this majority both grew stronger with each passing year. The majority soon found that it was not the written Constitution that stood in the way of national action in times of need. Instead, it was certain old decisions and ways of thinking on the part of the Supreme Court. The Court's own glosses on the Constitution in earlier years simply had to be removed and a fresh view had to be taken of the Constitution. An accumulation of doctrines and decisions from the days of Tauney to those of Brewer had to be overturned. As soon as this had been accomplished it became clear that the framers of the Constitution and the Supreme Court under Marshall had done very well by the national government. They had in fact authorized practically all the national actions that were needed, and no new amendments were required. As a result, various amendments that were proposed in the 1920s and in the depression of the 1930s to enlarge the powers of Congress to regulate commerce, and to authorize it to legislate on child labor, simply fell by the wayside as unnecessary baggage. The whole theory of dual federalism went the same way.

In 1936 the Court made a sharp distinction between the powers of the national government in external or foreign affairs and those in internal or domestic affairs. The Court's reasoning on external powers, which was based upon some earlier decisions, can be seen by piecing together a number of its statements on the subject, not exactly in the order used by the Court but in a fairly logical order, as follows:

> As a result of the separation from Great Britain by the colonies, acting as a unit, the powers of external sovereignty passed from the Crown [of Great Britain] not to the colonies severally, but to the colonies in their collective and corporate capacity as the United States of America. Even before the Declaration, the colonies were a unit in foreign affairs, acting through a common agency—namely, the Continental Congress, composed of delegates from the thirteen colonies. That agency exercised the powers of war and peace, raised an army, created a navy, and finally adopted the Declaration of Independence. . . . Sovereignty is never held in suspense. When, therefore, the external sovereignty of Great Britain in respect of the colonies ceased, it immediately passed to the Union. . . .

> It results that the investment of the federal government with the powers of external sovereignty did not depend upon the affirmative grants of the Constitution. The powers to declare and wage war, to conclude peace, to make treaties, to maintain diplomatic relations with other sovereignties, if they had never been mentioned in the Constitution, would have vested in the federal government as necessary concomitants of nationality. . . . As a member of the family of nations, the right and power of the United States in that field [foreign affairs] are equal to the right and power of the other members of the international family. Otherwise, the United States is not completely sovereign.

As to the distinction between the internal and external powers the Court said:

> The two classes of powers are different, both in respect of their origin and their nature. The broad statement that the federal government can exercise no powers except those specifically enumerated in the Constitution (see Kansas v. Colorado), and such implied powers as are necessary and proper to carry into effect the enumerated powers, is categorically true only in respect of our internal affairs. In that field, the primary purpose of the Constitution was to carve from the general mass of legislative powers then possessed by the states such portions as it was thought desirable to vest in the federal government, leaving those not included in the enumeration still in the states. . . . That this doctrine applies only to the powers which the states had is self-evident. And since the states severally never possessed international powers, such powers could not have been carved from the mass of state powers, but obviously were transmitted to the United States from some other source.

That source has already been noted above. One effect of this opinion was to make explicit what to many had been obvious before, that the doctrine of the national government's being limited to enumerated powers (Kansas v. Colorado) was applicable only to the internal powers of government. The scope of applicability of the Tenth Amendment, and that of the doctrine of dual federalism as long as it lasted, were both correspondingly reduced. In the entire field of external affairs the national government stood free of these restrictive theories, and was limited only by the express provisions of the Constitution itself, such as those assigning treaty-making to the President, subject to Senate consent, and express provisions for the protection of individual liberties. In short, as to external affairs one looks in the Constitution not for express grants and enumerations of power but only for express restrictions upon an otherwise unlimited power.

In addition the Supreme Court developed in the following years a doctrine already known to the justices, namely, that as a nation among nations the United States has "the power to make such international agreements as do not constitute treaties in the constitutional sense" in general accordance with international law and practice. This refers, of course, to the power of the President to make "executive agreements" with other countries, and, indeed, to have these enforced as laws. This power is not mentioned in the Constitution, but is something in addition to it. This power helps to round out the national powers in external affairs to substantially the same scope as the external powers of any other nation. Hence the fact that the national government has a power to make treaties as stated in the Constitution is no bar to its having powers to make other international agreements, and in other ways.

How these broad powers in external affairs affect national-state relations becomes fairly clear when it is remembered how close the relationship is between external and internal affairs. This is particularly noticeable in times of all-out wars, when the national government proceeds to regulate all production, transportation, and sale and distribution of goods, to take man and woman power almost without limit, and to raise money and take the lands and goods needed for war purposes in tremendous amounts, to the great embarrassment of state and local governments. The powers of the states to borrow and to acquire personnel, supplies, and equipment for their purposes are all subject to national restrictions in wartime.

The developments from 1936 on in Supreme Court decisions concerning internal affairs also tended to remove hampering restrictions on action by the national government. In the regulation of interstate commerce, for example, although a considerable liberalizing trend had been evident for some years, definite limitations had been imposed by Court decisions. It had been held, for example, that the "production" of goods such as sugar was not commerce, and hence was beyond the power of Congress to regulate, and that an act of Congress to penalize the shipment in interstate commerce of goods made by child labor was not a regulation of commerce but an unconstitutional attempt, under the guise of regulating commerce, to invade the states' power to regulate manufacturing. Both of these restrictions imposed by the Supreme Court on the power of Congress to regulate commerce were, in effect, only different applications of the dual-federalism theory. Both were overruled by the Supreme Court that staged the "revolution" in the years after 1936. That Court upheld the power of Congress when regulating commerce to control production, whether on the ground that it was "production for commerce" or on the ground that it "affected" commerce. Congress had itself provided the appropriate phrases for the new interpretation in its legislation to regulate unionization and collective bargaining, the enforcement of fair labor standards with respect to wages and hours in industry, the prohibition of child labor, and the provision of unemployment compensation in most major industries except agriculture. From 1937 on, all such national legislation was upheld, with the result that the national government took priority over the states in the regulation of industrial relations and wages and hours in the major fields of production. Even the acts passed by Congress after 1936 for "agricultural adjustment" and the restriction of agricultural production to "balance the market" received the approval of the Court as far as their constitutionality was concerned. The AAA decision of 1936 involving the tax on the processing of agricultural production was not specifically overruled, but its conclusion against the power of Congress in that situation was effectively sealed off and by-passed by later decisions.

Mention has now been made again of the taxing power of Congress, and this raises the question of its spending power since the two are tightly bound together by the words of the Constitution. In the AAA decision mentioned above, the tax on processing was declared invalid as a part of an invalid scheme to spend money in such a way as to establish national control of agricultural production to the detriment of state powers of control in that field. This strange conclusion was not repeated in later decisions. It went out with other parts of the dual-federalism doctrine.

In addition the Supreme Court announced important new doctrines concerning the national spending power in decisions that upheld the constitutionality of various parts of the famous Social Security Act (1935). For example, several suits were begun to have the system of unemployment compensation held unconstitutional. Under this system the states that consented to cooperate were expected to enact taxes on the payrolls of the employers covered by the law and to set up state agencies to administer the law and disburse money to unemployed workers when unemployment occurred. In the states that agreed to the plan the payment by employers of the state payroll tax would result in canceling 90 per cent of the corresponding national tax on payrolls, leaving only 10 per cent to go to the federal treasury. On the other hand, the whole of the national tax collected in nonparticipating states would go into the national treasury, but workers in such a noncooperating state would not have unemployment protection because of the lack of a state law. Of course no state would or did remain long outside of this system.

The entire tax collected by each participating state was to go into a special trust fund in the national treasury, to be paid back to the states as needed for payment to the unemployed in accordance with state laws and federal standards. The 10 per cent of the federal tax mentioned above was also to go into the federal treasury but for undefined purposes. However, the national government agreed to pay to each state annually a sum not over the receipts from this 10 per cent, as appropriated annually by Congress, for the administrative expenses of state unemployment compensation systems. Thus a branch of the state government would become dependent upon annual appropriations from the national government and Congress would determine each state's administrative needs under the program. This was a most unusual system of national-state cooperation, especially notable for the strength of the inducements to the states to participate and for the strictness of the federal controls on expenditures and standards. It was small wonder, therefore, that employers who had to pay the taxes attacked the whole system as an unconstitutional scheme for national invasion of the powers of the states. State laws consenting to the plan were characterized as unconstitutional surrenders of power brought about by coercion and duress.

The Supreme Court decisions in the two leading cases on the unemployment compensation laws in 1937 show an almost complete reversal of the attitude of the Court's majority since the AAA decision of 1936 in the face of a somewhat different set of facts. Four justices who were of the majority in the AAA case were now the dissenting minority. A shift of one vote on the Court had made a significant change.

It was with these decisions and a few related ones that the Supreme Court put behind it practically all ideas of trying to impose limits upon the spending power of the national government. In upholding the provisions for old-age benefits (now called Old Age and Survivors Insurance or simply "social security") administered directly by the national government, the Court justified the program under the power of Congress to tax and spend for "the general welfare." It said that "the line must still be drawn between one welfare and another, between particular and general" but that the decision on this point was not confided to the courts. "The discretion belongs to Congress, unless the choice is clearly wrong, a display of arbitrary powers, not an exercise of judgment."

In these decisions also the Court denied that the very strong inducements offered to the states under the Social Security Act amounted to coercion on them, and asserted the right of the states themselves to make agreements with the national government. The charge that the states were thereby abdicating their "sovereignty" was also denied by the Court, and the right of the states under the Constitution to enter into cooperative arrangements with the national government was upheld. "Nowhere in our scheme of government—in the limitations express or implied of our Federal Constitution—do we find she [the state] is prohibited from assenting to conditions that will assure a fair and just requital for benefits received."

When the Commission on Intergovernmental Relations studied national-state relations in 1953-55, the majority of the members accepted the new doctrines of the Supreme Court on the national spending power as consistent with the principles of the federal system and the Constitution, and as sound if not indeed unavoidable in the light of the many developments that had changed the United States from an early confederation of states into one nation—politically, economically, socially, and technologically. The majority could see no possibility of turning back the clock.

A robust minority of the commission's members, on the other hand, felt that the Supreme Court's recent decisions on the national spending power have dealt a serious blow to the position and importance of the states in the Union and that a continued expansion of national spending on functions within the reserved powers of the states can lead only to a further decline in the self-government of the states. There is no better way to show the thoughts and feelings of the minority in this matter than to quote from the dissenting opinions that they entered on the record and that were printed in the commission's report:

> Governor Peterson makes the following statement in which he is joined by Governors Battle, Jones, Shivers, and Thornton, Senator Schoeppel, Congressman Dolliver, and Mayor Henderson:
>
> "It is a matter of regret that the Supreme Court of the United States in sustaining legislation designed to alleviate the effects of the depression of the 1930's has weakened the constitutional concept that the National Government is one of delegated and enumerated powers and that 'the powers not delegated to the United States by the Constitution, nor prohibited by it to the States, are reserved to the States respectively, or to the people.'
>
> "The effect of these decisions (Helvering v. Davis, 301 U.S. 619, and others) has been to create a situation under which the Congress may by the expenditure of money enter virtually any sphere of government. There exists little restraint on Congress other than that which it determines to exercise over itself. These decisions have fundamentally altered the balance of power designed by the architects of the Constitution."
>
> Governor Driscoll makes the following statement in which he is joined by Governors Battle, Jones, Shivers, and Thornton and Mr. Burton:
>
> "Since 1920 a number of decisions of the Supreme Court have drifted in the direction of an increasing liberalization of the power of Congress to spend money and impose controls in fields theretofore reserved to the State and local governments.
>
> "We regret that in some of these decisions the Supreme Court failed to indicate any restrictions on the use of the Federal expenditure power in areas historically within the jurisdiction of the States. Thus the Supreme Court in this field has largely abandoned its role as arbiter of the respective constitutional rights and responsibilities of the State and National governments.
>
> "The result of these decisions is a fundamental change in the balance of power between the States and the National Government as devised by the architects of the Constitution.
>
> "Where there is an overriding national interest we have approved grants-in-aid that did not involve a basic impairment of the traditional powers and obligations of the States. We cannot approve, however, the present situation in which Congress has very nearly become the sole judge of the activities of State and local governments it may choose to enter.
>
> "While we are confident that Congress will exercise great restraint in the use of the power that has become available to it, we are mindful of the pressures that are inevitably brought to bear upon the National Government to expand its activities. We express the hope that the Supreme Court at the first opportunity will reconsider its position and decisions and clearly define constitutional restrictions on the use of the National expenditure power consonant with the principles of our federal system."

These statements in a government report from important public leaders are but a small part of the evidence that the "revolution" in the thinking of the Supreme Court has not gone unchallenged. The charge has been made that the Supreme Court is arrogating to itself legislative powers instead of waiting for constitutional amendments. Indeed such criticism has increased significantly in recent years, following the Court's decision in 1954 declaring segregation in the public schools to be unconstitutional, and even more in later years following decisions that restrict the powers of investigation of congressional committees and the powers of states to punish for sedition and subversive activities. The Supreme Court has been openly accused of rewriting the Constitution to suit itself and of having become "activist" in deciding questions of public policy that should be decided by the legislative branches of the state and national governments. As a result of this resurgence of feeling against the Court, committees of Congress are seriously considering measures to reduce the Court's appellate jurisdiction and to clip its authority in other ways.

But while letting down some Court-created bars to action by the national government the Supreme Court since 1936 has also been generous to the states and their claims. The old "twilight zone" or "no man's land" was a poorly defined area in which, according to the decision in Kansas v. Colorado, neither government was permitted to operate—the national government because it lacked a specific "enumerated power," the states because the subject was one of national and not state concern. This concept and the zone to which it relates have now in effect disappeared from the armory of judicial weapons against national and state legislation. The new theory views every potential field of public action as belonging to either the national or the state government, or to both. The bias, if any, is in favor of public action and not against it. This change of attitude by the Supreme Court from an earlier position that in general favored laissez faire to one of accepting public action as the normal method of meeting public needs may be the most important element in the general revision of the Court's position in the past two decades. In a sense it shows the Court in a mood to uphold the acts of Congress and also those of state legislatures. This seems to be quite the opposite of the "activism" with which the Court is being charged, but a distinction must be made that will help to clarify the record.

The legislative acts that the Supreme Court has shown itself increasingly willing to uphold are those in the fields of commerce, general business, industrial relations, wages and hours, taxation, spending, and the rendering of public services with public funds. Such legislation deals largely with the economic and material aspects of life and the social order. In these fields it will be noticed that almost no national legislation has been held unconstitutional since 1936. State legislation in this field has also been dealt with more liberally than in earlier years. The right of a state to have its own economic policy so long as its legislation does not trench upon a field already occupied by national legislation, or does not go contrary to a clear national policy, has been repeatedly asserted by the Court. In matters of taxation, too, the Court has been rather generous to the states, although not to the point of allowing direct state taxation of federal instrumentalities. Among the taxes upheld have been state income taxes on the salaries of federal officers and employees stationed in the states; state sales taxes on materials and equipment used by contractors doing work for the national government; and taxes on persons and personal property located within federal reservations. The theory back of this tax policy is that in a federal system both levels of government render valuable services to the people and to each other, and that each should have access to adequate sources of revenue. There should be no implied tax immunities except in cases where a state tax might result in a material interference with a federal function. The mere possibility of some increase in the cost to the federal government of carrying on its functions is not sufficient ground for invalidating a state tax provided the tax is not discriminatory against the national government, its employees, or its activities. Some shifting of burdens between the two levels of government through taxation "is but the normal incident of the organization within the same territory of two governments, each possessing the taxing power." Similarly, a nondiscriminatory federal tax which impinges upon states along with private parties engaged in a certain kind of business is not unconstitutional merely because states as well as individuals must pay the tax, although a federal tax on some type of activity that the states but no private parties engage in, such as the maintenance of courts, would probably be held unconstitutional.

So much for the general philosophy of the Supreme Court in the field of economic or material affairs. The situation is much different when we consider more personal rights such as freedom of speech, press, religion, and conscience; the separation of church and state; equal protection and treatment for all persons in the processes of law enforcement, and access to and use of public schools and other public facilities, without discrimination on the grounds of race, color, religion, or other such distinctions; and due process of law in the arrest, trial, and punishment of all persons accused of crimes. The Supreme Court has in the past generation paid more attention than ever before to these rights and has in consequence declared a number of state acts, legislative, executive, and judicial, and even some actions of the national government and its agencies to be unconstitutional, or, alternatively, it has so narrowed the scope of some of the supposed governmental powers in this field as in effect to enlarge considerably the rights of individuals against the governments. The 1954 decision outlawing racial segregation in the public schools is only one of the most striking and sweeping examples of what I have in mind. In the field of judicial due process in criminal cases the Court has in general enforced higher standards in the activities of courts and prosecutors of the federal government than of the states but the latter are also being compelled by Supreme Court decisions to improve their standards of criminal due process.

In almost every area of governmental action, therefore, the constitutional rules on what the states may do and on what the national government may do have undergone important if not revolutionary changes in the past three decades. Important old restrictions on both national and state activity in the economic field have been removed by the Supreme Court's reversing some of its earlier doctrines. At the same time restrictions of new types have been applied to personal and social rights. In general it appears that the old restrictions that have been removed from the activities of the national government are more numerous than the new ones that have recently been imposed. This is true to a great extent also with respect to the states—but precise statements and comparisons are impossible to formulate because the loosening of bonds has been primarily in one field and the imposing of new restrictions in another. In most areas of governmental activity the state and national governments are both more free to move ahead, because the old attachment to laissez faire and the old suspicions against governmental action are less than they were and are largely ineffective. What is more, the growing trend toward cooperative action between the states and national governments, though not originated by the Court, has received its approval, and the fears that marked relations between the two levels of government are certainly on the decline.

I have dealt at some length with these great shifts in constitutional doctrine and interpretation because I think they are of considerable importance for every phase of national-state relations. The written Constitution as interpreted by the great national departments of government, and especially by the Supreme Court, defines the channels within which governments may act. These channels have changed significantly in our time.

CHAPTER 4

The National Government in Minnesota

Thirteen former British colonies along the Atlantic seaboard, from New Hampshire to Georgia, acting in unison, designated themselves to be states and declared their independence from Great Britain in 1776. Soon after this they formed a "perpetual Union" under the Articles of Confederation. These thirteen became the "original states" under the Constitution of the United States which in 1788 superseded and replaced the Articles. Since most of the works on the Constitution start with these thirteen states and treat the federal system historically from this starting point, it is not surprising that the status of the original thirteen and the ideas expressed by their leaders color most of the published views on the nature of the Union from that time to the present.

It should be kept in mind, however, that thirty-seven of the present fifty states, nearly three fourths of the total, did not share the experiences of the original thirteen, that thirty-six cannot claim ever to have been separate states except as states in the Union under the Constitution, and that thirty-three of them were carved out of the territories and public lands of the United States, designated as states, and admitted to the Union by act of Congress. Minnesota is one of these thirty-three.

More than fifty years before Minnesota was admitted to the Union, and forty years before the vague geographical expression "Minnesota country" began to be used, the national government had taken steps to exercise its authority within the area included in the present state boundaries. The area had been acquired by the nation in three stages: the part east of the Mississippi River in 1783 by the treaty of peace with Great Britain; the part west of the Mississippi in 1803 by Jefferson's purchase of Louisiana Territory from Napoleon; and the area in northwestern Minnesota by the Bulwer-Lytton treaty with Great Britain in 1818, which fixed the boundary between American and British possessions from the Lake of the Woods west at 49° north latitude.

In 1804 the military authorities at St. Louis, under orders from President Jefferson, sent Lieutenant Zebulon Pike up the Mississippi to explore the country to the source of the river. In September 1805 he raised the United States flag for the first time in the area at Pike Island in the Mississippi. Then he proceeded farther up the river. At Leech Lake he came upon a British contingent that had not yet withdrawn from the region, and he ordered it to leave. He also negotiated with Sioux Indian tribes for the acquisiton of extensive lands for an army post at the confluence of the Mississippi and St. Peter's (Minnesota) rivers. These probably were the first on-the-spot official acts of the United States government in any part of the present state area. The years were 1805 and 1806. What came to be called "Minnesota East" (east of the Mississippi) was then nominally under Indiana Territory, while "Minnesota West" was under Louisiana Territory. There was practically no white population in the region.

For the next forty-three years all the governmental actions performed in this as yet unnamed area were either those of the United States government acting directly through the War Department or the Army, or the Post Office, or some other central agency, or they were those of one or another of the successive territorial governments

(Indiana, Illinois, Michigan, Wisconsin, Louisiana, Missouri, and Iowa) that were responsible for part or all of the area. All these territories operated through territorial governors and other officials appointed by and responsible to the President of the United States.

In 1819 the United States Army began work on what came to be Fort Snelling near the present sites of St. Paul and Minneapolis. Other forts followed. In 1819 also a federal Indian agent arrived by appointment of President Monroe; he labored on in the area for twenty years. Other government explorations followed, notably those of Lewis Cass and Stephen H. Long. Treaties with the Sioux and Chippewa for the cession of lands came mostly from 1837 on. These opened the way to white settlement. The President, the Senate, the State Department, and the Indian agents of the national government in the area were all involved in making these treaties.

In 1840 Minnesota East, just beginning to get a considerable number of settlers, became a part of St. Croix County, Wisconsin Territory. Now there were three governments in the area, national, territorial, and county, but still no Minnesota. Also in 1840 came another civilian federal agency, the first regular post office in the present state area, at Lake St. Croix. Stillwater and St. Paul got post offices in 1846.

In the meantime land between the St. Croix and Mississippi rivers, now open for settlement, was being surveyed by federal surveyors. The first sale of government lands took place in August 1848 at the St. Croix Falls federal land office. In December 1848, with the "meandering" of White Bear Lake completed, the first government survey of lands had been accomplished, from the St. Croix to the Mississippi.

With Iowa (1846) and Wisconsin (1848) admitted to the Union as states, the Minnesota country (and now the name Minnesota was being used), reaching from Iowa to the British possessions in the north and from Wisconsin westward without limit, was without territorial government but ripe to become a territory under its own name. On March 3, 1849, President James K. Polk approved the territorial act for Minnesota. Its western boundary was set at the Missouri and White Earth rivers—far into the present areas of the two Dakotas.

In the next nine years the people of Minnesota increased rapidly in numbers while experiencing the trials and occasional excitement of pioneer life and the sort of limited self-government that territorial status offered. The chief executive and judicial officers of the territorial government were appointed by the President, but the legislative assembly was locally elected. An elected delegate to Congress, Henry H. Sibley, began to serve in fact in 1848. In 1849 Alexander Ramsey, a Whig, arrived to be the territory's first governor after being appointed by President Zachary Taylor and sworn in at Baltimore by Chief Justice Taney. The governor, the territorial secretary, and the judges of the higher territorial courts all represented the national government in Minnesota. In 1849 there were many "firsts": the first territorial legislative assembly, the first term of the territorial supreme court, the first county elections, the first general act for a public school system, the first county courthouse occupied at Stillwater—and the first organization in the territory of a national political party, the Democratic party.

In the meantime in Washington Delegate Sibley was working almost incessantly, and with marked success, to get federal lands and funds to assist the territorial government on its course. Congress had already set the pattern of giving aid to the territories to start them on their way. This policy was supported right down to the Civil War even by the then Democratic party, which was in principle opposed to federal aid for the states. With the policy thus set, it was up to every territorial delegate in Washington to see to it that his territory did not receive less than any other territory had received and if possible to try to get more.

Even before Minnesota had achieved territorial status in 1849 Congress had for many years appropriated money to buy out Indian land rights, to build Fort St. Anthony (later called Fort Snelling), to open roads, to improve waterways, to establish post offices, to regulate Indian affairs, and to survey and sell public lands, so as to make settlement safer and easier. It was no change of policy, therefore, that led it to appropriate land and money to the new territory for the expenses of its government, for a territorial capitol, for a university endowment, and for various public works. Such grants were wholly approved by the political mores of the time.

In short it is simply a fact that before Minnesota was, the nation was, and its national government was. And the latter was here, in the area, carrying on a number of its own functions and also preparing the way for the territory and the later state of Minnesota that were to follow. A greater contrast between this situation and that of states like Massachusetts, New York, and Virginia in the 1770s and 1780s would be hard to imagine. And when Minnesotans after nine years of territorial status came to seek statehood, there was no thought of antagonism to the national authorities, no opposition to the Constitution. What they wanted was to be a state <u>in the Union, under the Constitution</u>. They did not aspire to anything higher, or to any sort of independent international status.

Ignatius Donnelly summed up the feelings of Minnesotans in an address to Congress during the Reconstruction debates: "We who come . . . from the far west [Minnesota was far west then] have not that deep and ingrained veneration for State power which is to be found among the inhabitants of some of the older States. We have found that State lines, State names, State organizations, are in most cases, the veriest creatures of accident. To us there is no savor of antiquity about them. Our people move into a region of country and <u>make</u> the State. We feel ourselves to be offshoots of the nation. We look to the nation for protection. The love of our hearts gathers around the nation; and there is no prouder and gladder sight to our eyes than the flag of the nation fluttering in the sunshine over our frontier homes. We are willing to trust the nation. . . . We need erect no bulwark of State sovereignty behind which to shelter ourselves."

The setting up of Minnesota as a state and its admission to the Union involved a series of interdependent actions, some performed by leaders, officials, and voters in the designated area of Minnesota Territory in order to prepare themselves for statehood, and the others by Congress and the executive in Washington acting under their national constitutional authority to admit states to the Union. Since it was generally understood that the entire area of Minnesota Territory was too large (166,000 square miles) to be admitted as a single state, the territorial assembly did not petition Washington for statehood for the territory. Instead rival factions in the assembly, without official status, went forward with their divergent plans for the future state. In general one faction, mainly Republican, and centered in southern Minnesota in such communities as Winona and St. Peter, wanted to lop off the northern part of the territory from about 46° north latitude and make the southern half, from the Mississippi to the Missouri River, into the state of Minnesota, with its capital at St. Peter. A rival faction, predominantly Democratic, and centered in St. Paul, St. Anthony, and Stillwater, wanted to cut off the western half of the territory by a line north and south through Lakes Travers and Bigstone and northward along the Red River of the North to the Canadian line, and to make the eastern part the state of Minnesota, leaving St. Paul, St. Anthony, and Stillwater as the sites of the capital, the university, and the prison, respectively. The latter faction had in the person of Henry M. Rice, resident of St. Paul, Democrat, businessman, and the second Minnesota delegate to Congress in the crucial years 1856 and 1857, a strong tie with the Democratic administration and the congressional majority in Washington.

On December 24, 1856, Delegate Rice introduced into the House of Representatives a bill to enable the people residing in the eastern portion of the territory, as defined above, to express their wishes about becoming a state in the Union, and if their vote was favorable, to draw up and adopt a state constitution, and to apply for admission into the Union. Congress having approved the bill, on February 26, 1857, President Pierce signed it into law. Early in the same year a special federal census showed the population of the territory to be over 150,000, most of it within the proposed state.

Proceeding under this enabling act, with the aid of the territorial and county officials, the voters within the proposed state (and apparently also some who lived in the excluded western half of the territory), on June 1, 1857, elected delegates to a state constitutional convention. Scheduled to meet as a body on July 13, the delegates-elect split instead into two parts, one Republican, one Democrat, each of which organized as a convention and claimed to be the true constitutional convention, and each of which drew up a proposed constitution for the state. At the end, however, a compromise committee wove into one document various parts of the two drafts and this constitution, of which two official copies were made (one for the Democrats and the other for the Republicans to sign), went to the voters in October 1857 and was overwhelmingly ratified. It was transmitted to Congress as evidence of the people's compliance with the provision in the first section of the Enabling Act authorizing the people "to form for themselves a constitution and state government, by the name of the state of Minnesota, and to come into the Union on an equal footing with the original states, according to the federal constitution."

Interpreting the words about forming a state government and coming into the Union as authority for immediate action after the state constitution should be adopted, the framers put into the latter document provisions for the election of representatives to Congress and a full complement of state officers to take place at the same October 13 election as was designated for the vote on the constitution. In addition, they provided for the state legislature elected at that time to meet in St. Paul on the first Wednesday of December 1857, long before Congress could be expected to pass the usual act admitting the state to the Union. Some of the convention leaders seem to have assumed that, under the Enabling Act, as soon as the voters had approved the constitution, Minnesota would be a state, fully entitled to act as such, to make laws and to be represented in Congress like any other state, without waiting for the usual act of admission from Congress. But an attempt by General James Shields, who had been elected to the United States Senate by the December 1857 session of the state legislature, to have himself seated before the act of admission was passed brought the ruling from the Senate Judiciary Committee on March 4, 1858, "That Minnesota is not a State of the Union, under the constitution and laws." Not until after the act admitting Minnesota to the Union was passed and signed on May 11, 1858, were Minnesota's two senators and two representatives given their seats in Congress. In short, despite the yearnings of many Minnesotans for immediate statehood on October 13, 1857, when the state constitution was adopted, nothing in the Minnesota proceedings weakened in any way the constitutional principle that since the people of the original thirteen states ratified the Constitution of the United States, no state has become a state in the Union, or can become one, except through an affirmative act of admission by Congress.

The effect of an act of admission is, therefore, twofold: to create a state in the Union that was not such a state before, and to admit it to that Union. The consent of the people in the area has always been expressed in some form before the passage of the act of admission, but no such population can constitutionally make itself into a state in the Union by its own action. It takes the action both of Congress and of the people affected, and constitutionally the consent of Congress is all-important. The consent of the people concerned is implied but not required by the Constitution. These conclusions have some relevance to the question of the true status of states in the

Union under the Constitution. They do not come in as independent sovereignties accepting membership in an international league that lacks a central supreme government. They come in as equals with other states already in the Union, but subject to the supreme law of the land, consisting of the Constitution as written and officially interpreted, the laws made in pursuance thereof, and all treaties made or which shall be made with other countries under the authority of the United States. In short the states are autonomous equals under the Constitution, laws, and treaties of the United States. They are not sovereigns in the international sense or in any other sense that goes against the Constitution and its supremacy clause.

It is true that when Minnesota became a state in the Union in 1858 these propositions were still being debated to some extent and that the great decisions following on the Union victory in the Civil War, including the adoption of the three Civil War amendments, had not yet been made. But the Minnesota leadership placed that state's people solidly on the side of the Union as soon as secession and civil war threatened.

Minnesota's transition from territorial status to that of a state in the Union was such as to perpetuate the close relationship that had already been established with the national government and to hold to a minimum any thought of antagonism to the national government.

First of all there were the valuable grants to the state offered to it in propositions set forth for its acceptance in the Enabling Act, and accepted by the people of the state through a specific provision of the state constitution—Article 2, section 3. The offers made to the state by the United States were as follows: (1) In every township sections 16 and 36 of public lands, or their equivalent if these were unavailable, for the use of schools. (2) Seventy-two sections, the equivalent of two townships, for the use and support of a state university. (3) Ten entire sections of land for completing the public buildings or erecting others at the seat of government. (4) All salt springs within the state, not exceeding twelve in number, with six sections of land adjoining or near each one, to be used or disposed of as the state might direct. (5) Five per cent of the net proceeds of sales of all public lands lying within the state and sold after the admission of the state—this revenue to be used for public roads and internal improvements under the direction of the legislature.

The conditions imposed by Congress upon the state's acceptance of these grants were explicit and are worth quoting: "Provided, The foregoing propositions herein offered are on the condition, that the said convention which shall form the constitution of said state shall provide, by a clause in said constitution, or an ordinance irrevocable without the consent of the United States, that said state shall never interfere with the primary disposal of the soil within the same, by the United States, or with any regulations congress may find necessary for securing the title in said soil to bona fide purchasers thereof; and that no tax shall be imposed on lands belonging to the United States, and that in no case shall non-resident proprietors be taxed higher than residents."

The section of the state constitution—Article 2, section 3—by which the state "accepted, ratified, and confirmed" these offers and propositions also declares them to be irrevocable without the consent of the United States. Such clauses in state constitutions are sometimes spoken of as "compacts" between the nation and the states concerned. As a matter of fact there is nothing required of the state under the conditions fixed by Congress for the acceptance of the proffered lands and money that the United States could not insist upon under its own constitutional powers and supremacy without reference to these clauses. Furthermore, Congress did not insist that the state accept what was offered as a condition of admission to the Union. The offer was for the state's "free acceptance or rejection." A rejection would have affected only the ownership of the land and money offered. The United States was already the owner of practically all the lands of Minnesota, except as some lands had already been patented to settlers and other purchasers, and except, also, as the United States recognized the rights of the Indians and had already begun to set aside reservations for their use. The Enabling Act offered the people not only statehood but also nearly 4 per cent of the state's land area for public purposes, the lands to be selected by the state itself. This was in effect an outright grant to help the state get started, and quite in line with, as well as in addition to, the grants previously made to the territory. The conditional clauses served primarily as a reminder to officials and other citizens that the United States owned the land and could lawfully dispose of it as it saw fit, and that the state had no right to interfere with it or to tax it, and also that, under the "comity clause" of the United States Constitution, a state may not tax citizens of other states at higher rates than it taxes its own. In any case, the grants were so munificent and so much desired by the people that the framers of the state constitution would probably have made even more substantial pledges, if necessary, to obtain them.

In addition to these grants, however, there were the even larger land grants offered to the state by a separate act of Congress for the building of railroads. Under Delegate Rice's able and effective handling this act passed Congress in the same session as the Enabling Act. As a counterpart to the Enabling Act, it provided for a network of five railroads to link up all parts of the proposed state in order to speed its development. Four roads were to radiate from St. Paul and St. Anthony—one to the far northwestern corner of the state, one westward and a little northward to the later North Dakota line at about the present city of Breckenridge, one southwestward through St. Peter to about the present city of Worthington, and one due south to the Iowa boundary. The fifth line was to start at LaCrescent and Winona and proceed westward through St. Peter and thence due west to the present South Dakota boundary. This line crossed the two lines running south and southwest from St. Paul and St. Anthony. The lands for these railroads, to be selected in alternate sections on both sides of the rights of way for a distance of six miles on each side of each road, were to be granted by the state to the companies that would construct the railroads. The lands thus granted amounted ultimately to about eight million acres, or about 16 per cent of the state's area.

Being so far from the eastern markets for their produce and the eastern centers of supply for their needs in developing their homes, farms, industries, and public services, Minnesotans generally realized the importance of building railroads. A number of states farther east had suffered serious financial losses in trying to develop main roads and canals at their own expense. Some had had their fingers so badly burned in these ventures that it was becoming popular to amend state constitutions so as to forbid the states from engaging in works of "internal improvement." The framers of the Minnesota constitution put such a clause into section 5 of Article 9 of their document, but carefully qualified the prohibition by this clause: "except in cases where grants of land or other property shall have been made to the state" for the purpose. They clearly had the railroad land grant in mind when they made this exception. And how, under these circumstances, could the people of Minnesota reject the federal aid that promised to bring them the needed railroads without expense to themselves as taxpayers?

These unusually generous grants to the nascent state by the national authorities surely helped to keep the people and the public authorities of Minnesota in a mood of friendship for the national government. Other factors worked in the same direction. Take political partisanship, for example. While Democrats controlled Congress and the administration in Washington during the state's first few years, Minnesota also had a Democratic administration under Governor Sibley, and other Democrats represented the state in Congress. Minnesota's leaders were thus hand in glove with the leaders in Washington. The situation was changing in both nation and state by 1860; Abraham Lincoln had been elected as the first Republican President, and in Minnesota Alexander Ramsey, a Republican, was governor. Thereafter Republicans continued to dominate both the national and the Minnesota state administrations, while in Congress, Democratic representatives and senators from Minnesota were also soon replaced by Republicans, and the entire composition of Congress, affected in 1861 by the departure of the southern Democrats, became and long remained predominantly Republican. Thus, Minnesota went along with the national trend and had state administrations as well as legislatures and congressional delegations in political harmony with those in Washington; there was no reason for partisan antagonism between the national and state capitals—quite the contrary. This condition continued to be true as one Republican succeeded another (with the exception of the ill-starred President Andrew Johnson) in control of both national and state administrations, through several decades.

When viewed in retrospect, the period from the Civil War to the beginning of Woodrow Wilson's administration in 1913 was one in which neither the national government nor that of the state was actively or extensively engaged in the performance of what are now considered essential public functions. To the people of that time, however, this did not seem to be the case. Many publicists pointed to various increases in public services and to the rise of taxes as evidence of the early coming of socialism, a prospect which was generally viewed with great alarm. Actually the functions of the national government in Minnesota (as in the other states) at that time consisted mainly of the following: the postal service, which was extended rather widely but was mainly self-supporting; certain rivers and harbors projects, principally on the Mississippi River and at Duluth; the regulation of Indian affairs; the surveying of public lands and their minimum protection; the sale and patenting of public lands through the federal land office; a small amount of weather reporting and census work; the collection of customs and of excises like the liquor and tobacco taxes; the maintenance of the federal courts and of the United States marshal's office. Before 1900 Congress enacted laws to regulate the railroads and to prevent monopolies, and it also began the extension of postal deliveries to rural areas. Soon after 1900 it took steps to control the shipment of foods and drugs in interstate commerce and inaugurated a postal savings system (1911) and a parcel post service (1913). Theodore Roosevelt, preaching his doctrine of the New Nationalism, espoused various measures to regulate commerce, to conserve natural resources, and to promote better living conditions in rural areas. His presidency was a period of enthusiastic exhortations and some small beginnings but not of great additions to the national government's activities. All the measures that have been mentioned brought relatively few new federal officials into Minnesota or into any other state. Even the pensions and other benefits that were provided for Civil War veterans, and which were strongly espoused by that important nationalizing organization, the GAR, were handled almost entirely in Washington, and partly by members of Congress through private bills. I do not mean to imply that the national government was not important within the states in those days, for indeed it was increasingly important. What I do mean is that, when compared with more recent developments, to people living away from Washington the nation's government seemed rather small and remote.

At the same time the states were also, by more recent standards, relatively slow in their responses to public demands for new laws and services. In Minnesota there were significant beginnings, to be sure, in public health work, in the provision of state hospitals and asylums, in the conservation of natural resources, in the provision of state aids for public schools; there was even, in 1898, a piddling state grant for main highways, to be expended through the counties. All these measures were relatively small, however, so that the year 1900, and even 1910, found the state with but a small staff of civil servants, mostly located in St. Paul or at state hospitals and other such institutions, and with a relatively meager budget. Even the state government was, therefore, not close to the people in the sense of rendering many services throughout the length and breadth of the state.

Given this condition of relative inactivity at both the state and national levels, there was fewer occasions for official national-state relations than have been observed in more recent times. There was little or no talk of national-state cooperation or of cooperative government in those days. Intergovernmental relations there certainly were, then as now, but they had not risen to the level of a major issue of public policy. Most of the discussions of intergovernmental relations were still in terms of constitutional law and powers.

I have concluded that from the Civil War up to about World War I four major factors were closely related to the relative inactivity of national and state governments. These probably had a considerable deterrent or delaying effect upon proposals to expand governmental functions.

One—not necessarily first in importance or in time—was the general view that the United States Constitution set definite limits upon what the national and state governments could legally undertake to do, and that these limits forbade a number of measures that were proposed to expand governmental activities. The Constitution, to some, even guaranteed an absolute right of private property, beyond the power of governments to regulate. The legal profession generally and many other conservative citizens, including a good number of Supreme Court justices and members of Congress and some Presidents of that period, held rather strongly to this general view. The argument, particularly if it came from a lawyer, that a certain proposed governmental action would be unconstitutional seems frequently to have effectively prevented the government in question from even trying it.

A second and closely related idea was that of laissez faire, simply defined as the theory that, by some natural law or law above the Constitution, certain things are never proper for governments to do. Hence government should let many activities of men in society go uncontrolled and unregulated, on the theory that by natural processes evils will correct themselves, or will be corrected, without governmental intervention; and that the results will be better all around, for everybody, if "paternalism" or governmental intervention to correct evils or supply services is avoided. There can be little doubt that this argument as well as the constitutional argument was used by powerful interests to delay or defeat public actions that they considered inimical to their property rights.

A third related factor was the rising rural fear of the cities, and the resultant refusal of rurally dominated legislatures to reapportion representation according to population and thus chance urban control of the states that would lead to the passage of measures desired by many city dwellers but not by rural interests. Rural leaders did not stand firmly upon any general laissez-faire principle. Many of them and many of their rural followers were quite willing to have either the national or the state government or both undertake measures presumably beneficial to agricultural interests. It was measures designed to help urban people that were, in general, longest delayed; and the delays appear to have come about through a combination of rural interests and the more conservative interests, sometimes called antilabor interests, in the cities. In a period of steady urban growth these delays meant that a considerable backlog of unmet urban demands for remedial legislation was built up.

A fourth factor, and one that I believe was very important in the period, was the general inadequacy of the revenue systems of both the state and national governments for the support of anything like a present-day program of public services either in the social and educational fields or in public works, national defense, and foreign aid.

The national government, after dropping the income tax at the end of the Civil War, went along for nearly five decades relying upon the revenues from the tariff and from a few selective excises like those on liquor and tobacco. The tariff revenues were small and somewhat inflexible because of the highly protective and in some cases almost prohibitive rates. The probability of excessive evasion if excise tax rates were too high limited to some extent those rates and revenues. Such budget balances as the national government achieved during these decades resulted primarily from reducing defense expenditures to an almost fantastically low amount and from a failure to appropriate substantially for any truly expensive national functions. Finally, after having had an income tax of 1893 declared unconstitutional in 1895, the national government introduced a corporation excise or income tax in 1909, and four years later, with the adoption of the Sixteenth Amendment, began to levy also a personal income tax. These two income taxes, together with expanded excise taxes, have sufficed in the twentieth century to give the national government revenues commensurate with its wartime needs and the functional responsibilities it has assumed in recent years.

In the meantime most of the states relied mainly upon the so-called general property tax, which had to support also all the local governments in the state. This tax was unpopular, it was usually poorly administered, and it had built-in features of inequity since it failed to reach all forms of wealth and income. Numerous studies pointed out its weaknesses and its inadequacy, yet it was not until after 1900 that most of the states began to supplement it, and some to replace it, with other more lucrative or more equitable taxes. Only as the states introduced broader-based and more equitable tax systems, with the use of various excise taxes, corporation taxes, income taxes, and sales taxes, did their revenues begin to become adequate for the many public services that were being demanded.

Minnesota began its development of a more adequate revenue system with the adoption of the "wide-open" tax amendment of 1906. It gradually introduced various supplementary gross-earnings, road-user, and occupational taxes, but not until 1933 did it enact a state income tax, covering both corporations and individuals. A general sales tax is still not a part of the state's tax system, but there are frequent proposals for one, in order to take some of the burden off the income and property taxes, and to avert impending deficits.

In general it can be said that the national government and many of the states now have far more adequate revenue systems than they had before 1910, and that their assumption of new functions has gone along with their improved access to the needed revenues. Throughout the whole period from the Civil War almost down to 1913 there was stubborn resistance to almost every proposal to change the outmoded and inadequate revenue systems of the nation and the states; in these decades the dominant political forces were reluctant to give either the national or the state governments new taxes and revenue powers that would enable them to expand their public services and expenditures. The year 1913 may be set down as the great turning point. But the change was not an abrupt one; it came in several stages; and steps taken in the former period proved to have importance in what was to follow.

In Minnesota, for example, the political leaders did not forget the grants of cash and land made by Congress to the territory, and they did not cease to press for conveyance to the state of all the lands promised to it in the Enabling Act. The work of selecting suitable lands and of negotiating with Washington for their transfer to the state went on year after year and decade after decade. The state auditor's office handled this function for many years but later it was delegated to the department of conservation. There being some small acreages due the state even in the present decade, the state legislature in 1953 authorized the commissioner of conservation, with the approval of the state executive council, to select and accept on behalf of the state any available federal lands that were deemed suitable.

One curious evidence of the state's pertinacity in this effort to get all the land due it concerns the grants for university purposes. In 1851, as a result of Delegate Sibley's exertions, Congress reserved two townships of land for the use and support of a university "in the Territory." This land, though merely "reserved," was in fact hypothecated and dissipated by the early board of regents in an unfortunate attempt to get the university started in the early 1850s. After statehood was achieved and the land grant for the territorial university had been used up, Minnesota's representatives in Congress pointed out that the statehood Enabling Act called for a grant of two townships of land for a state university. Other members of Congress conceded the point and in 1870 Congress directed the land office to permit Minnesota to select two townships or seventy-two sections of land for the state university. This was done, and the lands so selected became the nucleus of the Permanent University Fund.

The entry of the national government into the fields of agriculture and agricultural education (subjects not mentioned in the Constitution) began in the 1860s and 1870s. The Morrill Act of 1862 granted a minimum of 90,000 acres to each state (30,000 for each senator and 30,000 for each House member from the state in Congress) as an endowment for establishing a state agricultural and mechanical college. Each state was expected to construct and operate the college itself, and to report to Congress annually on the investment and use of its endowment fund. Thus some of the features of the recent grant-in-aid system—cost sharing and reporting by the states—were being introduced.

Later came the realization of a related idea, annual cash grants to the states for research and experimentation in agriculture. In 1887, just a century after the adoption of the United States Constitution and twenty-five years after the Morrill Act, Congress authorized an appropriation of $15,000 annually to every state for the establishment and maintenance of an agricultural experiment station in connection with its agricultural or "land-grant" college. Three years later Congress passed another Morrill Act which authorized federal appropriations up to $25,000 per year for each state to help support instruction in the land-grant colleges. This, the second annual cash grant to the states in the field of agriculture, carried with it a new condition, namely the right of the federal department to withhold grants from states not performing their instructional duties according to the terms of the act. The enforcement of this condition necessarily required the federal authorities to keep themselves informed, by visits for inspection, by reports, and in other ways, as to how the states were using their federally granted funds.

It is interesting to note how little effect on these developments political partisanship had. The experiment station act of 1887 was adopted during the presidency of Grover Cleveland, who headed the first Democratic administration since the Civil War, and the Morrill Act of 1890 granting federal aid for instruction in land-grant colleges was passed while Benjamin Harrison, a Republican, was chief executive.

This was a period when agriculture was really coming into its own as a particular concern of the national government. Created by a Republican Congress in Lincoln's first administration in 1862, the United States Department of Agriculture was advanced to full Cabinet status as the eighth executive department of the national government in the closing weeks of President Cleveland's first administration in 1889. The pattern that was laid out for national action to promote agriculture was approximately this: In programs of direct aid to and regulation of agriculture generally, the national government would deal directly with farmers and with any special committees of farmers set up to cooperate with the national department. But in matters involving education and local research in agriculture, state priority of interest would be respected; Congress would provide grants-in-aid for the states but would leave the actual work of teaching and research to state and local authorities. In a general way this policy still prevails.

Of course, officers of the national government had been in all the states more or less from the beginning to carry out its own immediate functions such as the administration of justice through federal courts, the postal service, customs and excise collection, defense, and the maintenance of military installations. Where else but in the states could these officers operate? The measures connected with agricultural colleges and experiment stations in the late 1880s and early 1890s were different, however. They brought the national authorities into the states for a new group of purposes, namely, to cooperate with the state officials in carrying out federally aided state functions, and to keep informed about the way in which state authorities were fulfilling the federal laws and the agreements with federal agencies under which the states were receiving and expending national funds. Here was a new type of activity that was destined to grow and spread tremendously. With the older, more traditional types of national government activities also expanding in all the states, the national impact upon the states was increasing immeasurably.

The next steps along the road toward cooperative relations between the national government and the states also came under the auspices of the United States Department of Agriculture, in the fields of agriculture and forestry. An experimental program of providing county agents to help farmers take advantage of the latest findings in agriculture was given congressional approval and nationwide legal status in 1914 by the Smith-Lever Act. This law established the first fully modern grant-in-aid system, with (1) annual appropriations by Congress, (2) an equal matching of funds by each state, (3) a formula for distributing the federal funds among the states, and (4) agreement on a plan of operation in each state worked out by its authorities to meet its own needs and approved by the United States department. These features have become fairly standard in later federal grant-in-aid laws. In the meantime in 1911 Congress had approved the Weeks Act for national-state cooperation in fire protection for forests, a plan that was later modified and expanded into a grant-in-aid program.

By 1914, then, the grant-in-aid type of working agreement between the national government and the states covering functions of mutual concern had been developed, tried out to some extent, and approved. Thereafter a number of new grant-in-aid measures were added to the list: in highway construction, maternal and child welfare, vocational education, public health, public assistance, school lunches, airports, public housing, libraries, to cite a few. Important early programs in agriculture and highways came in the Woodrow Wilson administration; in the social security, labor, health, and housing fields in the Franklin Roosevelt administration; and others in the Truman and Eisenhower administrations.

In each grant-in-aid law from the very outset the emphasis was upon a specific public function. The problem was how to get certain public functions that fell within the scope of state powers, but were also of national interest and concern, performed as uniformly as possible throughout the nation without the national government's having to take over the function from the states.

The operative factors and the steps toward the goal were very similar in all cases. First there was some specific function that clearly fell within the scope of state powers—agricultural education, or highway construction and maintenance, for example, or the control of some communicable disease, or the extension of library service to rural areas, or aid to the aged or the blind. In most if not in all cases the function was one that would yield best results if performed throughout all the states, and would prove to be of national benefit if so performed. But the states were and are clearly unequal in their capacity to support public services, and besides they differ in policies as to how much to do and how to do it. Even though interstate compacts, uniform laws, and other such devices are utilized, a uniform and united advance by all the states in any single field that calls for considerable appropriations of funds, well-qualified personnel, high standards of service, and a stable policy appears to be out of the question.

As the felt need for a new service, or for an improved and nationwide enlargement of an established service, failed to be satisfied by the states, interested citizens formed national organizations to promote national action in some form. These organizations had members from many sources—professional men, state and local officials, men representing commercial interests, those expecting direct benefits from the service, amateur enthusiasts, and others. It is surprising in how many instances they found the answer to their problem in the formulation and sponsorship of a congressional act to establish another federal grant-in-aid. Members of Congress from both major parties could always be found to endorse such bills.

Promotion of the function was the end to be attained; the means was a federal grant-in-aid law backed up by annual cash grants to all states that would accept the terms of the law and cooperate in the program. The usual arrangement was for equal sharing of costs by the national and state governments. Congress through its annual appropriations fixed the amount of the national contribution for each grant-in-aid program for the next fiscal year. The states received only the amount that they matched with their own funds, but could go as far as they wished in appropriating for the service beyond the matching amount.

Because the sponsors of each grant-in-aid emphasized only the one function in which they were interested, and because they always began with rather modest sums to be contributed by the national treasury, the fiscal importance of all grants combined received little attention in the early decades of the movement. Later the total fiscal effect upon the state and local governments, and even upon the national budget, came to be of considerable importance. This was true for several reasons: very few grant-in-aid programs once begun were later abandoned; with new programs created from time to time, the total number of programs increased rather steadily; the amounts appropriated for each program tended on the whole, and with only occasional setbacks, to be increased from time to time. The cumulative effect over the years, although not planned, came to be considerable.

In the total expenditures of state and local governments federal grants had no great fiscal importance until the depression years of 1934-39. Then the emergency grants for WPA, PWA, FERA, and other programs, plus some new regular grants, jumped the totals to an average of over $2,000 million a year and provided funds for over 25 per cent, on the average, of all state and local expenditures. The dropping of some emergency programs from 1939 on and the curtailment of all federal grants during the war years cut the totals to less than half the former average and the percentage of state and local funds from federal sources to just over 8 per cent in 1946, when our studies began. Then began another spectacular rise in federal aids. due partly to the enactment of some important new regular aid programs, so that by 1952, just at the end of our field studies, the total of regular federal grants came to $2,393 million, which accounted for over 10 per cent of all state and local expenditures. Since then there have been substantial further increases in federal aids to $4,000 million in 1957 and over $5,000 million in 1958.

But while federal aids have been increasing, state and local government revenues from their own sources have also increased substantially in the postwar years, from $15,000 million in 1946 to $42,000 million in 1957. Thus the actual ratio between what state and local units receive from federal grants and what they raise from their own sources remains on the average below 10 per cent. This is, however, an important amount, and a stable element in state and local budgets.

The states differ greatly, however, in the budget percentages they receive from federal grants. Some states receive over 20 per cent of their revenues from federal aids, others less than 10, because the statutory formulas for distributing aids are more favorable to some states than to others, and also because some states raise and spend more than others.

Minnesota has, in general, received more than the average state from federal grants-in-aid. On the average since the mid-1930s, for every $100 collected by the state in taxes it has obtained over $20 from federal grants. This means that the nation has a substantial stake in Minnesota's public expenditure policies and in many of its major functions. Financially the national government is helping Minnesota state and local governments to the amount of about $80 million a year (1958), although a part of this sum does not qualify as regular grants-in-aid. This amount is likely to be increased considerably if and when the construction of the Interstate Highway System (the "freeways"), toward which the national government contributes 90 per cent, goes forward more rapidly.

As already pointed out, the national government has expanded its governmental role not only through subsidizing the states for the carrying on of many state and local functions but also by increasing the number and expanding the scope of the functions that it performs directly for the American people as a whole. Since 1900 the old-line functions—foreign affairs, defense, the regulation of commerce, postal service, promotion of agricultural prosperity, veterans' pensions and welfare, rivers and harbors improvement, and protection of the public lands—have been expanded to include such expensive items as foreign aid; scientific research in weapons, atomic energy, earth satellites, and the conquest of outer space; river basin developments like TVA and the Missouri River project; direct payments to farmers for crop controls and soil-conserving practices; and the nationwide system of veterans' hospitals—to mention only some of the more costly ones. New functions have been added, such as Old Age and Survivors' Insurance (social security), the railroad retirement system, the regulation of industrial relations, the promotion and regulation of aeronautics, and rural electrification. These are in addition to a wide range of grants-in-aid in public health, social welfare, public education, and other fields.

These functional innovations and expansions have brought with them significant new developments in the life of every state. Whereas at one time the administration of national affairs (the post office, revenue offices, land offices, and military posts and arsenals excepted) was confined very largely to Washington, D.C., since the early 1930s in particular the national agencies have expanded into every state and every major city in the country. In recent years the civilian employees of the national government within the continental United States have averaged over 2,200,000, of whom about 235,000, or one in nine, have been located in Washington offices. The Defense Department with its three branches and its many installations throughout the country accounts for over a million civilian employees, and the Post Office Department for over half a million. Other departments and agencies range from nearly a hundred thousand for Agriculture down through tens of thousands, thousands, and hundreds of employees each for the others.

Departments and agencies with responsibilities for the nationwide performance of their functions, and with thousands or at least hundreds of officers and employees to organize and supervise in the field, have had to face major decisions about regional and district organization for their staffs, and have had to select suitable centers in the various states in which to do their work.

The problems connected with this dispersion of federal agencies all over the country first began to be studied seriously during the 1930s. At that time the "alphabetical agencies" of the New Deal, the NRA, WPA, PWA, FERA, and others, were establishing regional, state, and district offices everywhere that their duties called for them. The confusion to the public and to the agencies themselves that resulted from this rapid increase of field offices, and from the uncoordinated mapping of separate region-and-district plans by each agency to suit its own needs, led to a great deal of discussion but little action toward integration of the various schemes. There was some talk of trying to have all federal agencies agree upon one standard set of some dozen or so regions for the nation as a whole, with a major sub-capital such as Boston for New England, San Francisco for the West Coast, and so on, in which all agencies would concentrate their offices for the better coordination of their work. These ideas proved to be rather unrealistic. They did not appeal strongly to administrators, or to politicians and members of Congress, or to business leaders in those communities that were not likely to be selected as sub-capitals, or to the upholders of states' rights. Some of the latter wanted no districts that did not conform strictly to state lines, and no regions larger than a state for federal administration. They wanted every state to be dealt with separately as a state by the federal agencies. Students of public administration who looked into various proposals for standardized regions tended to conclude that the idea was not feasible and not worth the effort needed to put it into effect. Other ways of coordinating the work of federal agencies in the field, and of coordinating federal services generally with those of state and local governments, would have to be explored.

Anyone who wishes to get an idea of how numerous and varied are the schemes of regional and district organization of the national administrative agencies can get some of the basic information he needs by skimming through the pages of the United States Government Manual (recently titled the United States Government Organization Manual) for any recent year that he chooses. The Manual for 1947 (second edition), published some months after our studies began, is a good example. Turning the pages for the Executive Branch (pages 53ff), one finds that the Bureau of the Budget had four field offices—at Chicago, Dallas, Denver, and San Francisco—but with no regional boundaries indicated (page 57). The Federal Housing Administration had seventy-two "insuring or service offices," including one or more in each state (pages 75-76). The Federal Public Housing Authority had eight "regional and area offices," no. 1 taking in the six New England states, with headquarters at Boston; no. 2 including New York, Pennsylvania, New Jersey, Maryland, and Delaware, with headquarters in New York City; etc. (pages 77-78). The Office of the Housing Expediter also had eight "regional offices," and the regions were apparently the same as those for FPHA, above, but in the southwestern region it used Dallas and not Fort Worth as its headquaters, and even where a region had the same city as its headquarters the local office address was different (page 80). The Department of State listed no regions for its work in the United States, not even for the Passport Division (page 110). The Department of the Treasury, Bureau of Customs, listed forty-seven "district offices" within the 48 states, partly by naming the states included as well as the headquarters city, and partly by simply naming the port of entry for the district (pages 120-22). The Bureau of Internal Revenue in the Department of the Treasury listed sixty-three "collection districts" within the states and their headquarters; a number of states had more than one district each, but the district boundaries were not shown (pages 123-24).

In this way one could go through one department and agency after another and observe how even bureaus and lower level divisions in some agencies had separate regional and district schemes—for example, the Mint, the Bureau of Narcotics, the Savings Bonds Division, the Bureau of Federal Supply, the Secret Service, and the Coast Guard, to round out the Treasury Department list (pages 125-52). But after the Treasury Department most of the book still lies ahead (pages 153-566), with dozens more of separate and different schemes of organizing the field into regions, districts, and subdistricts. One count showed over a hundred different systems in existence in about 1945.

Early in our research we thought of making up an entire volume on the national agencies located in Minnesota, with some historical background for each, a description of its organization, powers, and activities in the state, and our evaluation of its services. On second thought this seemed to be an inordinately difficult undertaking and one that would result in a work of little interest even to scholars except as a census or directory. It would have necessitated intensive studies in all the larger urban centers and at least a survey in every county similar to the detailed one made by Paul Ylvisaker for the Council on Intergovernmental Relations in Blue Earth County. The historical part of the study would have required not only the county-by-county approach for every federal activity in that county (place), but also a statewide study of each agency (organization and function) to show its beginnings and subsequent developments and changes in the state, its personnel, its relations to other agencies—all this on a time scale from the earliest days to the 1950s. In the absence of a series of monographs on the separate national agencies in the state, this project might have resulted in file upon file of detailed materials beyond our capacity to analyze and synthesize.

This ambitious project was, therefore, put aside. In its place I endeavor here to give, first, some indication of the sources that are available to anyone needing information and, second, a thumbnail sketch of the situation in Minnesota as I perceive it. My evaluation must be more or less on the basis of impressions gained from wide reading and numerous interviews and contacts over many years, and not a fully documented account.

The sources of basic information about the national authorities in Minnesota are largely in the central files of the various agencies in Washington, but something will be found also in the regional and district files of each agency—not all in Minnesota, however Leads and clues will be found in the annual and special reports of the different national agencies, but these are usually too brief to give much attention to the developments in each state.

Information about the regional and district organizations of all important national agencies that have field services is given very briefly and somewhat unevenly in the annual volume entitled United States Government Organization Manual (originally called simply the United States Government Manual). Changes in the organizations themselves and in their field organizations can be traced through the series of annual issues of this useful publication. A number of agencies issue their own manuals for in-service training and for the guidance of both central and field personnel. These usually describe the field organization of the agency. They are detailed and authoritative, and, being revised and reissued from time to time, are kept fairly up to date; but they are not all readily available.

The Bureau of the Budget in the national capital has a great deal of information about all agencies of the government; and so does the General Services Administration. The latter has a regional office at Kansas City, Missouri, which includes Minnesota and six other states in its jurisdiction; and there is a district office in Minneapolis which is in touch with the federal agencies in the state.

The St. Paul office of the former Office of Government Reports issued on March 1, 1940, a 64-page mimeographed pamphlet that was entitled Directory of Federal and State Departments and Agencies in Minnesota, of which 46 pages were given over to national agencies. This was revised and reissued in 1941 under the title Minnesota Directory of Federal and State Agencies. In January 1949, a Directory of Federal Departments and Agencies in St. Paul, Minneapolis and South St. Paul was issued by the Office of the Regional Director, Eighth United States Civil Service Region, then headquartered in St. Paul.

At about this time Gary P. Brazier of our research staff was covering the Minneapolis and St. Paul area in an endeavor to track down all national agencies that had headquarters, however transient, in the two cities. He made contacts with a considerable number of agencies but reported his inability to get in touch with several officials who used the cities primarily as a center from which they traveled widely in the course of their duties. His notes were written up in a 32-page typed report in 1952 by Francis E. Rourke, also a member of the research staff.

Anyone wishing to make a survey of federal agencies in the state might well start with the telephone directories of Minneapolis, St. Paul, Duluth, and other principal cities of Minnesota, and also get in touch with the local offices of the General Services Administration in the major cities.

So much for the more obvious sources of information. In what follows I shall survey briefly the recent and present agencies of the national government in Minnesota. The comparison to be made is not primarily between Minnesota and other states but between Minnesota now (say in the 1950s) and Minnesota then (say about 1900 to 1910). Two major criteria will be used for indicating the extent of the presence and the activity of the national government in the state. One will be the number of federal agencies that actually maintain offices in the state, and the other will be the number of federal employees within the state's area. The latter will be the more definite figure.

The number of agencies is hard to determine and may not be of great significance for several reasons: (1) It is difficult to define an agency. The term covers a wide range of organizations from whole departments and large "independent agencies" to smaller and smaller subdivisions thereof such as bureaus, divisions, and offices. A single officer may be the sole representative of one agency in the state, whereas the Post Office Department has thousands of employees, with some stationed in every county. (2) Although all agencies of the government are potential renderers of service in every state, some render services in Minnesota only through correspondence and traveling representatives, without having any employee or officer stationed here. (3) Federal agencies move offices into and out of the state, and consolidate or even abandon some of their local offices from time to time, but no agency, public or private, keeps up to date a complete register of all agencies or of such moves and changes. The local telephone books in the leading cities provide the best current local directories of United States agencies for the citizen.

The services of the various agencies also vary greatly. Some render direct services to citizens generally, as the Post Office and the Weather Bureau do, or to selected classes of citizens, as illustrated by the OASI offices and the Veterans Administration hospitals. Others render services only indirectly as through research, the gathering of statistics and other information, or assistance and guidance to state and local agencies in their use of funds provided through federal aid. Some collect taxes, recruit personnel, type letters, take care of federal buildings, or keep or audit accounts.

I am writing, of course, primarily of the administrative branch of the government. Minnesota has the usual complement of federal courts and judicial officers, while the state's senators and representatives in Congress do most of their legislative work in Washington. Time has brought changes in the size of the judicial and legislative branches of the national government sufficient to reflect the greatly increased activity of that government in the nation's affairs, but these do not match the expansions in number and size of agencies that have taken place in the executive branch.

On the basis of evidence from the sources noted above it would appear that in recent years every cabinet department of the national government has had one or more of its activities represented in Minnesota by officials stationed here. In addition, a number of independent and semi-independent national agencies have had regional or district offices, or at least local representatives, stationed in Minnesota. If we look at the January 1958 telephone book for Minneapolis and the June 1957 directory for St. Paul, we find that the former has over four and a half columns of entries, the latter about three and a half. All ten departments (State, Treasury, Defense, Justice, Post Office, Interior, Agriculture, Commerce, Labor, and Health, Education, and Welfare) are listed with nine represented in both cities, the State Department only in St. Paul. The three departmental divisions of the Defense Department, Army, Navy, and Air Force, were represented in both cities.

Among the independent agencies represented in one or the other or both cities were the Central Intelligence Agency, Civil Service Commission, Farm Credit Administration, Federal Civil Defense Administration, Federal Communications Commission, Federal Deposit Insurance Corporation, Federal Mediation and Conciliation Service, General Accounting Office, General Services Administration, Housing and Home Finance Agency, Interstate Commerce Commission, National Labor Relations Board, Railroad Retirement Board, Securities and Exchange Commission, Selective Service System, and Veterans Administration.

To attempt to list all the various bureaus, offices, and services connected with the ten departments and the sixteen agencies here named would carry this account far beyond what is needed to make the major point, which is that at this stage of the nation's development the national government is not, if indeed it ever was, concentrated entirely in the national capital. It is in every state, "at the grass roots." It is in Minnesota as it is in every state. It is not some remote "they" down there in Washington. It is interwoven with the web of life in every part of the population. It influences every major phase and activity of the people, here and everywhere, throughout the national domain.

It is not to be understood that Minnesota is entirely typical of the states in the extent to which federal agencies have established offices within it. The Twin Cities and their suburbs constitute an important metropolitan center for a large region in the Upper Midwest, the headquarters of the Federal Reserve Bank for the Ninth Federal Reserve District and of one of the twelve Farm Credit districts, as well as the center of an impressive network of railroads and other facilities radiating out in all directions. For these and other reasons it was once expected by many local leaders that the Twin Cities and, hence, Minnesota would become one of the major centers for regional organization of the national government's field services. This hope has not been fulfilled. Boston, New York, Chicago, Atlanta, and San Francisco have in general outstripped the Twin Cities in this respect, because of their strategic locations and the large populations in the areas that they serve; and even Kansas City, Denver, St. Louis, and a few other places have equaled or somewhat surpassed the Twin Cities as a regional center for federal administration. Some federal regional offices that once existed in the Twin Cities have been moved away to other centers. Nevertheless the Twin Cities are an important regional or district center for many purposes in the area that corresponds approximately with the Ninth Federal Reserve District. This includes western Wisconsin, northern Iowa, Minnesota, North and South Dakota, and Montana. Some cities that are larger in population, such as Detroit and Pittsburgh, are not so strategically located for federal regional purposes as are Minneapolis and St. Paul. Consequently there is in the Twin Cities a very considerable concentration of federal field offices of various levels of importance. A comparison with cities like Toledo, Buffalo, Milwaukee, and Louisville shows this—and a comparison with smaller centers makes the importance of the Twin Cities even more evident.

In trying to develop a full picture of the situation it is well to remember that Minnesota, like other states, is served also by many federal agencies that have no regional organization, so all questions not settled locally must be referred to Washington. Many other agencies have regional organizations in which the headquarters are located outside the state. Thus Minnesota is a part of Region 5 of the United States Bureau of Public Roads field organization with headquarters in Kansas City, Missouri, whereas the Forest Service has placed Minnesota in its Region 9, which has its headquarters in Milwaukee; the Civil Service Commission puts Minnesota in its Region 9 with headquarters in St. Louis, and a number of other agencies put it in regions with headquarters in Chicago or in some other city.

A better indication of the presence (even if only by agents) of the national government in a state is the number of federal officers and employees who are stationed in the state. Here the comparison in numbers will be between the employees of the national government on the one hand and those of the state and local government on the other.

In The Federalist papers, numbers 45 and 46, James Madison discussed the probable relative influence of the national and state governments and whether federal encroachment on the states was not less likely than the reverse. He argued that "The number of individuals employed under the Constitution of the United States will be much smaller than the number employed under the particular States. There will consequently be less of personal influence on the side of the former than the latter. The members of the legislative, executive, and judiciary departments of thirteen or more States, the justices of peace, officers of militia, ministerial officers of justice, with all the county, corporation, and town officers, for three millions and more of people, intermixed, and having particular acquaintance with every class and circle of people, must exceed, beyond all proportions, both in number and influence, those of every description who will be employed in the administration of the federal system." In support of his position, Madison reasoned that "The powers delegated . . . to the federal government are few and defined. . . . The powers reserved to the several States will extend to all the objects which, in the ordinary course of affairs, concern the lives, liberties, and property of the people, and the internal order, improvement, and prosperity of the State." Obviously, then, the state with its local governments would have to have many officers and employees. Madison went into considerable detail along the lines of this general analysis. By including all local officals both salaried and unsalaried with those of the state itself, and by assuming that the national government would stay rather strictly within the range of its expressed powers, he made a fairly convincing argument.

Alexander Hamilton came to a somewhat different conclusion. In discussing the respective national and state powers of taxation he reasoned that the most expensive functions of government (war, defense, foreign affairs, and commerce) would fall on the national government, while each state's expenditures would be limited "to the mere domestic police of a state, to the support of its legislative, executive, and judicial departments, with their different appendages, and to the encouragement of agriculture and manufacturers (which will comprehend almost all the objects of state expenditure)"—and that these expenses "are insignificant in comparison with those which relate to the national defence" (The Federalist, number 34). By Hamilton's line of reasoning, the entire group of thirteen states could easily get along on less than two hundred thousand pounds (or, say, a million dollars) a year at that time. This would obviously mean that the states would not have to support many employees to administer their functions.

Neither Madison nor Hamilton proved to be a perfect prophet in this case—but how could anyone have foreseen the ways in which American society and the American federal system would develop in the next century or two?

As already stated elsewhere herein, both the national and state governments proceeded very slowly in the early decades of the republic to enlarge their functions and their administrative staffs. Unfortunately no reliable statistics are available on the numbers of state and local government officers and employees for many decades after the Constitution went into effect, down to well after the time when Minnesota became a state. For recent years the state and local figures are now available, while fairly reliable federal figures go back to 1816. Of course the federal figures have fluctuated greatly because of wartime expansions and postwar contractions. The figures in Table 1, although they are taken from different sources and are not strictly comparable, give some idea of the trends. These figures include the period of our Minnesota studies. They show that in 1940 and 1949 the national government had almost double the number of employees that the states had, considerably more than double in 1951, and

Table 1. Government Civilian Employment in Selected Nonwar Years, 1940-57 (in Thousands)

Year	Total	National	State	Local
1957	8,047	2,439	1,358	4,249
1954	7,232	2,373	1,198	3,661
1951	6,734	2,446	1,041	3,252
1949	6,203	2,047	1,037	3,119
1940	4,378	1,014	529	1,515

again nearly double in 1954 and 1957. However, if state and local figures are combined, they were double the national figures in 1940 and 1949, somewhat less than double in 1951, and well over double in 1954 and 1957.

Omitting from the reckoning the federal employees who are stationed outside the United States and those who are working on strictly national affairs in and around Washington, D.C., we find that 80 per cent of the federal employees in 1957, or almost exactly 2 million, were distributed among the forty-eight states, where some 5.6 million state and local officers and employees were also engaged in public services. The distribution of these two million federal employees is not at all even or in proportion to state populations, or to state public employees. In the average state there were about three federal to two state employees. In a number of states the ratio was more than two to one—Alabama, California, Colorado, Georgia, Maryland, Nevada, New Mexico, Texas, and Utah. These are states in which there are large federal projects and installations for defense and other purposes that require the services of many civilian employees. From these figures the numbers range downward to a state like North Carolina, for example, where the state employees outnumber the federal three to one.

Minnesota had, in April 1957, 23,479 federal employees to 29,400 state employees, or about four federal to five state. It is, therefore, well below the average in percentage of federal employees to state employees. In short the impact of national government operations on the local economy and attitudes might seem, according to this criterion, to be far less than that in the majority of the states. But such a comparative statement misses the major point. The important fact is that nearly 23,500 federal officers and employees were employed in Minnesota in 1957, practically all on a full-time basis. On the other hand, many of the 29,400 state employees worked on a part-time basis, especially in education; the full-time equivalent for state employment was 25,087. Hence, if only state and national employees are considered, the national government in Minnesota nearly matches the state government, man for man.

Using 1954 figures (all 1957 figures being not yet available) we find that of 24,194 federal employees then in the state, 12,895, or over half, were in the postal service, 4,661 with the Veterans Administration, 1,610 with the Department of Defense (Army, Navy, and Air Corps). This left over 5000 others to staff the many other federal agencies in the state.

Some of the consequences of the presence of so many federal agencies and employees in the state remain for later discussion.

CHAPTER 5

National-State Relations

He would be a very bold and a very ignorant man who would attempt to describe all the relations between the nation and its government, on the one hand, and any state and its government, on the other, in a single chapter or even in a substantial book. No such description is offered here.

One thing we all learned during our Minnesota studies is that intergovernmental relations under conditions of intensive governmental activity are exceedingly complex and hard to set forth. Besides that, they are constantly changing. Our entire series of monographs elucidates some aspects of national-state relations as observed in Minnesota for particular functions and during a certain time period. As I show in a later chapter in this review, however, certain major functions are scarcely more than mentioned in our publications, while some topics that cut across a number of functions also receive relatively little attention. In that chapter I endeavor to call attention to some of these major omissions and to suggest a few inferences to be drawn from what we learned about the omitted functions and topics without making an intensive study of them. The present chapter on national-state relations should also make some contribution in this direction.

As I have suggested in another connection, the study of intergovernmental relations in the United States does not involve viewing an entire large entity such as the United States government sitting down to settle certain questions of policy with another entire large entity such as the Minnesota state government. Quite the opposite is true. Every government that we consider herein, except perhaps some of the smallest and simplest unifunctional local units, is composed of, or, so to speak, split up into, a number of different branches, departments, and individual officers. Each of these has contacts, few or many as the case may be, with "opposite numbers" and also with other authorities in other governments within the same system. Many of the dealings are between agency and agency, others between officer and officer. The lines of interrelations crisscross, parallel, by-pass, or conflict with each other, pierce through levels from highest to lowest, and cut across geographic and jurisdictional boundaries. As a result they form ever-changing and indescribably complex patterns when one attempts to view them as a whole. Some of the <u>intra</u>governmental relations, such as those between the state governor and the heads of state administrative agencies, are seriously affected by the <u>inter</u>governmental relations that each agency has with authorities in other governments. Conversely the intergovernmental relations are affected by the intragovernmental.

These interrelations, in every situation, are a factor that those who deal with politics and government can never afford to forget. Citizen reform groups, pressure groups, and party leaders are well aware of this fact. It enters into the thinking and the actions also of government officials at all three levels and in all three branches, legislative, executive, and judicial.

Let me attempt to give some samples, therefore, from the field of national-state relations, of various ways in which intergovernmental problems affect nearly all activities of state and national governments. I make no pretense to completeness, and neither do I assert that the intergovernmental considerations are dominant in all actions and decisions of these two levels. I merely wish to illustrate the fact that such considerations enter into many things that these governments do and that they obviously affect both the forms and the substance of public actions. The illustrations will be drawn in large part from Minnesota experiences, but evidences from other sources will also be adduced.

CONSTITUTIONAL RELATIONS

Being in a constitutional sense an equal of every other state in the Union, Minnesota's relations with the national government are formally the same as those of any other state. In practice, however, some distinctive characteristics are evident. Most noticeable, I believe, has been a tendency of the state to avoid taking an antinational position. Minnesota has been neither a strong advocate of states' rights nor a waver of the flag of state sovereignty. Certain original states, for example Maryland and Virginia, located in close proximity to the national capital and frequently, so to speak, allergic to national powers and activities, have raised a number of major constitutional objections to federal laws and other measures. A number of these objections have gone to the United States Supreme Court and have elicited decisions that have helped to dispose of important constitutional issues. Minnesota's attorneys general have on occasion joined other states in questioning the powers and the actions of the national authorities (e.g., the diversion of Lake Michigan waters at Chicago, and the assignment of the "tidelands" oil and other resources to the adjacent coastal states), but Minnesota does not appear to have initiated any important litigation against the exercise of federal powers.

This does not mean that Minnesota has had no important part in litigation before the Supreme Court on questions involving its own laws and powers. Minnesota has done considerable experimenting in taxation, railroad regulation, chain store laws and taxes, congressional apportionment and districting, regulation of the press, mortgage moratorium laws, and other fields of public policy. As a result many aggrieved persons have brought cases into the federal courts to prevent the enforcement of Minnesota laws, or in other ways to secure redress in the federal courts against the state. The name "State of Minnesota" appears, therefore, in a considerable number of federal Supreme Court cases—something like fifty by 1952. In the same period at least fifteen laws and other actions taken by the state were held unconstitutional by the federal Supreme Court. The decisions have involved primarily the federal constitutional provisions for the election of representatives in Congress, the contract clause, ex post facto, freedom of the press, the regulation of commerce, due process, and equal protection.

LEGISLATIVE RELATIONS

During the many years since the United States Constitution went into effect, Congress and the state legislatures have developed legislative forms and practices for various situations in which they must recognize each other's legislative powers, or adjust their respective legislative actions to those of the other governmental level. Instead of making its laws cover every aspect of the subject being legislated upon, Congress has in many cases simply referred to and in effect adopted for federal purposes the pertinent legislation and common law of the states. Property laws and the registration of property deeds and titles, marriage and dependency laws, the laws of wills and estates—these and many other state laws have been recognized by Congress as binding upon the national authorities in pertinent cases. Thus in passing laws concerning ships in foreign and interstate commerce, Congress early recognized the laws of the several states as controlling in matters of pilotage. Similarly Congress has in effect adopted for purposes of federal elections the election laws and procedures of the several states instead of enacting a complete and uniform code of federal election laws, as it may do at any time.

The states on the other hand have recognized and made use of federal laws in a great variety of ways. The federal census has been accepted in all states for many purposes of state legislation, and federal standards in many fields such as weights and measures, milk pasteurization, and foods and drugs generally have been accepted and woven into their legislation by the states. Lacking their own postal services the states have made the mailing of legal notices, documents, and remittances by United States mail sufficient to satisfy the legal requirements for a number of state and local purposes, and in this connection have given registered mail an especially high rating.

These are but a few examples of many that could be cited as evidence of a general two-way tendency of the state and national governments to recognize and depend upon each other's laws and services in various situations. Indeed the common law and even the basic statute laws of the states form an essential substratum for most federal legislation. Recent decades have brought the development by Congress of a number of rather specialized types of legislation that are designed to assist the states in carrying out their functions.

For example, one of the handicaps under which the states labor is the fact that while all citizens, whether law-abiding or not, are free to travel from state to state without special permits, the states' powers of law enforcement are limited to their own state areas. Hence the criminal often finds safety in flight to another state. For reasons to be discussed later, interstate compacts help in this situation to some extent but do not wholly fill the bill. Also the field of interstate commerce and the postal service through which crimes may be perpetrated or aided and abetted, interstate or locally, fall within the power of Congress and not within the powers of the states.

Heeding the requests of state and local law enforcement officers, as brought by them directly to Congress and also as relayed by individual congressmen, all of whom come from states and know something about their own states' problems, Congress began long ago to pass laws to cover the interstate aspects of certain crimes. An early act of this kind was one to forbid the use of the mails to defraud. Fraud in general is a matter for state legislation and state suppression, but since the states do not control the postal service the act of Congress made it a separate crime to use the mails to defraud, and placed the main responsibility for enforcement on a federal agency, the postal inspectors.

Later came similar laws on white slavery (the Mann Act forbidding the interstate transportation of women for immoral purposes), on kidnapping, on the interstate movement of stolen automobiles and of other stolen property, and more recently on flight to another state to avoid prosecution. These laws cover federal offenses that are federally punishable, and they bring national law-enforcing agencies like the FBI into cooperation with the state and local agencies that are responsible for enforcing the basic state laws against white slavery, auto theft, and so on.

Other laws of this type are based more or less on the national taxing power, on monetary and banking powers, war powers, and others, but the commerce power may also be involved. Such are the federal laws on narcotics (a strict code on illegal possession, use, and sale, based on a federal license tax), the federal gambling tax and license law, the firearms act, and laws on the robbery of national banks and banks with nationally insured deposits. All these laws call for national enforcing action, and bring federal officials into cooperation with state and local officers.

Congress has enacted a number of statutes to keep within state control various functions that, under earlier acts of Congress or Supreme Court decisions, seemed destined to fall under national control. An early example arose in the field of liquor control when the Supreme Court ruled that a state (Iowa) with a prohibition law could not forbid or penalize the importation into it of liquor from other states. The interstate shipment of liquor was something that the Supreme Court thought was of national concern and that only Congress could regulate. This wide loophole in the state's prohibition law, which could have affected every state with such a law, was closed when Congress legislated to divest such liquor shipments of their interstate character and to subject them to state regulation when they entered the state where they were to be sold or used. Hence the state prohibition laws would apply. The Supreme Court held this act of Congress to be constitutional, and the Twenty-First Amendment to the Constitution, 1933, which repealed the Eighteenth or Prohibition Amendment, in a sense perpetuates and even strengthens this principle of state control over the liquor traffic.

Other congressional acts of this general character include (1) an act to give each state power to prohibit the sale or use within its limits of prison-made goods, wherever manufactured; (2) an act guaranteeing state control over the insurance business under certain conditions, after the Supreme Court had ruled various insurance activities to be interstate commerce; (3) an act returning the "tidelands" with their oil and other resources to the adjacent states of California, Texas, and Louisiana, after the Supreme Court had declared them to belong to the nation as a whole; (4) various acts granting or restoring limited state taxing powers and law enforcement authority over private persons on federal reservations and other special jurisdictions (forts, navy yards, parks, etc.) within the states. These acts all concede certain powers to the states, and necessitate legislative or other action by the states that wish to make use of such powers. They do not call for any significant law enforcing or other administrative actions by the national authorities.

Congress has recently considered a measure to restore to the states an independent power of punishing subversives, after the Supreme Court had ruled that federal legislation was exclusive in this field.

Other congressional acts that are based upon a recognition of state legislative and administrative problems fall into different categories. There are several designed to protect the states generally against the few states that have tried or might try to gain advantages for themselves as low-tax havens by failing to impose estate or inheritance taxes, or by not providing for unemployment insurance. Congress itself in these cases imposes a tax sufficiently high to offset any such advantages but allows a credit to any taxpayer (up to, say, 90 per cent of his federal tax) if his own state has such a tax and he can show that he has paid it. Another small group of laws restricts the power of the federal district courts to interfere with state agencies by means of injunctions in such matters as state tax law enforcement and state regulation of public utilities. As in the case of insurance regulation such acts usually set minimum standards that the state legislature must accept (i.e., legislate) if the state is to get the protection of the federal act.

Another category includes all recent federal-aid laws. These are based on the theory that any state may accept or reject their terms and benefits, but that if it decides to accept it must so signify by passing legislation embodying the terms of the federal aid and binding the state to perform its part of the bargain. The result is that the national and state laws on each grant-in-aid are truly interdependent. They stand or fall together. If Congress repeals the federal law the state acts cease to have any force. If any state repeals its own law, the national government makes no more grants for that purpose to that state, but other states may continue to benefit.

These types of laws by no means exhaust the list of those in which national legislation makes reference to state laws or state laws refer to national. In its legislation of 1949 to de-control rents, for example, Congress held the door open temporarily for state and local governments to impose their own rent controls if they so desired. In the act of 1946 concerning federal aid for airport construction Congress allowed each state to decide whether to have all such grants within the state channeled through a state agency, or to permit direct dealings between the national and local airport authorities. But it is not necessary to attempt to list all the varied types of statutes that link national, state, and local authorities in some sort of relationship.

It must not be understood, of course, that all legislation by Congress affecting state laws, or state legislation affecting national policies or powers, reflects a spirit of sweetness and light and a desire for cooperation. The recent rash of legislation in some southern states to prevent the enforcement of the Supreme Court decision of 1954 requiring racial integration in the public schools comes immediately to mind. In this situation, of course, the forces opposed to integration have refused to recognize the Supreme Court decision as the law of the land, and have resorted not only to litigation to test the decision's validity but also to state legislation and state court decisions to circumvent the enforcement of the decision. There are numerous other instances as well. For example, California's legislation on wills and bequests, as construed by the California supreme court, in effect forbids a person to bequeath property to the United States, although he may do so to the state of California, to municipalities, and to other public bodies and associations. The United States Supreme Court upheld the power of California to establish this law discriminating against the nation.

While our study was going forward a 1949 edition of Minnesota Statutes was published in two volumes. I scanned these volumes section by section for references to the laws of the United States. All told I found 273 distinct passages (and I may have missed some) that refer clearly to laws, services, grants-in-aid, property, and activities of the United States, or to the state's relations with the nation and its government. These passages cover such a wide range that it would be tedious and confusing to attempt even to summarize them. Soon after this the state published also the state laws enacted at the 1951 session of the legislature, popularly called the Session Laws of 1951. A careful scanning of these laws yielded 44 statutes that dealt in whole or in part with some aspect of Minnesota's relations with the national government. A number of these merely amended previous statutes, while others were new laws.

In addition there were eleven resolutions of the 1951 legislature that either touched upon national-state relations or made recommendations to Congress for action on issues of national policy and legislation. Some of these resolutions memorialized Congress to proceed with the St. Lawrence Seaway, to establish with Canada a reciprocal arrangement for the duty-free transshipment of crude oil and natural gas, to establish a national cemetery at Birch Coulee Battlefield in Renville County, to continue to supply Europe and Asia with food, feed, and fibers as a means of resisting communism, to oppose changes in the tax status of cooperatives, and to withdraw from the taxation of gasoline.

Such resolutions or memorials to Congress, and sometimes to the President and even to particular agencies of the national government, have a long history in many states, if not in all. I have long shared with other students a feeling that most of these memorials, even when laid before Congress and read into the Congressional Record, have little effect on congressional action. It has appeared that, in yielding to the pressures of groups asking Congress to enact the "Townsend Plan" of grants to the aged in the depression period, or for a "25 per cent limit" on federal income taxes, or for a federally guaranteed "cost of production" plan for farmers, and in memorializing Congress to approve such schemes, state legislators have merely shifted to Congress the burden of rejecting something that many state legislators would not themselves have approved. In so doing the state legislatures may have debased the currency value of their memorials to Congress generally and made congressmen indifferent to all such pleas.

But these are mere conjectures. No one has ever made a careful study of this phase of national-state relations in the field of legislation. Such a study in a few leading or representative states, with a follow-up on the work of Congress and its committees, might reveal trends and influences not yet fully brought to light. What the Minnesota legislature's many resolutions memorializing Congress, and its many laws that refer to the national government, positively do show over the years is that the legislators in this state have had Congress and the national government in mind more or less continuously as they have dealt with state problems. A scanning of the 1957 Session Laws reveals no lessening of this attention. To be effective state legislative action on many subjects simply cannot be taken without reference to the laws and services that emanate from Washington.

By the same token, Congress, along with the other two branches of the national government, needs to make frequent references to the states in what it enacts and in the national services and activities that it establishes and finances. Congressional legislation that touches upon national-state relations refers most frequently to the states in general and not to particular states by name. However, in numerous statutes of a private or local nature, such as those that transfer the title to pieces of land to the state or to a local unit of government within it, the acts of Congress do name the particular state. Minnesota has been so designated in numerous statutes. Thus there is an unimpeded reciprocity of recognition between state and national legislative bodies. These numerous acts reveal not only the multiplicity and variety of the contacts between nation and states, but also the predominantly cooperative quality of their relations and the mutual respect in which the levels generally regard each other. Even the states whose governments are resisting in every way they can the integration of the races in the public schools suffer no noticeable neglect or discrimination in their other relations with the national authorities.

One of the interesting facts about national-state legislative relations is that they have been developed at both the state and national levels without an obvious need for any new device or organization to facilitate them. There has been no need for a central clearinghouse or drafting bureau to prepare such legislation. Different committees of the two houses of Congress and of the state legislatures, including that of Minnesota, have prepared their own bills with such aid from attorneys general and appropriate government agencies as they deemed necessary. The results seem to have been, on the whole, satisfactory to both the state and the national authorities.

Of concern primarily to students of constitutional law is the question whether in this increasing trend toward the interdependence of state and national legislation the states have not in effect been delegating some of their constitutional powers to the national government, and the national legislature, that is Congress, delegating some of its constitutional powers to the states. When a state legislature legislates, as some did during the 1930s, to authorize state agencies themselves to accept future federal grants-in-aid with the conditions attached thereto, without having to go back to the legislature, is it not in effect turning over to Congress, which sets the terms of such grants, a part of its own legislative power? When Congress legislates to authorize the states to control certain phases of interstate commerce, or to exercise powers of taxation and law enforcement within federal areas devoted to forts, navy yards, and arsenals, for example, is it not delegating to the state legislatures powers that appear to be vested by the Constitution exclusively in Congress?

It has long been a theory of various purists and strict constructionists among constitutional lawyers that delegations of power either by Congress to the states or by the states to Congress are unconstitutional. Except in the field of admiralty and maritime law, however, where the exclusive power of Congress has been insisted upon, the Supreme Court has had no great difficulty in upholding apparent delegations of power or in finding that they were not delegations in law. At any rate, the borderlines between state and congressional powers of legislation have become more uncertain and more fluid than many would like to see them. None of the important fields of interdependent legislation have been seriously reduced by the application of the supposed rule against delegation. The power of Congress to define, within the limits of the Constitution, the extent to which it will legislate in the fields open to it, and the power of both Congress and the states to cooperate on programs and policies for the general welfare, have prevailed over stricter views of the Constitution.

This is one aspect of a great change that has been taking place in both official and public attitudes toward the Constitution. It is looked upon more and more as an instrument to facilitate action for the common good, and this requires that it be continuously adaptable to changing needs instead of being a rigid framework to separate national from state powers. But in view of the fact that the highest national authorities, Congress, the President, and the Supreme Court, are the only ones that can truly determine national policy, it follows that the states simply cannot, either separately or as a group, be the deciding authorities on any major national policy. The states may point to their powers under the Constitution, but the fact is that more and more their powers are being defined by acts of Congress. It is true that the Supreme Court has in recent decades been far more liberal in interpreting and upholding state powers than it was for several decades before and after 1900, but the recent favorable decisions in this field have not been on major questions, as it now appears. On the other hand a number of important decisions in fields of insurance, labor legislation, sedition laws, railroad regulation, and commerce have turned on the question whether congressional legislation has not pre-empted the field to the exclusion of state laws. The more Congress legislates the more it occupies certain fields of action, and thus sets practical limits beyond which the states may not go, no matter what the powers of the states might have been in the absence of congressional legislation. Even various grant-in-aid laws set actual standards and limits which the states must observe or lose the grants.

To have Congress in effect setting the limits for state legislation in a number of major fields of state powers is something new and significant in the constitutional relations of the nation and the states. It represents a change in the actual position of the states in the Union in a direction that the framers of the original Constitution seem not to have foreseen—and yet a change that is arguably foreshadowed in, and that seems to flow logically from, the national supremacy clause. If Congress ever uses all its powers to the hilt, and continues to be supported as at present by a Supreme Court imbued with a liberal doctrine of implied national powers, the powers that the states can actually use may be found written more largely in congressional legislation than in what can be spelled out of the Tenth Amendment.

As I pointed out in Chapter 1, Professor K. C. Wheare in his widely used work on Federal Government distinguishes sharply between true federal systems like that of the United States on the one hand, and those quasi-federal or pseudo- or para-federal systems, like that of South Africa, in which the state or regional governments are subordinate to the general or national government. This is a distinction that needs to be made, though with some qualifications, but the basis on which Professor Wheare makes it is one that I cannot accept. He contends that vis-à-vis the national government the states are coordinate and independent. The states are certainly not independent in any defensible meaning of that term; and since, by the second paragraph of Article VI of the Constitution, the laws and treaties of the United States are "the supreme law of the land, any thing in the constitution or laws of any state to the contrary notwithstanding," state powers are certainly not "coordinate" with those of the nation. What I contend here is not that the states do not still have their basic powers from the Constitution rather than from the acts of Congress, but simply that in fact more and more fields of state legislation are becoming defined in and dependent upon legislation enacted by Congress under its own supreme constitutional powers. Furthermore, the states have generally come to accept this situation. Even in the current controversy over racial integration in the public schools various opponents of integration are in effect saying that they object to accepting the Supreme Court decision as a mandate, but that if Congress would pass a law requiring integration they would accept it.

ADMINISTRATIVE RELATIONS

Much of the legislation that has been mentioned above deals with various forms of collaboration between the national and state governments in the performance of functions that are of interest to both levels. In our research in Minnesota we dealt with only a selected group of major functions, and we did not try to list all the others in which both state and nation were concerned. A recent compilation by a Special Committee on Intergovernmental Relations appointed by Governor Orville L. Freeman from among staff members of state agencies supplies much valuable information on Minnesota federal-state programs in early 1958. From the information provided it appears that all but a few of the programs listed were in operation during the period of our own study. Therefore the data supplied by this report are pertinent to our study and will be used here.

Areas of National-State Collaboration. The report lists 81 "separate identifiable programs involving about $75 million of federal funds per year. This does not include additional amounts reported by state departments as expended [by the national agencies] in programs paralleling theirs." The $75 million figure was based on 1957 receipts by the state from federal funds. The list also does not include cases of informal cooperation between United States and Minnesota authorities in which no money is granted or received.

The 81 programs listed are by no means all of the grant-in-aid variety. Many are based on contracts or even on less formal agreements between a national agency and a state agency to engage in a joint enterprise to which each will contribute what it can in manpower, money, and facilities. A few examples of such programs are barberry eradication, cooperative grading services for the poultry industry, the dairy industry, and other branches of agriculture, topographic mapping (Geological Survey), a cooperative audit program in income taxation. In addition the list includes various research projects at the University of Minnesota for the national government under contract arrangements. In some of these cases no money passes from the national to the state treasury, while in a few exceptional instances state money is turned over to a national agency for services rendered. Because of their great variety, a quick description of these many contractual joint or cooperative efforts is out of the question here.

Among the areas of cooperative activities not listed in this report, let me mention tion just four: cooperation in law enforcement, police training, fingerprinting and identification of criminals between the Federal Bureau of Investigation, the Secret Service, and the federal Bureau of Narcotics on the one hand, and the numerous state and local law enforcement agencies in Minnesota on the other; services of the United States Post Office to state agencies engaged in enforcing laws concerning shipment into the state of uninspected seeds, noxious plants, and other illegal materials; the extension of federal Old Age and Survivors' Insurance (social security) to state officers and employees, including those of the university, as a supplement to their retirement allowances; cooperation between the Interstate Commerce Commission and the state Railroad and Warehouse Commission in certain phases of railroad regulation and grain inspection.

Grant-in-Aid Programs. Much attention has been given in recent years to the national-state relations that have developed around programs based on federal grants-in-aid. The grants in which the state of Minnesota participates are listed in the 1958 report mentioned above. These grant-in-aid programs provide for national aid to the state in almost every major field of state activity, including education, conservation, public health, social welfare, agriculture, highways, airports, military affairs, civil defense, and employment security (which is not strictly a grant-in-aid). In most of these fields there are a number of distinct grants, so that the total number of programs is some forty or more—the count depending to some extent upon the definition of grant-in-aid that is employed.

Not listed in this report are a few grants under which local governments receive money directly from the national treasury instead of its first passing through the state treasury. Various federal payments directly to individuals, such as veterans benefits, social security payments, and agricultural benefits, are also not included in the report.

More than $65 million of the $75 million mentioned in the report as state receipts in 1957 came to the state through federal grants-in-aid and closely related programs such as employment security.

Some of the major federal grants-in-aid received by Minnesota are described in earlier monographs in this series. Also in Monograph 8 I have devoted Chapter 7 to "Federal Grants-in-Aid as a Revenue Source in Minnesota."

The impact of the grants-in-aid in any particular state upon its economy, its finances, its laws, and its administration presents an important subject of inquiry to which various scholars have given their attention recently. Our own studies have turned up some interesting observations and conclusions, to which I now wish to add a little concerning the impact on Minnesota's government and administration, both state and local.

In summarizing briefly what appear to be the administrative consequences of federal grant-in-aid programs on state and local administration I wish to avoid the implication that I am drawing a direct and unqualified cause-and-effect relationship. In short I do not say that any time a central government in a federal system sets up a grant-in-aid program the administrative consequences or sequences of events will be those that seemed to follow in the United States in recent decades. Neither do I assert that none of these changes could have occurred without the federal grants. I would say, however, that if I am right in describing what happened in the United States, then the fact that these things happened here suggests the possibility that they could happen under similar conditions at other times and places. Indeed if the conditions were highly similar at some other time and place I would venture to assert the probability that distinctly comparable results would follow.

On the other hand, it is not unlikely that certain developments would have come in time even without the federal grants and conditions. The latter did, however, provide at least an early and extra push, and the changes to be noted did come along with the state's acceptance of the grants-in-aid and apparently in large part because the federal offer of the grants was made conditional upon the state's acceptance of certain administrative standards in the expenditure of the grants. Some of these conditions came with the original grants; others were added later by act of Congress or by Federal administrative action with the approval of Congress.

Taken as a group, federal grants-in-aid and certain closely related national measures seem to have brought with them or been accompanied by the following changes in state governments:

1. New and enlarged state functions.

2. Direct state administration of functions formerly delegated to counties, towns, and municipalities—in short, increased centralization in the state.

3. The creation of new state agencies and the strengthening and enlargement of older ones, with considerable increases in state personnel.

4. The adoption of new state merit systems and the expansion and improvement of old ones, with considerable professionalization of the state services, and some reduction of political party pressures on state agencies. A new state emphasis upon the importance of qualified personnel.

5. New and increased contacts between state administrators and the district and regional administrators of federal programs.

6. The establishment of new national organizations of state and national officials in the functional fields covered by the grants.

7. Considerable standardization among the states in service levels, methods, and rules under the grant-in-aid programs.

8. A new or increased emphasis upon the planning of state services in the aided fields, and upon adequate reporting of the work done.

9. A new or increased emphasis also upon interstate cooperation in the administration of the aided service programs.

10. With general public acceptance of the grant-in-aid programs, a considerable increase in state revenues and expenditures, usually going far beyond the matching requirements of the federal aids received.

11. Along with their many new contacts and joint responsibilities, an increase also in the points of potential friction between state and national administrators over personnel standards, service regulations, audits and inspections, together with some difficulties in state budgeting of the federally granted funds.

12. Despite these difficulties, no general demand to decrease or eliminate the grants but instead a general and usually successful pressure from state agencies to get increases in the grants and liberalization of the rules controlling expenditures.

Minnesota's experiences with federal grants-in-aid have been very much the same as those of other states, although in general, unless I have been misinformed, the national-state relations seem to have been unusually amicable in this state. As in other states the fields of highways, social welfare, and employment security have received the largest amounts of federal aid, but conservation activities, public health and hospitals, airports, and some educational activities (e.g., vocational education, school lunches, agricultural extension and research and other university functions) have also received substantial federal support. Because of the continued reluctance of Congress to grant general aid for primary and secondary education, the state department of education has been outstripped by other state agencies as a recipient of federal aid; and aid to rural libraries has only just begun. Similarly the state department of agriculture, although it has many cooperative programs with the United States Department of Agriculture, does not receive ordinary federal aid in any large amounts. The national guard, civil defense, and disaster relief stand more or less by themselves; each one is under strong national influence, and each lacks some of the features of a grant-in-aid program.

Some students of intergovernmental relations once expressed concern that the non-aided state departments would fall seriously behind those that were receiving federal aid. As federal aid has come to be extended more or less to all state departments except the regulatory bodies this fear has tended to subside. Cooperative relations have developed between state and national agencies concerned with the same general fields, such as general law enforcement, industrial relations, and the regulation of railroads, telegraph and telephone lines, banks, and dealers in securities; and wherever there is even a little cooperation in performing a common task (even if there are certain differences in policy and some competition and antagonism), there is likely to be increasing mutual understanding and the raising of the levels of administration.

Personnel Relations. National-state relations in public administration affect more or less the entire range of administrative problems, such as legal powers, organization, personnel, planning procedures, budgeting, auditing, reporting, and public relations. Of all the problems it seems to me that personnel is fairly central and calls for a little more discussion.

Congress and the national administration have come in recent decades to put a great deal of stress on the importance of a thoroughgoing merit system for the national government itself, and in connection with the federally aided functions of the states they have also come to emphasize the need for politically neutral state personnel. Those who are to expend federal funds in the states and to administer the state functions that Congress subsidizes should also be persons of competence and personal merit.

To achieve this result the national government has proceeded along two lines. On the negative side Congress has tried to discourage partisan misuse of federal funds by the so-called second Hatch Act, 1940, which provides in effect that no state officer (with certain exceptions) who is paid in whole or in part from federal funds shall take any active part in political party management or political campaigns. The United States Civil Service Commission investigates alleged violations of this law and where it finds any violation it recommends that the state dismiss the offender. If the state does not do so, the penalty prescribed by the law is the withholding from the state's current grant of a sum equal to twice the annual salary of the offender. This law is being enforced, and it appears to be having some effect in eliminating the designated abuses. Minnesota does not appear to have had any important case arise under this law.

With so many state departments in all states receiving federal grants, this law means in effect that the national government is using its influence and powers to set the standards of political conduct for state officials. In so doing it is also neutralizing the state departments politically, and to that extent separating them from the partisan political influence of the governors. Many United States senators no doubt had this fact in mind when they voted for the law, because state governors are always potential and sometimes actual rivals of the senators for political leadership in their states and even for a senator's seat. Another result may be, however, and some governors have complained of this, that the heads of federally aided state departments have become less amenable to the governors' leadership and supervision in matters of state policy.

On the positive side of state personnel administration, federal policy for several decades has been strongly in favor of merit systems for the recruitment of persons who are to administer the federally aided programs in the states. The pressure in this direction was not strong in the World War I period when the federal-aid highway program was initiated, but much has been done since then by the United States Bureau of Public Roads and its several predecessors to help bring the states up to a high level of professionalization of the engineering and research staffs of highway departments.

The field of social welfare presents a different example. When the Social Security Act was passed by Congress in 1935 the national administration and Congress were already at work extending and improving the merit system in the federal service, and several national organizations were agitating strenuously for merit systems in the states. The original Social Security Act made no adequate provision for state merit systems in the welfare programs under that act, but by 1939 Congress became convinced of the need. In that year it authorized the then Social Security Board to define the personnel requirements for state and local welfare employees and, in effect, to establish a merit system for them. In that same year Minnesota enacted its own general civil service law and merit system. The latter law has been accepted by the federal authorities as adequate enough in general for state welfare personnel, but this does not tell the whole story. Regional representatives of various bureaus of the Social Security Administration and its several predecessors kept in close touch with the state welfare department and showed especial interest in departmental staff appointments and promotions. This caused some irritation and indeed no little confusion in the state agency, because several different federal bureaus in the welfare field were checking up on state staff changes in an uncoordinated way. In such matters no outsider like myself is in any position to pass a judgment, and very few insiders are likely to be wholly unbiased observers. In any case, however, there can be little doubt that despite certain irritations and differences of opinion, standards rose significantly in the early years of the welfare department and that they have been kept high. A show of genuine interest by influential outside agencies like the bureaus of the national Social Security Administration that were seeking improved welfare service could not have been seriously detrimental to the state service, whatever frictions may have developed in the process.

Because Minnesota lacked a general merit system law for the counties but chose to administer major categories of the welfare services for which federal aid was received through those units, it was necessary to set up a separate merit system under the state welfare department for the county welfare systems. This arrangement began soon after the congressional act of 1939 and it still continues. Thus a federal requirement brought into the counties of the state a merit system for welfare employees such as is still lacking for other employees of the counties generally.

It is interesting to note that in the seventy-five years since New York (1883) and Massachusetts (1884) established general merit system laws for state employees comparable to the federal Pendleton Act (Civil Service Act) of 1883, nearly half the states have failed to follow their example. On the other hand sixteen states without general merit system laws have merit system councils to cover the grant-in-aid programs, while still others have merit systems for certain services covered by grants-in-aid like public welfare services. As a result there is today no state that is wholly lacking a merit system for any purpose; and it is interesting to note how many states have set up special merit systems for various federally aided services.

What can we deduce from these data, with all the state-to-state variations that they reveal? It seems to me clear that federal inducements through grants-in-aid have brought many states at least to the halfway mark of merit systems for the federally aided services, while other states have added merit systems for the federal-aid functions to the limited merit systems that they already had. In short the influence of federal aid in bringing state legislatures to enact merit system laws is rather clearly revealed.

CHAPTER 6

Interstate Relations

Judged by the ordinary criteria of the amounts of money involved and the public attention they receive, the relations between state and state do not loom as large upon the horizons of federal systems of government as do the relations between the national government and the states. Interstate relations are ever present and unavoidable, however, and if worked out with intelligence and good will they can do much to facilitate the smooth and constructive operation of each federal system as a whole.

For reasons that would take long to present and explain, interstate relations have received much more attention in the United States than in the other important federal systems—and more in recent decades than in earlier times. State legislators and administrators, students of American institutions and political processes, nationwide organizations interested in the public services, and other classes and groups of individuals have contributed to this increasing interest and attention. As a result there have been notable changes in this category of relations, especially since about 1900. Many who are fearful of the consequences of centralization in Washington have looked to interstate cooperation as a substitute for national action.

Each author of a functional monograph in this series devoted considerable time and effort to working out the interstate relations in his field, but the developments varied so much from one function to another that their treatment of these relations in their reports had to vary accordingly. Anticipating that this would be the case I planned at one stage to have a separate report prepared and published on the interstate relations of Minnesota. Considerable work was done toward this end, and our collection of materials grew to be rather sizable. It became evident, however, that a full-length report could not be managed within the resources of the project. I decided, therefore, to prepare this summary chapter for inclusion in the final monograph, along with chapters on national-state and on state-local, national-local, and interlocal relations. These chapters if read together should give the reader at least a conspectus of the various types of vertical and horizontal relations that appear to bind together the American federal system.

In this chapter the general constitutional arrangements for interstate relations, which were in effect since long before Minnesota entered the Union, will be dealt with first. Then will follow a discussion of the changes in legislation, administration, and informal practice that make interstate relations today appear so different from what the framers of the Constitution seem to have expected. A few tentative conclusions and hypotheses will terminate the survey.

THE CONSTITUTIONAL ARRANGEMENTS

The framers of the constitution of the United States did not favor a complete consolidation of all public powers and functions in the hands of the national government, although this is in effect what the "Antifederalists" charged them with planning to do. Instead they left the states and their governments in existence, gave them work to do in the revised governmental system, and by implication left them in autonomous control of an undefined and unenumerated mass of governmental powers that were not delegated by the Constitution to the national authorities. James Madison covered this point adequately in The Federalist, Number 14, where he also pointed out that if the states had been abolished by the Constitution, "the general government would be compelled, by the principle of self-preservation,—to reinstate them in their proper jurisdiction." He implied that the national authorities alone simply could not have carried the burden of legislating and providing for all the regional and local public needs of a country so large and diverse.

A few years later, to allay the fears and terminate the importunings of numerous leaders in the states, Congress proposed and the states soon ratified (1791) the Tenth Amendment to the Constitution, which provides that "The powers not delegated to the United States by the Constitution, nor prohibited by it to the states, are reserved to the states respectively, or to the people." This clause made explicit what had been implied from the outset, that besides the Union and the government of the United States there were to continue to be states—thirteen at first, and more as new ones were formed and admitted—and that the states were to be autonomous units of government under the Constitution to carry out their vaguely implied "reserved" powers. The amendment gave the states a constitutional assurance for their continued existence, and a definite constitutional source for their powers.

To allow a number of states to exist and to govern the people in many things within their respective portions of the national area was to invite and to guarantee the right of diversity in policies, laws, and public services from state to state. Each state presumably could, under the Constitution, make and enforce its own laws in its own way, without regard to what other states were doing. Diversity seems to be a sort of law of nature among political units, and even the vague provision of the Constitution that "The United States shall guarantee to every state in this Union a republican form of government" could not ensure any real uniformity in laws and policies among the states, or set any limits to their diversities.

The same Constitution granted powers to Congress and made other provisions that foreshadowed a single national economy and a single society throughout the national area. It also guaranteed to every citizen the right to move freely throughout the national domain and to carry on lawful occupations anywhere, without regard to the state boundaries that might have to be crossed.

The many problems presented by such a combination of diversity and local control in many things with uniformity and central legislation in others, for a highly mobile and expanding population, were familiar matters to the people of the early states of the Union. They had lived under such conditions in the colonial period, when the British Crown and Parliament controlled or regulated a number of major public functions while each colony made and tried to enforce its own laws in other matters. Similar problems were with them under the Articles of Confederation, after national independence had been achieved but before a strong central government had been established.

The experiences of the colonists under a combination of British central rule in a number of common affairs and local rule over other matters in the several provinces or colonies had not only revealed a number of governmental problems but also produced various practical methods of composing intercolonial differences. The Continental Congress wrote some of these methods into the Articles of Confederation as guides for adjusting interstate relations, and these in turn, with some changes and additions, were incorporated in the United States Constitution in 1787.

The more important of these constitutional provisions fall into five categories:

1. Equality and territorial integrity. The Constitution in effect guarantees the constitutional equality of every state with every other state. It does so by failing

to designate any state by name and by not giving any special powers or exemptions to any one. All states are treated as equals in both the powers reserved to them and the restrictions placed upon them. The grant of equal representation in the Senate, two senators for each state, is evidence of an agreement not to give states that are large in area, population, or wealth any special constitutional privileges as against the smaller ones.

In addition the Constitution gives every state the same guarantee of a republican form of government and its own territorial integrity. "New states may be admitted by the Congress into this Union; but no new state shall be formed or erected within the jurisdiction of any other state; nor any state be formed by the junction of two or more states, or parts of states, without the consent of the legislatures of the states concerned as well as of the Congress." (Article IV, section 3, paragraph 1.)

At its first opportunities to do so, the Supreme Court came out strongly for the equality of the states in the Union, and for their indestructibility as members of the Union. These views have not been changed. Constitutional equality is the basis upon which the states approach each other in all their interstate dealings. Differences in area, population, and wealth make no constitutional difference.

2. Peaceful settlement of disputes, by court and compact. To prevent the states from resorting to war to settle interstate disputes, and thus possibly destroying or annexing each other, and to provide an alternative peaceful, judicial method of settlement, the Constitution makes the following provisions: "No state shall, without the consent of Congress . . . keep troops, or ships of war in time of peace . . . or engage in war, unless actually invaded, or in such imminent danger as will not admit of delay." (Article I, section 10, paragraph 3.)

"The judicial power [of the United States] shall extend . . . to controversies between two or more states; between a state and citizens of another state; between citizens of different states . . .

"In all cases . . . in which a state shall be party, the Supreme Court shall have original jurisdiction." (Constitution, Article III, section 2, paragraphs 2,3.)

These provisions of the Constitution are as a rule taken so much for granted that little is said about them. It is nevertheless true that the danger of interstate armed conflicts has sometimes arisen, especially in the early days of the Union, while on the other hand the Supreme Court has settled many difficult cases involving interstate legal controversies. Minnesota has been little involved in such interstate litigation. The case brought by North Dakota against Minnesota over the alleged flooding of some North Dakota lands by irrigation works on the Minnesota side of the Red River of the North failed in the Supreme Court in 1923 for lack of adequate proof of damage.

At this point the so-called compact clause of the Constitution should be discussed, since it also provides a means for settling interstate disputes peaceably. It is, however, a topic of sufficient importance to be discussed separately, as it is below (see pp. 72-76).

3. Preservation of nationwide free market. The dozen years from 1776 through 1787 saw the beginnings of interstate tariff walls and other interferences by the states with the principle of internal free trade to which the people had become accustomed under British rule in the colonial period. Men engaged in commerce and manufacture were much disturbed by the probable effects of these restrictions upon their markets in the future as well as by the immediate inconveniences. These fears provided much of the motivation for the movement to create a strong national government with the power to regulate interstate commerce and preserve the freedom of the internal market.

To this end the new Constitution was so drawn as to grant to Congress the power to regulate commerce not only with foreign nations but also "among the several states, and with the Indian tribes." At the same time Congress was forbidden to tax exports from any state, or to give any preference to the ports of one state over those of any other. To round out the guarantees against interstate trade barriers, the Constitution also imposed prohibitions on the states, as follows: "No state shall, without the consent of Congress, lay any imposts or duties on imports or exports, except what may be absolutely necessary for executing its inspection laws; and the net produce of all duties and imposts, laid by any state on imports or exports, shall be for the use of the treasury of the United States; and all such laws shall be subject to the revision and control of the Congress." (Article I, section 10, paragraph 2.) I read this language to mean imports into a state and exports from a state from or to any other state, as well as from or to any foreign country. It was the rising threat of interstate trade barriers that was most disturbing at the time.

In spite of these constitutional prohibitions, many states have found ways to "protect home industries" against products from other states. There was a widespread rash of such interferences with interstate trade during the depression years of the 1930s, when the effects of out-of-state competition upon ailing local industries were keenly felt. A vigorous campaign of public education by governmental and private agencies at that time made much headway against the "interstate trade barriers." It was, however, the return of a more active pace in business generally in the 1940s that apparently reduced the emphasis on state protective devices.

Two types of such devices are still being used. One includes the setting up by the states of excessively high standards for the quality of food products that may be sold locally, on the grounds that the public health is being protected, and perhaps enforcing these rules more strictly on goods brought into the state than on locally produced articles. Excessively high insepection fees may accompany such a scheme. It is said that a number of states now in effect exclude Minnesota dairy products by such schemes. Another scheme is to legislate a strong preference for the use of things produced in the state in all state and local public purchases and construction. Minnesota once engaged in such practices, legislating a strong preference for Minnesota quarry products for public buildings in the state, and ensuring the use in public institutions of butter (produced in Minnesota) as against oleomargarine (produced from materials originating outside the state). It is hard to prove that such practices fall under the prohibitions of the Constitution, and therefore it is difficult to eliminate them by litigation in the Courts. Congress has passed very little legislation to discourage such actual interstate trade barriers.

One recourse open to the states discriminated against is to adopt retaliatory measures of a similar nature against the states that originate the trade barriers. This is what had happened in many cases before and up through the 1930s. It was found, however, that having a larger share of the in-state market may not offset the losses in markets elsewhere resulting from retaliatory measures. This problem in interstate relations is one that may never be fully eliminated. Congress probably has ample power for constructive legislation here but finds few pressures to stimulate it to action. But even without congressional legislation, Supreme Court decisions on the basis of private suits sometimes provide relief. The states themselves have not adopted any general code to ensure against their own interference with interstate free trade, and are not likely to do so.

In the meantime in one field, that of liquor control, the Twenty-First Amendment (1933), which repealed the Eighteenth or Prohibition Amendment, appears to have encouraged interstate trade barriers in the liquor industry. The second section of that amendment reads: "The transportation or importation into any state, territory or possession of the United States for delivery or use therein of intoxicating liquors, in violation of the laws thereof, is hereby prohibited."

The early Supreme Court decisions under this section seemed to hold that it gave each state full power to exclude all imports of liquor into its territory for delivery or use therein, and that since this was true, a state could do anything less than making a complete prohibition. It could keep out liquors made in other states, or impose special taxes and burdens upon them. It is doubtful, however, that Congress in proposing the Twenty-First Amendment or the state conventions in ratifying it really meant to abolish the control of Congress over interstate commerce in liquor. If Congress were to enact a general law on the subject that still left the states free to have their own prohibition laws, such a law might be upheld under the powers of Congress (1) to regulate interstate commerce, and (2) to pass laws necessary and proper for carrying into effect the provisions of the Constitution. Such a conclusion would be in keeping with general developments of constitutional doctrine, and some more recent decisions on the states' powers over liquor have tended in this direction.

4. According comity to citizens generally. It was the state legislatures that passed citizenship laws during the War for Independence and under the Articles of Confederation. Hence the framers of the Constitution were thinking of the citizens of the several states when they provided in the Constitution that "The citizens of each state shall be entitled to all privileges and immunities of citizens in the several states." (Article IV, section 2, paragraph 1.) This clause, usually called the "comity clause," represented an important step toward the establishment of a national citizenship and nationwide citizenship rights. Another step toward a national citizenship was contained in the clause authorizing Congress to enact a uniform law of naturalization.

The comity clause continued in effect the fundamental rights that all British subjects had enjoyed throughout the thirteen colonies, which in turn had been guaranteed to the citizens of the states by Article IV of the Articles of Confederation. The clause in the Constitution has been interpreted by the Supreme Court as forbidding the states to discriminate against the citizens of other states in favor of their own citizens in "fundamental" matters, that is to say, in those privileges and immunities "which belong, of right, to the citizens of all free governments; and which have, at all times, been enjoyed by the citizens of the several states which compose this Union." These include the right to enter and leave a state, or pass through it, for lawful purposes like employment, trade, and agriculture, to have the protection of the state government and access to its courts, to acquire and dispose of property like any citizen of the state, without discrimination, and without being subjected to discriminatory taxes and other burdens. These rights are all subject to nondiscriminatory regulation by the states under their police powers. In addition the equal privileges accorded do not include the right to vote or to hold office in the state, or to practice any profession or engage in any trade where it is reasonable to require that a man be a responsible or specially trained local citizen. Neither do they include the right to hunt and fish in the state or to get education in a state's schools and universities on the same terms as are provided for citizens of the state. The game and fish and the state institutions are in a sense the property of the people of the state concerned, and hence these rights are not considered to be as fundamental in the constitutional sense as those mentioned above.

The adoption of the Fourteenth Amendment in 1868 has somewhat changed the situation concerning these privileges and immunities. That amendment introduced a category of "the privileges or immunities of citizens of the United States" (as distinct from state citizens) which the states are forbidden to abridge, but the Supreme Court has failed to make any significant constructive use of this provision. The amendment also provides that "All persons born or naturalized in the United States, and subject to the jurisdiction thereof, are citizens of the United States and of the states wherein they reside." The last clause simplifies the problem for any United States citizen to become a citizen of any state. The same amendment also says that no state shall "deprive any person of life, liberty, or property, without due process of law; nor deny to any person within its jurisdiction the equal protection of the laws." These equal protection and due process clauses have a broader scope and have served more purposes than the comity clause of Article IV. But the comity clause is still in effect and still available for the protection of citizens of any state from discriminations against them in other states.

5. One state assisting another in civil and criminal law enforcement. (a) Interstate rendition. It is a general understanding among nations that no nation will enforce the criminal laws of another. By parallel reasoning it is generally held that no state in the union will enforce the criminal laws of another state. Each state must carry its own burdens in this field. A criminal should be tried and punished in and by the state in which he committed his crime.

To carry out this principle the criminal who has fled from the state of his crime into another state, before or after his trial and conviction, should be apprehended and returned to the state of the crime. For this purpose the Constitution provides that "A person charged in any state with treason, felony, or other crime, who shall flee from justice, and be found in another state, shall on demand of the executive authority of the state from which he fled, be delivered up, to be removed to the state having jurisdiction of the crime." (Article IV, section 2, paragraph 2.) This is sometimes called the interstate rendition clause. The process is similar to that of extradition between nations.

Congress in 1793 passed a brief statute to implement the constitutional principle. It designated the "executive authority" or governor of the state as the person to carry out this duty by turning over the accused person to an authorized agent of the governor of the demanding state upon the showing of an indictment or an affidavit stating the name and the alleged crime of the person in question. It also authorized the agent to transport the prisoner back to the demanding state.

The Supreme Court in 1861 declared that the duty thus imposed on the state governors by this act of Congress is merely a moral duty and not one that is legally enforceable upon the governors, but this decision has made little difference in fact. Governors have at times refused to return alleged criminals to other states for trial, asserting, for example, that the person accused could not get a fair trial in the other state, but a state thus denied can easily retaliate by a like refusal in its turn. Such a policy tends, therefore, to be self-defeating. Shrewd criminals can easily take advantage of such a situation. The return of accused persons, when apprehended, to the state of the crime has, therefore, been a fairly automatic process for many years. In 1926 the National Conference of Commissioners on Uniform State Laws proposed a Uniform Criminal Extradition Act that all states were advised to adopt. A later revision of this act made by the Interstate Commission on Crime and accepted by the National Conference has been adopted, though with some variations, by most of the states, including Minnesota. This uniform act, which is now in regular use, is complete with standard forms and recommended procedures. There are also numerous state and federal court decisions interpreting various aspects of the interstate rendition process. A member of the governor's staff usually handles the routine steps in the procedure, perhaps with help from the attorney general's staff, but the final decision in each case is that of the governor.

(b) Full faith and credit. In civil as distinct from criminal cases the states do not follow the rule that a state will not help enforce the law of another state. Beginning their political careers within the jurisdiction of the British crown and the English common law, the American colonies cooperated with each other, primarily through their courts, in enforcing civil judgments, contracts, and other legal obligations under British law wherever they were rendered or entered into. Appeals to the higher courts in England gave some uniformity to the rules of law that were applied. To carry forward the practices thus begun among the colonies, the Articles of Confederation and later the Constitution made suitable provisions for the guidance of the states. One important constitutional provision is the "full faith and credit clause," which reads as follows: "Full faith and credit shall be given in each state to the public acts, records, and judicial proceedings of every other state. And the Congress may by general laws prescribe the manner in which such acts, records, and proceedings shall be proved, and the effect thereof." (Article IV, section 1.)

This also is a sort of "comity clause" and one of broad scope. It expresses or at least adequately implies the sort of friendly and understanding reception that the public acts, records, and proceedings of every state ought to receive in the other states. This in turn implies the sort of assistance that state officials including judges in each state should give to other states, for what would be the point of full faith and credit to other states' records if no help were to follow?

The observance of full faith and credit has fallen in the main upon the courts in the states. Uncounted thousands of procedural rulings and equally uncounted numbers of state court decisions must have been made in cases where judicial proceedings, court judgments, and laws and records from other states have come before state courts. There is so much movement of persons and transaction of business across state lines that courts must be almost constantly considering situations in which some transactions took place in other states. In the process of deciding what state's law applies, how the applicable law of another state is to be construed, and so on, judges have built up a tremendous body of case law that goes under the name "conflict of laws." This is one of the most complex bodies of law that students in American law schools are expected to learn. The existence and importance of conflict-of-laws problems in the United States are traceable almost entirely to the federal system and to the great multiplicity of interstate transactions.

Full faith and credit questions come up in many ways and in many branches of substantive law. Marriages and divorces have recently held the center of the stage of public attention in this field because many people who are married and domiciled in one state go to some other state for a quick divorce and then return to the state of domicile where one or the other or both marry other persons. Was the out-of-state divorce valid? Did the parties (one or both) acquire residence or domicile in that state so that the local court had acquired "jurisdiction" over them to grant the divorce?

Another field of considerable recent interest is that of workmen's compensation for injuries received in the course of employment. Take the case of a telephone company lineman working in several states. Let us say the employer is domiciled in one state but does business in several. The contract of employment is made in one of the states, not necessarily that of the employee's residence, and the injury takes place there or in another state. In which state and under which state's law does the injured workman collect compensation for his injury? Does he have a choice of state and law? The laws and the benefits may differ a great deal from state to state. If he collects in one state can he also collect in another where the benefits are higher, or does the "full faith and credit" accorded to the award in one state exclude his getting another award? These are but examples of many questions that arise, and upon which there is no uniformity in the decisions. Among the hundreds of different courts scattered throughout the states there can be and are considerable diversities in opinions.

In 1790 Congress passed a brief statute defining how state laws and the records and judicial proceedings of state courts should be authenticated (by seals and certificates) for acceptance in other states, and then went on to provide for the full faith and credit that such documents should receive. As slightly amended from the original form the act says: "Such acts, records, and judicial proceedings or copies thereof, so authenticated, shall have the same full faith and credit in every court within the United States and its territories and possessions as they have by law or usage in the courts of such state, territory or possession from which they are taken."

To this day the statute does not say that when a state court gets an authenticated copy of a civil court judgment from another state it shall, after being satisfied as to its authenticity, simply issue a court order to the sheriff or other police authority to "execute," that is, to carry out the judgment. On the contrary, a new judicial proceeding must, in effect, be begun, if the defendant objects to paying the judgment. He may raise various questions, including the main one, whether the court that issued the judgment had "jurisdiction" to try the case, a "defense" that is very common in out-of-state divorce cases. In short full faith and credit need not be given, at least until the lawyers have argued their various points and the court has become satisfied that the judgment from the other state is unassailable as far as the arguments and evidence before it are concerned.

All this means is that full faith and credit is not a principle that provides a simple, inexpensive, and semiautomatic process for collecting in one state a judgment gained in the courts of another. In fact, various delays and complications are possible, and justice may well be defeated, or, at least, bought too dearly, because of the existence of many states, which operate their own judicial systems, each according to its own rules. That this is one of the current costs as well as possible values of having a federal system can hardly be denied. And yet the states and their courts cannot be blamed for the difficulties that have developed. Each court is in duty bound to exercise its own judgment in cases that are brought before it, and not let itself become a mere registry office or a rubber stamp.

That Congress could do a great deal more to regulate full faith and credit between the states and to put it on a sounder basis seems to be generally admitted. Congress might define, for example, under what conditions an out-of-state divorce must be given full faith and credit in all states—but this is only one example of a number of problems. It happens, however, that in this case there is no strong pressure group to help bring about congressional action. Even the legal profession does not stand strongly united on what needs to be done, and the clients served are a scattered, amorphous class without any visible organization.

INTERSTATE COMPACTS

To discourage groups of states from impairing the strength of their "Confederation and perpetual union" the Continental Congress when framing the Articles of Confederation for the original thirteen states agreed that "No two or more states shall enter into any treaty, confederation or alliance whatever between them, without the consent of the united states in congress assembled, specifying accurately the purpose for which the same is entered into, and how long it shall continue." (Article VI, paragraph 2.)

The framers of the United States Constitution in 1787 took up this idea, and incorporated it in the Constitution in the following modified form: "No state shall, without the consent of Congress . . . enter into any agreement or compact with another state, or with a foreign power . . ." (Article I, section 10, paragraph 3.)

These successive phrases were directed against a real danger. There was talk of splitting up the original union under the Articles into three regional confederations—northeast, middle, and south. Despite the prohibition in the Articles against such action the states adjacent to the Potomac and the Chesapeake considered a plan of interstate regulation of navigation on those waters, since Congress lacked the power to act. Wise leaders like Washington and Madison turned these restless gropings into a movement to strengthen the central government through a revision of the Articles.

It is one of several unanticipated developments of American constitutional practice that the clause quoted above directed against interstate agreements and compacts has come to be looked upon as an important grant of powers to the states to make compacts with each other with the consent of Congress. A qualified negative has become a positive authorization. Before this fundamental change in interpretation could take place, however, the security of the Union against the secession of groups of states had to be established by the Civil War, and by the making of a strong nation out of an original loose confederation of states.

The early compacts under the Constitution dealt almost entirely with interstate boundary problems and adjustments. Other subjects began to creep in by 1900 but not until the 1920s was much constructive use made of compacts. About then the interstate compact device began to be put forward by sanguine publicists as at least a partial substitute for national action, especially in cases where the subject matter, like labor regulation, was deemed to belong to the states and to be beyond the competence of Congress. A substantial literature has been built up around this theme, and some very interesting proposals have been made for interstate cooperation via the route of compacts. There has been at least one failure, involving an attempt in the 1930s at setting standards for the regulation of labor by interstate compact, but there have been a number of distinct successes. The Book of the States for 1954-55, published by the Council of State Governments, which covers the problem for the approximate period of our study, lists seventeen compacts that were of sufficient importance to be described at some length and includes comments on several others. A monograph published by the same council just at the end of our period of active research provides an excellent review of the interstate compacts from 1925 to 1950, a period of great activity and of significant reappraisals of the compact device.

No one can review the record of these recent developments and deny that interstate compacts are important factors in the intergovernmental relations of our times. It would appear, also, that the compact method gives real promise of new and constructive uses in adjusting the relations between states and in handling some of their common problems in the future. Already compacts are being used by groups of two and more states for the cooperative development of the great Port of New York, for the allocation between states of the waters of common river systems, for stream pollution control, for the conservation of fisheries, for forest fire protection, for interstate parks and interstate bridge construction and administration, for the regulation of oil and gas production, for metropolitan area planning, for cooperation in maintaining higher education, for the supervision of parolees and probationers, and for civil defense purposes. For some of these functions, such as that of parole and probation, there is only one compact for all states to join; in others the compact is designed for joint action in a single metropolitan area by only two states; in still others the compacts embrace potentially all the states in a river basin or in a region defined by other distinguishing factors. For the principal oil and gas compact the states need not be contiguous.

Joint ownership and administration of common facilities is characteristic of some interstate compacts; in others there is collaboration of the states in administration of a function without joint ownership of facilities; while other compact organizations can do little more than study a common problem and try to induce the member states to cooperate in action. There are, in short, great variations among compacts. No two are even nearly identical, because each one is negotiated to meet a single problem or a unique complex of local problems in one area.

It would be interesting to go into the ways in which compacts are developed, negotiated, and ratified, and to consider the legal standing and legal effects of compacts as distinct from state laws, national laws, and international treaties. To do this at all thoroughly would take the discussion far afield. The simple fact is that the states are not equipped with separate departments of interstate affairs as the nation is for international negotiations, and the state constitutions do not designate which branch of the government, whether the executive or the legislative, is to handle interstate negotiations. There is considerable variety in the proceedings, therefore, although the ideas for a particular compact usually arise among state administrators in the functional field concerned, whether that is highways, or conservation, or some other. Preliminary negotiations may be carried fairly far among the functional officials before the governor, attorney general, or appropriate legislative committees are brought actively into the making of the decisions. Legislative approval is the final step.

Although approved by Congress, either before or after it is negotiated, an interstate compact does not become a law of the United States. It is essentially an exercise of state powers by the contract method. At the same time, since two or more states are involved, any legal dispute concerning the compact, whether it arises within a single state or between two or more states, raises federal questions that only the United States Supreme Court can finally decide. No single state supreme court can determine the meaning of the contract or decide on its constitutionality, since the decision would affect all the states in the compact.

How much have Minnesota's interstate relations been affected by or expressed in the form of interstate compacts? A list compiled by the Legislative Reference Service of the Library of Congress late in 1953, which carried through August of that year and hence covered the years of our study, showed congressional approval of the following compacts affecting Minnesota:

In a first group are two acts that ratified boundary adjustments, one between Minnesota and Wisconsin in 1918, and one involving Minnesota, Wisconsin, and Michigan in 1948, which affected their common boundaries on Lake Superior. A third act of ratification in this group concerned a bridge over the St. Croix between Minnesota and Wisconsin in 1942.

By a second group of acts, Congress gave its consent in advance to compacts to be made among groups of states that were named in the acts (Minnesota being one in each case) for the following purposes: 1917, for the conservation of the boundary waters of Minnesota, North Dakota, and South Dakota and the control of pollution therein, but all works to this end were to be approved and supervised by the secretary of the army; 1938, for the apportionment of the waters of the Red River of the North and its tributaries, among the same three states; 1938, for the control of fisheries on the Great Lakes, Congress consenting in advance to compacts for this purpose between any two or more of eight states, New York, Pennsylvania, Ohio, Indiana, Illinois, Michigan, Wisconsin, and Minnesota.

In a third group of laws Congress authorized any two or more states in the union to make compacts with each other for (1) forest conservation and forest fire protection (Weeks Act of 1911); (2) the development and maintenance of parks and recreational areas (1936); (3) mutual assistance in the prevention of crime (1942); and (4) the conservation of water and the prevention and control of water pollution (1948).

These are all important and interesting pieces of legislation to enable states adjacent to each other, or at least coexisting within the same federal union, to cooperate with each other on essential public services. I submit, however, that even the entire list of laws does not cover or provide for the whole of any major function of government. What these laws do is to authorize the states to utilize one method of interstate cooperation for the handling of some part only of the several functions mentioned. Also, while authorizing the states to proceed by the compact method of cooperation, these laws do not exclude the states from trying other methods of interstate action.

As far as Minnesota is concerned, the compacts entered into under the foregoing enactments of Congress probably represent over the years but a small fraction of 1 per cent of all the work of state government, whether calculated in terms of personnel involved or in dollars spent. Indeed, the activities under compacts represent but a small part of all of Minnesota's interstate relations, on whatever basis the comparison is made—and interstate relations as a whole are dwarfed, in monetary terms at least, by national-state relations and by state-local relations.

A question that cannot lightly be dismissed is why the method of interstate cooperation through compacts is so much discussed. The compact method has a peculiar fascination for students of public law, with the result that some very interesting and persuasive analyses of the law of interstate compacts have appeared in print. But as a matter of practical government what are the advantages of compacts as compared with other methods of interstate collaboration? To the uninitiated, at least, the method appears to be unduly cumbersome and rigid.

The answer seems to be that no one method of interstate collaboration is equally suitable for all purposes. Various methods have been developed and each one seems to be suitable for meeting certain requirements. A strong argument can be and has been made that in situations where large public interests are involved, where important facilities are to be acquired and operated, or major resources like water are to be allocated, and where, consequently, stability and a high degree of security, legal enforceability, and moral force are important, a compact worked out with due care and solemnly accepted by the parties and approved by Congress is better than any other device yet developed. A compact cannot be changed by the action of a single state, but it can be changed with the consent of all parties. It can further be shown that the compact device is highly flexible since the contents of each compact can be drafted according to the needs of the situation to be met.

Another question may well be raised, however, and that is whether compacts have not been used in some instances where simpler methods would have sufficed. A separate compact is certainly not needed for every interstate bridge, as Minnesota's experience reveals. Most of its dozen or more interstate bridges have been constructed without separate compacts. The same is true potentially if not in fact with regard to interstate cooperation on conservation projects, interstate parks, forest fire protection, higher education, and civil defense.

In the matter of bridging interstate waters, which are usually navigable and therefore under congressional supervision, present national legislation authorizing such works subject to the approval of the Army Engineers, supplemented by general and reciprocal state legislation authorizing highway departments to negotiate with each other and the federal Bureau of Public Roads on particular bridge projects and to enter into contracts on behalf of their respective states, is certainly adequate in most cases. The state legislatures still retain the general power of approval and veto on the location of interstate bridges and on the priorities in point of time of one bridge project over another, and yet leave all the arrangements to be agreed upon in the responsible administrative departments. For extra safety a state may provide that the governor or a state commissioner of administration must approve all interstate contracts, but any such checks become part of the regular administrative procedures and it is not necessary to draw the entire state legislatures of both states and both houses of Congress into the approval of an interstate compact for each project.

Under such a philosophy and arrangement interstate contracts and agreements of various kinds will be authorized by general enabling legislation, both national and state, made in advance, and will be negotiated and carried out in regular administrative channels under the usual checks and controls to protect each state's interests. The more formal compact method will then be reserved for the more important and unusual types of agreements that may become needed more and more to deal with interstate metropolitan problems and river basin water control and water allocation problems. There will also probably always be a place for some interstate compacts in the early and experimental stages of new types of ventures in interstate collaboration. Since interstate boundaries have now become fairly well settled, compacts for interstate boundary adjustments will probably be rarely needed.

LEGISLATIVE RELATIONS

I turn now from reviewing the interstate relations that have been specifically provided for by the Constitution to consider various relations that have developed in practice without express constitutional mention. First let us consider the relations between state legislatures and also between their products, the written laws of the states.

Lack of Uniformity in State Laws. The highest written law peculiar to each state is its constitution, but this is only in part the product of the legislature. The original constitution of Minnesota, for example, much of which is still a part of the written constitution of today, was put together, as we have seen, by a compromise committee set up by the two fractional bodies, Republican and Democratic, into which the delegates elected to form one constitutional convention had split. Each one had proceeded to draft a constitution and each had prepared various articles and sections before the agreement was reached to submit only one constitution to the voters. The compromise committee selected articles and sections from the work of each group and itself prepared some additional ones to round out the whole. The document thus put together was adopted by the voters.

From what sources did the many provisions come? Some were taken over from the United States Constitution but many more came from the written constitutions of the thirty-one other states at the time. This copying or borrowing is, in fact, true of all state constitutions, and it is also true of many state statutory provisions, although copying is not always verbatim.

But when one state copies provisions from other states' constitutions and laws without knowing the history or the purposes of such provisions, the courts of the several states can be far apart in interpreting them. For example, there are two "due process" clauses in the United States Constitution and most state constitutions contain one each. The state provisions are not given the same interpretation in the several states, and the United States constitutional provisions have also had their own distinctive interpretations. Every state's supreme court will pay respectful attention to the interpretations given in other states to similar or identical clauses, but will not feel bound thereby. Even the United States Supreme Court's interpretation of the federal due process clauses is not wholly binding on the state supreme courts. A state enactment might be held constitutional by the United States Supreme Court under the federal Constitution's Fourteenth Amendment, and yet be held unconstitutional by a state supreme court's decision under an identical clause in the state's constitution. The reverse situation is theoretically possible but in that case the state court decision would be ineffective, since the federal Supreme Court's ruling under the Fourteenth Amendment would invalidate the act and no state decision could then validate it.

At one time or another, and in some form, all but a few of the states adopted the English common law as the basis for the decisions of their courts, and all have to some extent copied or borrowed constitutional and statutory provisions from each other—but uniformity of laws on the same subject among the different states has not been achieved. Far from it!

In a country that is a single area for industrial, commercial, financial, recreational, travel, and other purposes, this nonuniformity of laws is always something of an inconvenience and in some cases it is a serious burden. For nearly a century, from 1842 to 1938, the United States courts with the approval of the Supreme Court made attempts to develop a system of rules of "common commercial law" for the whole country in cases that came before them. But the state courts did not have to conform to these rules, and the result was that in the same state the federal courts might be following one rule on any given subject and the state courts another. Two rules of law on the same subject in the same state gave lawyers a sort of "choice of law" and led each side to try to get the case into the court that followed the rule it considered the more favorable. Of course if the state courts had consistently decided to follow the federal rule on the subject, some uniformity would have been achieved in the areas covered by the federal decisions, but many chose not to do so.

In 1939 the Supreme Court tried to put an end to the resulting confusion. It said that under the United States Judiciary Act the federal courts deciding cases between persons of diverse citizenship were bound to follow not only the statutes that obtained in the state in which the case was being tried but also that state's court decisions. This ruling did not make for greater uniformity in laws between state and state—in fact it actually worked against that result; and its success in achieving uniformity of rulings within any state is still in doubt.

Uniform State Law Movement. Long before this episode the states themselves, led by the American Bar Association, had been trying to achieve more interstate uniformity in laws, primarily in the laws affecting commerce and business. A movement was begun in 1889 to set up a National Conference of Commissioners on Uniform State Laws, and to get each state to create a corresponding state commission to work with the national organization. Minnesota joined this movement relatively early, and it has had such a state commission for a considerable number of years. At the same time the state has been very economical with its appropriations for this service to the point of cutting off the appropriation entirely in some years.

Every state legislature is entirely free to adopt or reject any "uniform law" that is drafted, proposed, and circulated among the states by the National Conference. By 1951, when the intensive period of our study was drawing to a close, the National Conference had fifty-eight such legislative proposals on its active list, of which Minnesota had adopted twenty-two (1952-53 Book of the States). This put Minnesota near the average for all states. In addition the National Conference had drafted and proposed to the states sixteen "Model Acts." Of these Minnesota, along with nineteen other states, had adopted none.

In the country as a whole only two uniform laws, those on negotiable instruments and on warehouse receipts, had been adopted by all the states and territories (52 in all), but the stock transfer act with 51 adoptions was not far behind. Others trailed with 42, 38, 37, 36, 33, and smaller numbers of state adoptions down to one and none. It is generally the acts on commercial subjects that are most widely adopted, probably in part because there are commercial interests that encourage such adoptions. After so many years of effort by state and national commissions, the figures on adoptions seem rather disappointing—but even these data do not tell the whole story. A proposed uniform law is not a compact that every state must adopt or reject as a whole and without change. Local legislative draftsmen in many states have amended uniform laws even as the states were preparing to adopt them; and when incorporated into a state's own body of laws a so-called uniform act becomes subject to legislative amendment like any other statute. Moreover, it is subject to different interpretations by the courts in the various states, so that what starts out to be a uniform act soon varies considerably from state to state.

The ideal of uniformity of laws for all states must be measured against the ideal of having each state's laws suited to its own needs and ideas. Given the diversities in people and in the conditions that are found from place to place the latter may be the more desirable. Uniformity is a convenience, not a necessity, although in nationwide business and other affairs a high degree of uniformity of laws is practically a necessity.

It is in the nature of a federal system to permit diversity in laws and policies on those subjects wherein it is deemed to be advisable or at least tolerable to have diversity, and to provide for uniformity on those matters in which that is deemed necessary. The practical mechanism provided to achieve these ends is the delegation to a central legislative body of the powers needed to make uniform laws of nationwide application on the subjects of greatest national concern, and to assign to all the state governments the right of making laws for their own states on the subjects wherein diversity of laws is desirable or at least bearable. To find the states now engaged in a general movement to make uniform laws on subjects reserved to their discretion suggests strongly that the original division of powers was not wisely conceived, or that conditions and needs have changed so greatly as to outmode the original allocation of powers. In the fields where powers overlap to some extent, and where both the national and state governments have power to act, the states may simply be trying to achieve enough uniformity of laws to satisfy minimum public needs, and thus head off any serious demands for uniform national legislation by Congress. The latter might oust the states from certain fields of power.

I have little doubt that on the major commercial subjects, as well as on some others, Congress has the power to enact legislation of nationwide application that would be more nearly uniform in operation than anything that fifty states acting through their own legislatures can achieve. The balance of political forces that results in leaving it to the states to try to achieve uniformity of laws, when it is obvious that the states fall far short, in capacity and willingness, of being able to attain the goal, presents one of the interesting puzzles for the student of American politics.

As it now appears to me, uniformity of laws cannot be attained, except to a small and uncertain extent, by state action. It could be achieved very much better by the legislation of a single body, the United States Congress. Nevertheless public leaders generally, including members of Congress, continue to give lip service and a somewhat halfhearted support to the uniform state law movement in preference to urging and supporting legislation by Congress to attain uniformity. I can only conclude that uniformity of laws per se is not as highly valued as is a restriction of the scope of congressional activity.

I honestly think that the movement for uniformity in state legislation is based upon a number of questionable premises: (1) that uniformity of laws over as large an area as the United States is really attainable (although even federal legislation is accommodated in various ways to the regional and sectional differences that exist); (2) that uniformity can be attained through the actions of X state legislatures and as many state judicial systems (now each fifty in number); (3) that the many state legislatures and judicial systems can be spurred and motivated to achieve uniformity of laws in certain subject-matter fields without impairing their autonomy and spirit of independence in other fields. In short the premises assume that the states can and will pursue uniformity as a goal in a number of matters without adversely affecting the position of the states in the federal system.

I do not wish to be understood to say that no important results have been achieved by the uniform state laws movement. The movement has called attention to an important defect in the federal system, a defect that is more obvious as the United States becomes more and more a single nation with a single national economic system. It has produced a closer approach to uniformity of laws in several important fields, and has aroused many people to a realization of the responsibility of the states to help make the federal system work better. By pooling the legislative drafting resources of many states in a single national movement numerous excellent model laws have been produced for the states to adopt, some of them much better than many of the states would have been likely to produce if each state had had to rely solely on its own resources in legislative draftsmanship. These are by no means unimportant achievements. A continuation of present efforts is likely to extend these gains, even though the goal of completely uniform state laws on any important number of major legislative subjects appears to be unattainable by present methods.

It is possible that something more could be done toward uniformity of state laws if the principle of the interstate compact were applied to this field. If the states adopting uniform laws would make a compact, first, to adopt any uniform laws that they do adopt without verbal change, and not thereafter to change the wording thereof unilaterally and, second, to accept as binding on their own courts the interpretations of an interstate high court or panel of jurists drawn from the state supreme courts as to the meaning of the uniform laws adopted by them, with a sort of reference or appeal to this panel from the states' highest courts available to the parties in state cases, there would be a closer approach to real uniformity of laws among the states, and the officially recognized uniform laws would attain a distinctive and somewhat higher status.

Such a suggestion will sound not only unconstitutional but truly revolutionary to many students of the Constitution. The constitutional issues that could be raised about it would make those in previous cases on the compact clause appear to be relatively unimportant. Several points should be noted, however. This is not a suggestion either to turn questions of state statutory construction over to the United States Supreme Court, or to deprive that Court of the final word on all federal questions. The suggestion leaves the power over state statutes in the hands of the state legislatures and an interstate tribunal of state judges. The purpose is simply to make uniform state laws more nearly uniform in words and in meaning—and to prevent unilateral changes in them by the action of any state legislature or court.

The High Court of Australia and the Supreme Court of Canada in the federal systems of those two countries already have a general appellate jurisdiction over state court decisions on state statutory and common-law questions. This jurisdiction goes far toward enabling those two supreme courts to give a certain uniformity to state law generally. I believe, however, that in the United States it would be better to reserve the Supreme Court for the decision of federal questions. Any attempt to impose on it the burden of making decisions interpreting the nonfederal laws of the fifty states, even the so-called uniform laws, would require a drastic revision of its structure and of its role in the federal system. Certainly the slow development up to now of uniform state laws hardly calls for major changes in the Supreme Court in order to make the uniform laws more uniform and more effective.

Reciprocal and Retaliatory State Laws. As we have seen, state legislatures copy laws from each other, and they also enact a number of laws that have been drawn up by national organizations to serve as uniform laws in the states that adopt them. They take note of the work of other state legislatures and of the problems of interstate relations also in adopting so-called reciprocal and retaliatory laws. Perhaps the majority of these have been promoted by national organizations interested in advancing particular public services or the welfare of particular professions, or by semiofficial organizations like the Council of State Governments that are endeavoring to improve intergovernmental relations generally, or even by federal administrative agencies that are responsible for supervising the services rendered by the states using grant-in-aid funds.

A reciprocal law is one in which the enacting state offers certain advantages to such other states and their people as enact laws giving similar advantages to the enacting state and its people. A retaliatory law either withdraws some reciprocal advantage or imposes an actual burden upon nonreciprocating states and their people. These two types of laws are closely related to each other, and there are various subtypes of each one.

In the study that I made in 1951 of Minnesota Statutes of 1949 I turned up twenty-seven laws that provided for reciprocity with other states, or retaliation, in one or more sections each. These provided for a wide range of reciprocal privileges including the interstate sale of certified nursery stock without prior registration; the reciprocal rights of in-state and out-of-state insurance companies; court jurisdiction on boundary waters; the examination and licensing of professions (doctors, dentists, pharmacists, chiropodists, architects, surveyors, engineers, and certified public accountants); motor vehicle registration and drivers' licenses; fresh pursuit across state lines in criminal cases; the exchange of insane persons; reciprocity in old age assistance and in cases of unemployment compensation; the use of state courts for out-of-state collection of taxes due; and the municipal acquisition of lands for airport use across state lines. This list, if not complete, provides at least some indication of the wide usefulness of the principle of reciprocity.

In six of the twenty-seven laws examined, the act authorized a state administrative agency to negotiate with its "opposite number" in other states, so that written agreements at the administrative level would become the basis for the actual reciprocity. How many of these negotiated agreements were in effect at the time I did not ascertain.

The uniform laws discussed in the preceding section resulted in little or no contact between the states that passed them. Any two legislatures enacting the uniform negotiable instruments law, for example, would not have to negotiate with each other or follow up their legislation in any way. Neither would any administrative agency be called upon to do anything about it. The courts alone would be concerned, and their decisions in one state or the other on what the law meant would call for no legislative or administrative action in any state, and no interstate conferences of legislators or administrators. Litigants under the law and their lawyers in later cases would be interested in the courts' interpretations of it, but primarily as private parties.

This is not true of reciprocal and retaliatory laws as a rule. They call for state administrative actions in most instances, and, since two or more states would be involved in a licensing controversy or in reciprocal actions involving old age assistance, for example, the appropriate state officials would find it desirable to get in touch at once with the corresponding officials in the other states concerned.

As a means of drawing state legislators together from all states to discuss common problems, the American Legislators Association was organized about a generation ago. When the Council of State Governments was created in 1925 the legislators' organization was drawn into the council's orbit. The latter arranges for special legislative conferences from time to time and organizes drafting committees and research projects on particular legislative problems. A legislative reference service is also provided.

It is nevertheless true that the approximately 7,500 state legislators do not have regular means for meeting. They are too numerous; they are not as fully professionalized in their interests as judges or administrators are; and their problems not only are diffused over a wide range but are also peculiarly those of their own several states. They have little to gain from intensive interstate legislative contacts.

ADMINISTRATIVE RELATIONS

As we turn from legislative to executive and administrative interstate relations we enter an area of far more interstate organization and greater and more varied interstate activity. It is in this branch far more than in the legislative and judicial branches of state government that the large expansions of governmental functions have been taking place in modern times. Furthermore, the daily operations of practically all state functional activities call for frequent decisions and actions that involve relations with officials and ordinary citizens of other states.

For convenience I have arbitrarily chosen to speak of governors, top budget officers, and attorneys general as the main state executive officers (those having the entire state administration within their purview) and to speak of the heads of various functional departments such as highways, conservation, health, education, welfare, and law enforcement as administrative officials. Admittedly the line that separates these two groups is blurred and indistinct in a number of places.

When compared and contrasted with the interstate relations of state legislatures, the interstate relations in the executive and administrative field are notable for the existence of a number of active interstate organizations of officials. These are formed on the basis of office titles and general official position at the executive level, and on the basis of function without much regard to office title or type of organization at the administrative level. These differences call for some explication.

The best known and one of the oldest interstate organizations is the Governors' Conference. It was organized in 1908, in the administration of President Theodore Roosevelt and with his blessing, and has met with great regularity ever since. Its secretariat is the Council of State Governments. All state and territorial governors are members. Partly because the public expects him to be the spokesman for the state as a whole, this is the role that each leading governor tends to play in the annual governors' conferences. The conference agenda cover a number of subjects that relate to the internal policies, organization, and administration of the states, but these tend to become subordinated to others—or at least such is the general impression that is left upon the public. What the news media play up, and what the people read and hear about the governors' conferences, are the speeches of those governors who demand that the states unite and take a firm stand for states' rights and against the encroachments of the national government. Although the governors cannot really speak for their respective state legislatures, they take the lead in demanding the turning over of certain functions by the national government to the states, the elimination of certain federal taxes, and sometimes the dropping of specified federal grants-in-aid. In these efforts they have had only one clear success, namely, the return of employment security administration to the states after World War II. Thus their interstate dealings in their annual conferences are usually directed in large part not to the promotion of interstate collaboration per se, but to the uniting of the states for the ulterior purpose of resistance to the national government and its policies. It is primarily in times of war that this attitude changes, and then it must be said to the great credit of the governors and their conference that they unite to give firm support and assistance to the war effort.

The National Association of Attorneys General was organized two years before the Governors' Conference, in 1906. It meets in annual convention and, through the Council of State Governments, which is the secretariat for a number of national organizations of state officials, it conducts an informational service on state legal problems and an interchange of legal opinions. Like the governors, however, the organized attorneys general have become more noted for another activity. That is the uniting of the states (not always unanimously) on briefs before the Supreme Court in opposition to certain national measures like the control of rivers and other waters for the production of power. Thus the governors in the political field and the attorneys general in the legal field stand more or less united in trying to protect what Dr. Weidner in Monograph 9 in this series calls "expediency values," the rights and powers of the states against the national government.

Other over-all state officials such as state auditors, budget officers, and secretaries of state also have national organizations that hold meetings annually or occasionally, exchange information, and even arrange for some interstate cooperation. This cooperation is not likely to be of great importance. In general the states have little occasion for financial transactions with each other. There are very few interstate loans or grants-in-aid, for example, so that state auditors and state budget officers when they meet tend to concentrate on their common problems of accounting, reporting, and dealing with the national government instead of on truly interstate matters. The budget officers have taken strong stands on the right of the states to budget the grants-in-aid received from the federal government, and on federal practices in remitting the money. Like the governors and attorneys general they use their national meetings in part to try to improve the position of the states vis-à-vis the national government.

It is when we come to the functional departments of state administration such as public health, social welfare, highways, conservation, and employment security that interstate cooperation as such becomes very important to the successful performance of the functions. In these fields there are a number of specialized nationwide organizations of state officials. In addition there are regional organizations in New England, the Midwest, the South, and the West that make for closer relations between adjacent states. In some cases these nationwide and regional organizations include local officials, also, and in most there are national officials with the same functional interest who either are regular members or regularly meet with the organization members to discuss common problems. There are such common interests, obviously, because many of the state and local functions concerned are the recipients of substantial federal aid and operate under federal as well as state laws and standards.

Thus we find national, state, and to some extent local officials integrated in nationwide organizations that tend to include the word national in their official titles. In each one there is a common bond of interest in a single function, and even a single professional orientation like engineering, medicine, education, or social welfare, that to some extent tend to transcend the prosaic fact that the different members are employed by different levels and units of government. The unifying interest in a function induces them to explore ways of getting their several units of government to work together more effectively, both vertically (national to state to local, up and down) and horizontally (state with state, and locality with locality). There can be no doubt that "expediency values" also come into play, that the state people use the organization meetings to induce the federal officials to allow the states more leeway in methods and standards of work, and to grant them more funds, and so on. Interlevel tensions have developed at times, but this tendency is less pronounced than in the organizations of governors, state attorneys general, and state budget officers.

To bring the facts about these national organizations of state officials down to Minnesota, I can report that a study we made in 1948 revealed thirty-nine such organizations in which Minnesota as a state or some of its appropriate officials held memberships. In at least fifteen of them officials of the national government also held memberships or had some regular part in the organization, while in five or more that were based on individual memberships officials of cities and counties also were included.

Supplementing the work of these many organizations of state officials, serving as a clearinghouse of information for all states, acting as a secretariat for some of the interstate organizations, and working to promote both interstate and national-state cooperation, is the Council of State Governments, whose headquarters are in Chicago. The members of this organization are the states themselves, and its principal financial support comes from appropriations voted by the state legislatures.

A directory of Public Administration Organizations published in 1954 (soon after the conclusion of our basic research) by the Public Administration Clearing House provides in 150 pages the basic information about most of the organizations I have been considering, as well as about certain unofficial organizations.

Why do I stress these interstate or national and regional organizations of state administrative officials in the various functional fields? I do so because they are agencies that both help to satisfy the needs for interstate contacts that led to their establishment and to churn up and take action upon new developments, new needs, and new ideas concerning their functions and their interstate relations. As the state officials in the several functional fields tend to become more and more expert and specialized, their national organizations take on also some characteristics of professional societies, with their own national officers and headquarters, news bulletins, annual meetings, and nationwide acquaintanceship. As the members meet to discuss common problems together they tend to develop not only a professional spirit but also a national as distinct from a state viewpoint. They tend also to draw away from other functional groups, and that means to some extent away from their fellow officials in their respective state administrations. This is true whether their work is in highways or public health, in vocational education or in agricultural extension, in social welfare or in the conservation of natural resources.

These tendencies in the national organizations of state functional officials are obviously reinforced by the federal grants-in-aid that help so much to support the state services, by the acts of Congress in the several fields that provide a framework and a stimulus for their work, and by the participation of the appropriate federal administrators in the activities of the various interstate organizations. Such support by the national government has clearly a very reassuring effect upon state officials. It helps to improve their status and security. Is it necessary to recall that such a condition does not prevail among the state legislatures, or between them and Congress? Or to mention that the state courts and judges have no such regular contacts with each other or with the United States Supreme Court justices or the federal Courts of Appeal? Or that even the governors, with their generalized, nonprofessional functions and their emphasis on "expediency values," have no such specialized functional ties to bind them to each other nationally or to maintain contacts with national departments? Despite the frequent attendance of Presidents and heads of federal departments at the annual conferences of the governors, this show of national-state unity is only a fleeting one. When the annual meeting is over, each governor must continue to operate by himself, in accordance with his own and his party's policies, and essentially within his own state.

To round out this sketch of interstate and national organizations of state and local functional officials I should logically proceed now to list and explain the many varieties of interstate services and transactions that take place in the regular course of state administration. This I cannot do. No full list of such activities ever has been made, and perhaps none ever could be. I call attention to the partial lists that appear under appropriate chapter headings in Monographs 2 through 7 in this series and to the 1954 directory of Public Administration Organizations mentioned above. It should be noted, however, that our strictly functional studies cover only six fields, important ones though they are. Activities in general law enforcement, the regulation of railroads, utilities, banking, insurance, and the sale of securities, the conservation of natural resources, state hospitals and institutions for the sick and the handicapped, for dependents, delinquents, and criminals, workmen's compensation and labor relations, and a number of other functions, would add a great many other types of routine interstate transactions to these lists.

CONCLUSIONS

To summarize my own conclusions and those, I believe, of the several authors of monographs in our series, I offer the following propositions or hypotheses on several points related to interstate relations:

1. With the great increases in commerce, travel, and communications across state lines, and the multiplication and expansion of state and local public services, there have come to be innumerable problems of an interstate nature that are not covered by laws passed by Congress. These problems arise in practically every field and function of state governmental activity. Under a broad definition of interstate commerce as including all interstate intercourse, it is probable that Congress could legislate to regulate most of these interstate interests and activities, but it is unlikely that Congress will hasten to do so.

2. The formal means and methods of interstate action set forth in the United States Constitution (full faith and credit, interstate rendition of criminals, interstate compacts, for example) cover only a part of the field of interstate problems. They have had to be supplemented by numerous other arrangements, both formal and informal, in order to give effectiveness to the laws and the intrastate services of the various states. In these newer areas the state legislatures play an essential role as the authorizers and legalizers of interstate agreements, but the administrative agencies in the different functional fields (law enforcement, highways, education, public health, social welfare, and others) provide most of the leadership and make the necessary decisions.

3. A considerable apparatus of nationwide and regional organizations composed of national, state, and local administrators, many of them of high professional attainments, has been built up, through which information is developed and spread from state to state, official acquaintanceships across state lines are established and continued, and ideas for interstate cooperation are developed, to be implemented by the several states through legislative and administrative action.

4. These organizations and official associations also become agencies for passing along proposals to Congress and the national administration for national action to assist the states in their work, both intrastate and interstate. Such proposals are frequently accepted and implemented by Congress and the national administrative agencies.

5. In some regulatory fields like that of insurance, and in some service functions like those of highways and public health, interstate cooperation has become highly effective. The difficulties experienced by the states in the regulatory fields are partly due to the territorial limitations on state jurisdiction, and partly due to the fact that interstate commerce is involved, the regulation of which belongs to Congress. But there are other difficulties in the way of effective programs of interstate cooperation such as, for example, the different standards and policies set by state laws and administration, and the failure to provide enough funds and well-trained personnel to do the necessary work. Partly for the latter reasons some state regulatory agencies find it difficult even to cooperate with federal agencies in the same fields. The activity and influence of special-interest pressure groups are sometimes given as the immediate causes of these deficiencies in state regulatory bodies.

6. The roles of Congress and the national administration in interstate relations are important in most of the major state functions, and practically indispensable in certain fields, such as general law enforcement, the protection of the public health, and highway planning, financing, and construction. For many decades both the "political" branches of the national government, without being either aggressive or meddlesome, have been favorable to increases in interstate cooperation. Although no important laws

have recently been passed for the direct regulation of interstate relations, even in the fields where the Constitution permits such legislation specifically, Congress has been able to promote interstate cooperation in a number of fields by providing federal services of direct value to the states, by encouraging and helping to finance the expenses of interstate conferences, and by setting standards of service under grant-in-aid laws that encourage the states to engage in voluntary cooperation. Evidences of such assistance to the states are to be found in the fields of general law enforcement, health protection, stream pollution control, the regulation of the interstate shipment of seeds, planting stock, and other agricultural supplies through the mails and interstate commerce, and interstate control of the production of petroleum.

7. Because interstate cooperation seems like such a reasonable idea, there have been those who have thought of it as a feasible substitute for national action in a number of functional areas. This has not proved to be the case, despite the fact that in certain fairly local and regional matters arising within the range of state powers there have been some distinct successes. For matters of nationwide importance, and especially in those on which states may well have different policies and on which their individual policies may change decisively from time to time, interstate agreements, whether formulated as compacts or in other ways, simply cannot match in effectiveness a single national law carried out by a single national administration. Even on matters that are clearly within the legal competence of the states, interstate cooperation appears to work best when the national government participates with supporting legislation, financial inducements, and other forms of encouragement and assistance. Such national participation appears to raise the level of interstate cooperation and to provide it with a measure of continuity and stability. For any of the major functions that were specifically assigned by the Constitution to the national government, or into which it has entered without specific authorization of the Constitution and in which it has been long engaged in formulating a national legislative and administrative policy, a return to state action with interstate cooperation under something like a new set of Articles of Confederation seems to me to be practically unthinkable.

CHAPTER 7

State-Local Relations

Intergovernmental relations in the United States are not confined to the national and state governments. Within every state in the Union there are many units of government that possess most of the general characteristics of both the national unit and the state units. They are corporate or quasi-corporate in legal organization; autonomous or semi-autonomous in the management of their own affairs; authorized by constitutions, statutes, and charters to perform certain public functions as agents of their respective states; and possessed of at least minimum financial powers and resources to make it possible for them to carry on their work. The identification of the various classes and individual units of government and the study of their characteristics go hand in hand with the study of their interrelations.

The relations of the local units of government with their respective states, to which this chapter is primarily devoted, concern every phase and aspect of their existence. Their operating relations with the national government are also extensive and varied, but are primarily financial and functional. In addition, interlocal relations are exceedingly complex. It hardly needs to be said that the relations among national, state, and local units depend upon many factors. Their respective positions in the governmental system, their functions, and their finances are perhaps of highest importance in this connection. Also important are their relative numbers and competence and their organization for carrying on fruitful cooperation. In the next few pages I will try to present a sketch of the system of local governmental units and of their relative capacities, powers, and influence as a background for more specific considerations.

THE UNITS OF LOCAL GOVERNMENT

When in the early 1930s I first attempted to define and enumerate the units of local government in the United States, with the aid of academic and official consultants in most of the states, I arrived at a total of 175,369. This figure was probably a little too high even at that time, but it was lower than earlier estimates. School districts (127,108) made up over 72 per cent of the national total; towns and townships (20,262) over 11 per cent; incorporated places like cities and villages (16,366) over 9 per cent; counties (3,053) less than 2 per cent; and other units, mostly special districts for other than school purposes (8,580), nearly 5 per cent.

By states the smallest total number was in Rhode Island (93), the largest in Illinois (17,336). The rank order of the states below Illinois at that time was Missouri second (11,626), New York third (11,184), Kansas fourth (11,072), Minnesota fifth (10,544), Wisconsin sixth (9,762), Michigan seventh (8,905), Texas eighth (8,676), Nebraska ninth (8,455), and Iowa tenth (7,497). These ten states, all but two in the Upper Midwest, accounted for almost exactly 60 per cent of all the local units in the nation. In all ten of the high states school districts accounted for most of the local units, but in five of the midwestern states from 1,268 (Michigan) to 1,973 (Minnesota) townships added substantially to the totals. Indeed, three factors combined in the Midwest to give this area the highest concentration of local government units in the nation: (1) very large numbers of small school districts, (2) large numbers of organized townships, and (3) hundreds of villages and small cities recognized under laws that allowed incorporation of places having no more than fifty or a hundred inhabitants.

In the twenty-five years since my first study of local units was conducted, the Bureau of the Census, which has made a series of enumerations down to and including 1957, has reported very substantial changes in the total numbers and the distribution of local units. The total number has gone down from my figure of 175,369 to 102,328, a drop of 73,000, or nearly 42 per cent. The greatest decline has been in school districts, which, primarily as a result of a nationwide consolidation movement, decreased from 127,108 to 50,446, or more than 60 per cent. Towns and townships have decreased by 3,000, or about 15 per cent, the only other category of units to show a significant drop. Counties have remained almost unchanged in numbers, incorporated places have increased by about 800 and special districts other than those for school purposes have gone up nearly 6,000.

School districts, which once accounted for 72 per cent of all units, in 1957 were just under 50 per cent of the total and were still declining in numbers. Municipalities and townships were just under 17 per cent each, special districts 14 per cent, and counties under 3 per cent.

Among the states Nebraska, with less than 1 per cent of the 1950 national population, led all the states in local units of government in 1957 with 6,658. Nearly three fourths of these were school districts. Nebraska had over six times the average ratio, on the basis of population. Illinois was next in numbers with 6,494, and Minnesota third with 6,302, or about three times the normal ratio. The Upper Midwest from Ohio, Michigan, and Indiana to the Dakotas, Nebraska, and Kansas still had the greatest concentration of local governments in the nation. The twelve states in this region had 62,216 local governmental units, or 60 per cent of all local governments for less than 30 per cent of the nation's population. It should be added, however, that California, Texas, New York, and Pennsylvania also had high numbers of local governments. At the other end of the scale, Connecticut with considerably more population than Nebraska had only 383 local governmental units, and Virginia with more inhabitants than Minnesota had only 368. The eastern, southern, mountain, and western states in general had low numbers.

The changes in local units in Minnesota during the past quarter-century are fairly typical of the nationwide trends, and even more so of those in the Midwest. Between 1932-33 (the approximate date of my first enumeration of units) and the federal enumeration of 1957, the Minnesota changes have been as shown in Table 2. The net decrease was 4,242, or 40 per cent. Minnesota's decrease is thus just under the national average of 42 per cent.

Table 2. Local Governmental Units in Minnesota

Unit of Government	About 1932-33	Census of 1957	Decrease	Increase
Counties	87	87	0	0
Cities and villages	728	826		+98
Towns or townships	1,973	1,828	-145	
School districts	7,755	3,469	-4,286	
Other units (special districts)	1	92		+91
Total	10,544	6,302	-4,431	189

From what has been shown by these figures or may be inferred therefrom, there is, first, a great multiplicity of local units, not so much among the counties as among the "minor civil divisions" like organized townships and towns, villages, and cities, and especially among school districts and various types of other special districts such as housing authorities, soil conservation districts, and airport authorities. Second, although the numbers are very large nationally, they vary tremendously from state to state. Third, these local units do not constitute a single class, but are divided by law and in practice into a number of types. The various classes of units coexist among a people, perform different but overlapping services, but to some extent compete and also cooperate with each other. Fourth, it is also clear that the numbers of local units are always changing to some extent. This occurs partly through the purposive efforts of men to make units that are more suitable for performing the functions assigned to them, or more amenable to the control of selfish interests, and partly through mere attrition or erosion—the moving away of the population, the flooding of the land for water storage projects, etc.

There are some other facts that are not so evident from the data given. These units vary greatly one from another in area, in population, in wealth, and in other characteristics. This is true not only for all units over the nation as a whole, but also within each class of units, and within each class in every state. Diversity in characteristics and disparity in size no matter how they are measured are characteristic facts about local government units. They differ also in forms of organization, in rosters of officials, in legal powers and duties, and in the constitutional status they enjoy in their respective states. Some of these points will be spelled out a little more in what follows. With so many local units all differing so much in so many ways, it is perhaps inevitable that by any reasonable standards of performance, many local governments should be found inadequate for the performance of their duties and, I might add, inadequate for carrying on effective relations with other local units, with the state, and with the national government.

One consideration that is exceedingly important for the student of intergovernmental relations as well as for the citizen in general is the extent to which these units seem to lie in one layer upon another, with or without conforming to the same local boundaries. The Bureau of the Census has prepared a map of the United States showing all the counties and revealing how they cover the whole country. Suppose this map is transferred onto a large clear tracing cloth. Then suppose another such transparent map of the same size is made to show the organized towns, townships, cities, and villages, or what are called minor civil divisions. On this map the northeastern quarter of the United States, where towns and townships are most prevalent, would be heavily filled in, but the rest of the country would show primarily the many scattered incorporated cities and villages. A third similar map might show the school districts, which would make a network of fine lines and areas throughout most of the United States except in some southern, mountain, and New England states. Fourth, fifth, and other maps would be needed to show the boundaries of the various classes of other special districts. To show the units in certain metropolitan centers a considerable number of such maps would be required.

If all these maps were then laid one on top of another on a glass table and illuminated from below, the picture presented would seem to be one of utter confusion. In some places in the southern states nothing would show but the boundaries of the counties and of the scattered small areas representing incorporated places. Each resident in a rural place would have but one local government to concern him, his county, but the city dweller would have two, city and county. From these areas of relative governmental simplicity the situation would grow more and more complex in the northern and western urban places, and especially in and around large metropolitan centers where the boundary lines of the dozens of different units would be so numerous and so interwoven and overlaid that the light would hardly shine through the several layers of maps. In such places only the leaders in local government and specialized students would at all comprehend the complexities of the local government structure or, as some call it, the local chaos. The mythical average citizen would not know the many different local governments with which he should be concerned.

The relations among the many local units in these great urban clusters would also beggar all description, as would their relations with the state and national governments. For whatever the laws might say as to what these relations should be, the practices would be considerably different. Even though working for the welfare of the same general population, the different units in an urban area have separate governing bodies and officials, and are responsible for different functions, so that they cannot be expected to see all things eye to eye. I for one shall not attempt to sketch out the maze of intergovernmental relations even in the Minneapolis-St. Paul metropolitan area, which I know fairly well. Charles R. Adrian made an excellent start on the problems of this area in a study of metropolitan government that he conducted for our project, but there was not enough time to complete the study.

It follows from this preliminary sketch of local government that the intergovernmental relations of local units are impossible to describe for the nation as a whole and difficult to summarize for even a single state. I am reminded of something an English writer on municipal charters wrote over two centuries ago: "[W]hoso desireth to discourse in a proper manner concerning corporated towns and communities, must take in a great variety of matter, and should be allowed a great deal of time and preparation. The subject is extensive and difficult."

What I shall try to do, then, is to select a few of the leading headings of the subject, and outline under each some of the relations between national, state, and local governments that most affect the local governmental units. First I shall consider some constitutional and legislative problems for the United States as a whole but with Minnesota always in the forefront of my thoughts.

LOCAL UNITS AND THE NATIONAL CONSTITUTION

Although the discussion of the actual operating relations between the national and the local governments is reserved for the next chapter, it seems best to present the constitutional position of the local units under both the national and state constitutions in a single connected account. I begin that account with this section on their position under the United States Constitution.

From the constitutional point of view the states always seem to stand between the national and local governments, but this is not necessarily so in practice. There are direct national-local constitutional relations as well as operating relations. We begin with the fact that the highest written law of the land, the Constitution of the United States, does not mention local governments within the states. The division of powers implied in the original text of the Constitution, and expressed in rather vague language by the Tenth Amendment, is entirely a division between the national government and the states. From even the pre-Constitution period it has been understood that it is the states and not the national government that have the power to create, alter, and abolish local governments and to regulate their affairs. In this respect local government corporations are like private corporations, the great majority of which have been created by the states.

Basic questions concerning the status of local governments under the United States Constitution arose to some extent under the contract clause of the original Constitution. After the adoption of the Fourteenth Amendment new questions arose, and especially so after the rights of private corporations as legal "persons" had begun to receive the protection of the Supreme Court under the due process and equal protection clauses. These provide, as we have seen, that "No state . . . shall . . . deprive any person of life, liberty, or property, without due process of law; nor deny to any person within its jurisdiction the equal protection of the laws." Why should not local government corporations as well as private ones receive the protection of these clauses? This question arose from the 1870s on.

In 1923 the Supreme Court decided the leading case of Trenton v. New Jersey. The state had in effect taken away from the city a property right that the city had legally acquired from the state through the purchase of a private water company's property and its franchises, conferred by the state, to take all the water it needed for municipal purposes from the Delaware River. When the state began to charge for the water, the city appealed to the courts on three federal grounds, the impairment by the state of the city's contract, the deprivation of property without due process, and the denial of equal protection of the laws. On all three points the Supreme Court by a unanimous decision denied the city's claim. Said the Court: "The relations existing between the State and the water company were not the same as those between the State and the City. The company was organized and carried on its business for pecuniary profit. Its rights and property were privately owned and therefore safeguarded by the constitutional provision [the contract clause] here sought to be invoked by the City against the legislation of the State. A municipality is merely a department of the State, and the state may withhold, grant or withdraw powers and privileges as it sees fit. However great or small its sphere of action, it remains the creature of the State exercising and holding powers and privileges subject to the sovereign will."

The decision against Trenton under the due process and equal protection clauses followed the same course of reasoning. And what was decided concerning cities in the Trenton case would clearly hold true of any county, town, village, school district, or other local unit. According to this decision the United States Constitution gave such local units no protection against the state. The importance of this decision and others like it for state-local relations can hardly be overemphasized. Local governments had to get the powers and rights they wanted from their states, and could never be sure that they were protected.

The principle of the Trenton decision has never been expressly overruled. But recent decisions in other cases, also involving local governments and water rights, reveal how a different result was reached when the principle of national supremacy came into conflict with that of the Trenton decision. In a recent decision of the Supreme Court involving the city of Tacoma, Washington, the city was upheld in a controversy with the state over water rights on a navigable river. Congress had passed the Federal Power Act for the control of floods and the development of power on navigable streams. Under this act the city of Tacoma, a municipal corporation created by the state of Washington, had applied for and received from the national government a license to build several dams on the Cowlitz River in the state and to develop water power at the dams. This meant the flooding of some state-owned lands and a state fish hatchery. The state proceeded in one lawsuit after another, in its "sovereign capacity," to oppose the Tacoma power project. Its attorneys argued that the city as a creature of the state and subject to the state's sovereign power could not exercise any power not conferred upon it by the state, and that the state had not granted it any power to take state property like the fish hatchery even though they conceded that the state had granted to the city broad powers to engage in the production of electric power by means of dams and other works in streams.

The federal Court of Appeals, which made the real decision in the case, the Supreme Court later affirming and also overruling a contrary state supreme court decision, based its rejection of the pleas of the state upon the proposition "that the Federal Government under the Commerce Clause of the Constitution . . . has dominion, to the exclusion of the States, over navigable waters of the United States." Congress having acted through the Federal Power Act to authorize the building of power projects on navigable streams by municipalities and other persons, and the Federal Power Commission, after full hearings, having licensed Tacoma to do what it was doing, the national government had in effect conferred on the city the federal power of eminent domain to take and remove properties like the state fish hatchery. No action of the state was needed to authorize this taking, and no state action could obstruct the federal licensee in carrying out its power.

In short the city, though not created by the national government, had received certain powers from it and had become its agent under the license to build the dams and power plant. Nothing the state could do could legally obstruct the city's action. The state's creature and agent had become also an agent of the national government, and this capacity of the city is in a sense superior to the city's position as a subordinate creature and agent of the state.

This elevation or sublimation of the city makes it not only an agent of the nation but puts it also into the situation of being an agent of two principals, the nation and the state, and having to choose between them in cases of conflict. This is not an unusual situation in federal systems. Each state government is itself an agent not only of the people of the state but also to some extent of the national government and the nation. Many state officials such as game wardens are also federal officials, while local sheriffs, assessors, and other local officers serve both the state as a whole and their own communities.

If the national government in the future enters more and more into the problems of local government—in urban renewal and planning, soil conservation, public housing, hospitals, and other fields—local units and officials may become even more bound up with the national government and to that extent be weaned away from the states. I cannot foresee the time when the basic dependence of the local units upon the states will be ended, but I can foresee increasing complications in national-state-local relations. The penetration of national powers and activities into more and more areas of local government functions has the effect of blocking out the states from some areas and of increasing their activity in others. The potentialities for continued change in this area are impressive.

LOCAL UNITS AND THE STATE CONSTITUTIONS

The position of local governments under the state constitutions is so involved with problems of state legislation for them that the two topics must be considered together.

Every state has a written document called a state constitution that defines the governmental organization of the state and includes various provisions covering a state bill of rights, state taxation and finance, education, local government, and many other things. These documents tend more toward prolixity than brevity, and toward constant change instead of rigidity or permanence—but there are exceptions to all generalizations when fifty different states are being discussed.

Vis-à-vis the United States Constitution and the supremacy of the national government, the written constitution of a state has no higher standing than a state statute or any other form of state action, although many persons have misconceptions on this point. Within each state, however, and with respect to state and local powers and organization, the written constitution of the state has legal superiority over state statutes and administrative regulations, as well as over all actions of local governments. How strictly the state constitutional provisions are enforced against the public authorities depends in large part upon the attitudes of the members of the state supreme court, and they also change their minds from time to time.

Under the federal Constitution, as we have seen, all states are equal in powers; and we look not only to that document but also to the United States Supreme Court's decisions to learn what powers the states in general have and the limits thereof. If the United States Constitution is the source of each state's powers, as I think it is, the written state constitution serves the state primarily as a limitation upon the powers of its own legislature. In the absence of any words to the contrary in the state constitution a state legislature may exercise all possible powers of the state under the federal Constitution. A state constitution may not forbid the state authorities to exercise their federal duties, but in all matters that are of indifference to the nation as a whole, a state can impose limitations on its own authorities through its written constitution. It can say to them, in effect, that although under the United States Constitution a state is permitted to exercise a certain power (levying a state income tax, for example), the state constitution forbids its authorities to do so. Each state constitution does this in the name of the people of the state, as if the people had imposed the restriction. Most state constitutions and amendments thereto have, of course, been approved by the voters of the state.

In view of the Supreme Court doctrines in the Trenton and Tacoma cases I would say that, insofar as there is no conflict with the superior powers of the national government, or with proper actions taken by the national authorities, a state has complete power in all matters concerning local government within its area. The state and the state alone may create local units of government and systems of local government, and it alone may consolidate, alter, and abolish local units, grant and withdraw their powers, and regulate their affairs. In the absence of any state constitutional provisions to the contrary, the state legislature would exercise all the state's powers over local government, but in practice the state constitutions impose many different restrictions upon what the legislatures may do in this field. For the state legislature, therefore, the state constitution is a limitation of powers, but for other state authorities, like the governor, it is more in the nature of a grant of powers. A power granted to the governor is in effect denied to the legislature. This difference is frequently of importance in the relations of the state authorities to local governments.

The earliest state constitutions imposed very few restrictions upon the powers of the legislature over local affairs. One consequence was the development of legislative practices that could hardly be described otherwise than as abuses of power. Almost everything was done by special laws relating to particular cities or counties, often without notice to the place concerned and in some cases without publication until long afterwards. Local taxes and assessments were imposed, local streets were opened, street franchises granted, and buildings ordered to be built, at local expense, without local consent or even knowledge. It was the rising urban places that suffered most from such legislation.

Such abuses of power brought about a widespread demand to restrict legislative powers over local affairs, and to give the people of each community greater powers of local self-government. Since many legislators as well as other citizens recognized the evils that had developed, and believed in the principle of local self-government, many state constitutions were changed in response to the new demands. The new constitutional safeguards took many forms: (1) provisions in the constitution itself setting up certain types of local units like counties and towns; (2) prohibitions against specific legislative abuses like grants of street franchises and acts opening streets in local communities; (3) general and sometimes sweeping prohibitions against any sort of special legislation for local governments; (4) provisions that local bond issues and other measures required the approval of the voters in the place; (5) constitutional grants in about a third of the states to permit cities to frame, adopt, and amend their own city charters in conformity with the state constitutions and laws—a right later extended in a few states to counties also.

LOCAL GOVERNMENTS AND THE STATE LEGISLATURES

The various prohibitions against special legislation for local governments obviously had a certain amount of moral and legal effect. State legislators who were reluctant to yield to the demands for special laws to benefit particular interests at the public expense could point to the constitutional prohibition against special and local laws. It appeared, however, that some of the constitutional prohibitions against special legislation went too far. Local units operating under earlier special laws or charters found themselves saddled with archaic and unworkable charter provisions and yet unable to obtain legislative relief because general laws could not easily be obtained to fit the case, while special laws were prohibited.

To get around the constitutional prohibitions against special laws, state legislatures developed a variety of practices. Some simply passed special acts in disregard of the prohibition, naming in each act the place to be affected, on the theory that no general law could fit the case. If no citizen contested by court action the enforcement of such laws, the desired result had been obtained. More generally the legislatures took hints from lawyers and courts that the same results could be obtained by a system of legislation based on classifications of local units by population, area, assessed valuation, outstanding bonded indebtedness, and other pertinent criteria. On the reasoning that "general" legislation does not mean legislation of all-inclusive application but simply legislation that applies to all members of a genus or class, legislative draftsmen found many adroit ways of classifying local units, not, as a rule, by a single criterion like population, but by the more selective process of combining two, three, or even more criteria so as to include the one community to be affected and to exclude all others. Then the legislator from the place affected could assure legislators from other districts that their counties or cities would not be affected, and thus he could overcome any reluctance they might have about voting for the measure. In many states it was not long after special legislation had been constitutionally forbidden that the annual or biennial volumes of session laws began to be dotted with acts worded something like this: In every county of this state having from 10,500 to 12,000 inhabitants, and an area of not less than 600 and not more than 750 square miles, and an assessed valuation of not less than $8,000,000 nor more than $9,000,000, the county board may "do so and so," or "The county auditor's salary shall be" so many thousand dollars per year or "the county may borrow" so much for improvements on the courthouse.

Practically all such acts were actually special. They could apply to no more than the one county or city that came within the narrow limits of the two- or three-fold criteria of classification. Indeed, for most such acts the criteria were strictly *ad hoc*, being devised for this one act so as to include the particular place to be affected and to exclude all others. Another law in the same session or a later one might use different criteria and still apply to the same place. Most of these acts went into effect because no one contested their validity. An occasional decision of the state supreme court that one of these acts was unconstitutional, that it was really a forbidden special act, did not shut off the flow of such legislation. Many of these acts were, in fact, either harmless or needed and desirable in the public interest.

One defect in all such legislation is that none of these acts names the county, city, or other unit to which it applies. Lawyers and officials trying to search out all the legislation affecting some local government have to spend a great deal of time checking areas, populations, and other figures and criteria to ascertain which laws are legally applicable.

While many violations of the constitutional prohibitions against special legislation can be cited, it should be pointed out that such prohibitions have not been wholly ineffective. It appears that they have had some influence in inducing legislatures to enact more general legislation for local governments. Such laws are more carefully scrutinized during passage by the legislators, since they are likely to have effects in many communities. The general laws that get enacted usually enlarge the powers of local governments instead of putting new restrictions on them, and in that sense they increase local self-government. Indeed, a considerable measure of local autonomy can be achieved under well-drafted and reasonably liberal general laws.

It may be pointed out, also, that in the states whose constitutions do not forbid the enactment of special laws the volume of special legislation for local governments continues at a high level. In some states even the annual budgets and tax rates of certain communities are enacted by the state legislature. Since this seems to be the very opposite of local autonomy it calls for some analysis of the state-local relationship that is involved.

The Local Legislative Delegations. A consideration of the constitutional position of local governments within the states has brought this discussion into the realm of the attitudes of legislators toward state-local relations, and the legislature's role therein. This is an area in which we did some exploratory research and interviewing, but not enough to justify any very confident generalizations. Our questionnaires went primarily to administrative officials, local, state, and national, and to the members of local governing bodies, not to state legislators or members of Congress. This omission from our questionnaire list was not due to either an oversight or an underestimation of the importance of legislators in the intergovernmental processes. We simply could not explore everything in the time we had and with the resources available to us. Despite these limitations of our research, a few comments on the local role of state legislators seem to be in order.

State legislative leaders appear to have realized from the early days of the republic the strategic position and important role of state legislatures in the American federal system. By the very nature of its functions, each state legislature is responsible for the whole policy and all the laws of its state, and for substantially all relations with the national government, even when these are to some extent delegated to state administrative agencies. In the beginning, when state populations were small and those of the local units still smaller, there was no clear theory of the importance and the distinctive role of local government within the states. Even in New England with its pride in towns and the town-meeting system, local governments were looked upon as primarily agents of the state and certainly not as equal in importance with the states. Powers were doled out to them with a very sparing hand. Looking after the interests of the several towns, cities, and counties and the taxpayers thereof fell mainly to the lot of the locally elected individual members of the legislature, and these members found this work rewarding because it increased their usefulness, prestige, and power in their own districts, and gave them some assurance of re-election. Because there were not enough general laws to guide the local units in their work, and practically no state administrators or administrative departments to aid the local authorities, individual legislators easily slipped into the role of agents at the state capitol for the towns, cities, counties, and other local governments in their districts—and indeed in many cases a member represented only one town or county. Hence the legislator carried the local government needs of his district with him to the sessions, and introduced special bills to meet those needs. Since every member had the same type of responsibility for local legislation, no member was inclined seriously to question the bills introduced by others; and rules were worked out for passing such bills in batches and with relatively little debate or inquiry. Thus the locally elected members of the state legislature, one or more house members and one senator from a district, as a rule, and more from counties that were entitled to more representation, became a local county delegation in the legislature. This arrangement of local legislative delegations to look out for the legislative needs of local governments has become established in many places throughout the country. The larger cities and counties in particular seem to have become dependent upon them, but not so much the numerous small school districts, towns, and villages. Here is a factor in state-local relations that may deserve more study than it has received.

The local delegation is not required to sponsor or try to promote the passage of every local bill presented to it. The local officer, official body, or citizen group proposing the legislation may be strongly opposed by others; the measures proposed might result in too large an increase in local expenditures and taxes to suit many; there might be partisan reasons for not supporting them. The local legislative members have to make up their own minds what to support and what to oppose. Thus in many places the local legislative delegation has become a sort of standing local charter commission and a controller of tax rates and functions for the local government—in short, a body in some respects superior to the local governing authorities in the district. In the absence of general legislation of sufficient flexibility to cover most local needs, local governing bodies are often compelled to make terms with the local legislative delegation in order to get the laws they need.

And considering the power that lies within their grasp as long as local and special legislation is so greatly needed, what legislators would rush to draft and promote the necessary general laws to take care of local needs?

In some states, and especially for certain larger communities, the local legislative delegations have become well organized under definite rules to handle local bills, and the legislature has recognized their authority. Not only that, but the houses of the legislature do not wish to pass upon the merits of local bills or to decide between one faction or party and another in a controversy over a local bill. They do not desire to get embroiled in local controversies or to devote time to them that could be better spent on statewide problems. Hence, it is important (some legislatures seem almost to insist upon it) that each local delegation in the legislature present a united front and unanimously support any bill from that locality so that it may be passed without a struggle.

On what basis local legislative delegations decide which local bills to support and which to oppose it would be impossible to say. No doubt the factors that enter into consideration cover a wide range. Among the important ones have been the probable effects of the proposed laws upon the local tax rate and debt burden; the desire to promote and not discourage local industry; the rival claims and views of the central city and the suburbs in metropolitan areas; the opposition or support of special interests like those of the public utilities, liquor dealers, and organized labor in the cities, and of various farm groups in the rural areas. Because their own constituents' tax burdens will be affected by increased expenditures, legislative delegations have tended to keep a close watch on all measures that call for increased expenditures and taxes.

What seems to be important here is the almost organic nature of the connection that has been developed between the state legislature and many important local governments through the local legislative delegations. If this sort of connection is to continue, it would seem to be in the public interest to have a more formal recognition and organization of the delegations and provisions for regular open hearings, as if the delegation were in fact a committee of the legislature for local purposes, at the same time that it serves as a sort of superior local authority.

In stressing the work of the local delegations in approving and promoting bills for their local counties and municipalities, I do not intend to slight the general legislative committees on municipal affairs, on education (including school districts), and on other units of local government and their problems. Such committees exist in all state legislatures primarily to deal with general legislation for local units.

Local Dependence on State Legislation. How can local governments avoid the necessity for constant recourse to the state legislatures for new local legislation? Complete avoidance is obviously out of the question. Urban places in particular continue to grow and change. Old charters and laws get out of date. Inflation upsets or makes obsolete old tax systems, tax and debt limits, budgetary and expenditure restrictions. Technological changes and public demands make new public services a necessity. Offers of new federal aid call for new matching by state and local governments. The legislature of the state is the body to legislate for such local needs, and recourse to it is regarded as natural and logical.

Nevertheless, many leaders in local government and in other local public affairs have been striving for more than a century in the United States to reduce the dependence of local units upon the legislatures and to mark out a broader field of local autonomy. The ideal of local self-government in local affairs for all local communities has become a part of the American ideal of government. It is, however, far from complete realization in practice.

For one thing the difficulty of defining what are local affairs and of distinguishing them from state affairs is almost insuperable. It has not been possible to work out such a division with any precision between national and state affairs, as we have seen, but the interdependence of state and local affairs seems to be even greater. Everything that local governments do, in education, public health, social welfare, law enforcement, streets and highways, parks and recreation, and other public services, falls within the reserved powers and responsibilities of the states.

Furthermore at the most important point, namely, where they impinge upon and affect the lives and well-being of individuals, all functions of government, national, state, and local, blend together. This is the "government locally" that is discussed in Monograph 7 by Paul N. Ylvisaker. If law enforcement is the problem, or the protection of public health, or the education of youths and adults, or the conservation of natural resources, the work of all levels of government must be coordinated in one general direction. There can be no sharp division of functions, no demarcation of areas in which any governmental unit can do absolutely all that is needed, or can do exactly as its people please without regard to adjacent populations and other levels of government. Temporary conflicts there will be, of course, and divergencies of policy on many matters, and these may even help to clarify policy; but in general and in the long run units of government in the same governmental system cannot follow conflicting policies.

It is not practical, therefore, and it has not been the policy of the American states, to grant complete freedom to local governments to do anything locally that they may choose. Broad blanket grants of power and discretion are very rare in this field. State legislatures have instead granted to each city that they charter, and to each class of local units, a number of well-defined, specific, and limited powers, and the state courts have cooperated by holding the local governments fairly close to these enumerated grants when legal questions about local powers have arisen in court cases. When the powers granted to any unit or class of units of local governments are studied along with grants on the same general subject (e.g., public health or law enforcement) to state departments and to other units of local government, it will be found that all the provisions are fairly well integrated and interconnected, so that what one unit or official has power to do meshes in with but does not seriously conflict with the responsibilities of other units or officials.

This piecemeal way of dividing up governmental functions and powers among the different units and levels may seem at first glance to be excessively unimaginative and restrictive. It keeps the initiative of local governing bodies and officials within limited and definite channels. As the problem is normally handled it also keeps local governing bodies and other officials pounding at legislative doors for changes in local laws that will permit them to provide new public services, or to change the organization, powers, procedures, and financing of the local governmental units. This means in effect that the local units are kept in leading strings under legislative control and that the ideal of genuine local self-government is only partially realized.

On the other hand the system works to reduce conflicts and to promote cooperation among local and state authorities, and to prevent the near-chaos that might result if every local government had authority to provide for all "local affairs" according to its own definition thereof. Furthermore the citizens and taxpayers are saved from not only the fact of unwarranted and unwanted services, expenditures, and taxes, but also from the fear of them. With the legislature available annually or biennially as the court of appeal on all local affairs, there is, also, no danger of unduly long delays in satisfying urgent public needs. That is to say, the legislative needs will be met by the legislature but at a price, namely, the continued subservience of the local units to legislative control.

Resentment against continued state legislative domination over and interference in the affairs of local governments began to develop, as I have indicated above, over a century ago. It was particularly strong in the rising urban places, and the cities are still the centers of the strongest demands for "home rule" or freedom from legislative control. It was in the cities that the demands arose for state constitutional amendments to forbid special legislation and to authorize the local drafting and adoption of "home-rule" charters. Rural leaders and legislators were usually content to go along with legislative control of local governments because, in general, the rural governments needed less special legislation than the cities did, and the rural populations were becoming increasingly dominant in the legislatures and hence had less to fear from legislative control. During the past century, owing to faulty original apportionments combined with later refusals of legislators to reapportion according to population, most cities have become badly underrepresented in the state legislatures while rural areas have continued to dominate them despite their relative or absolute declines in population. Hence local leaders in urban places have continued their demands for freedom from legislative control over their affairs while the rural and small-town attitude has been to uphold legislative power because it has ensured their own power not only to pass such legislation as their own communities have desired but also to prevent urban places from getting anything out of the legislature such as increased state aids or shares of state taxes that might be in any way or degree at the expense of the more rural areas.

This analysis must not be understood as meaning that exclusively rural blocs of legislators have dominated legislative policies in every state. The situation varies from state to state, but in general the urban leaders and legislators have themselves been divided, frequently along party lines but also along economic lines. The more conservative property-owner-and-taxpayer-defending legislators from urban areas have stood with and have often led the conservative forces generally in opposition to the more liberal or progressive urban mayors, councilmen, and local reformers who have tried to increase the powers and the independence of the cities with a view, among other things, to enlarging their public services. That the more generally conservative rural legislators should fall into an alliance with the more conservative legislators from urban places to maintain strong state legislative controls over cities is not surprising.

What are the alternatives to the type of legislative control over local units of government that has kept local governments so directly and continuously subordinate to the state legislatures? I have already dealt briefly with the attempts to restrict legislative interference in local affairs through constitutional prohibitions against special legislation. These attempts were almost entirely negative and they provided no constructive substitute to meet local needs. Since growing communities always seem to be in need of changes in their basic laws, and legislators either wish to influence the result or cannot avoid doing so, the prohibitions against their actions proved to be only partly successful. Legislatures everywhere found ways to get around them, while many urban leaders who disliked the system of legislative control were perforce constrained to accept it.

The obvious alternatives to special laws are general laws, that is, laws that deal uniformly with the needs of whole classes of local units. While the apparent evolution of state legislation for local government has been from the special to the general, actually both general and special are to be found together even in colonial days. Counties, parishes, and towns were usually provided for in early times by rudimentary general laws, while incorporated urban places were created by special charters, as a rule. The trend for many decades has been toward more and more emphasis on the provision and improvement of general laws on an increasing number of subjects.

In subject matter, the general laws on local government are of three main types: those that provide for the creation, incorporation, governmental organization and officers, changes in boundaries, annexation and detachment of territory, consolidation, and dissolution of the local units; those that provide for necessary means of operating their governments and services, such as elections of officers, taxation and other revenues, special assessments, the taking of property for public use, budgets, purchasing and contracts, personnel, and public buildings; and those that establish and regulate the functions and services of the local units, including education, welfare and relief, public health, housing, building codes, local planning and zoning, parks, recreation, libraries, highways and other public works, fire protection, law enforcement, and local courts.

Until the recent enactment of laws for the consolidation of school districts the legislatures had done little to modernize their legislation in the first category. Laws that permit the incorporation even in metropolitan areas of small populations on tiny patches of land that are obviously inadequate to shoulder effectively the work of a city or village are still on the books in many states. Legislatures have done very little to "rationalize" the basic geographic structure of local governments. This is notorious in the case of counties many of which continue to exist in spite of declining and obviously inadequate populations and resources. Here is some evidence of the effects of the representation of counties as units in the state legislatures; they have, as it were, a built-in protection against any sort of rational consolidation of their areas.

In the second and third categories, namely, those laws that provide for the means to carry on local governments and those that establish and regulate their services and functions, there has been an almost nationwide ferment of legislation for the past forty years or more. It can be assumed, I believe, that the existence of the new bodies of general legislation has considerably reduced the need for special legislation in many fields. Most of the recent general laws have been carefully drafted by competent lawyers with the aid of subject-matter experts in the various fields. This makes them better in draftsmanship than most local governments would be capable of producing for themselves, and being general they are broader in scope than many local leaders would think of making them.

This leads me to one rather broad generalization on this aspect of state-local relations: If state legislatures could be induced to enact adequate modern codes of general laws for local governments covering all the major subjects and following the principle of allowing the local authorities a substantial amount of leeway in settling local problems, the legislative aspects of state-local relations would be greatly improved and the need for special legislation would be substantially reduced. Even the need for home-rule charters and charter amendments in cities would be in large part obviated.

Home-Rule Charters. And now just a few paragraphs on municipal home-rule charters. After the early prohibitions against special legislation had been on the books for some decades without much evidence of success in producing municipal autonomy, it was found that the charter problems of the larger cities in particular remained as trying as before. In 1875 a state constitutional convention in Missouri was confronted with the knotty question of how to modernize and rationalize the city government of St. Louis. After considerable discussion by a committee of local delegates to the convention it was decided, in effect, to refer the problem back to its source. This was done by means of a constitutional amendment to authorize each city of over 100,000 population in the state (St. Louis and Kansas City) to frame and adopt a charter for its own government as a city consistent with and subject to the constitution and laws of the state. The mechanisms provided for this purpose were a local board of freeholders called a charter commission to frame and propose the charter, and a referendum to the voters to reject or ratify it. Later amendments were to be made by the same procedure. Clearly this constitutional provision endowed each of these cities with a power and a procedure for making a city charter parallel to that by which each state in the Union may adopt and change its own state constitution in harmony with the Constitution of the United States. The scheme implies a sort of federalistic relationship like that of nation and state between the state and each major city—a relationship that has not been pressed any further, although in connection with legislative reapportionment the county leaders in many states are arguing for a parallel relationship between the counties and the state.

The Missouri plan for St. Louis and Kansas City, which was approved by the voters of the state, came to be called constitutional municipal home rule. A similar but broader scheme was soon adopted in California and other states followed suit. Today more than a third of the states from New York to Washington and California have such constitutional provisions, but there are none in New England or in the southeastern states. To meet the needs of urbanized counties a small number of state constitutions now provide also for county home rule, but there has been no significant demand for county home rule in the great majority of the states or generally in the more rural counties.

The constitutional municipal home-rule provisions vary considerably from state to state. At one end of a scale based on relative powers are several states that specify rather fully the powers that a city may claim under its charter while at the other end are states whose home-rule provisions leave it up to the legislature to define the scope of the home-rule powers. In practice there are some resultant differences in the powers of cities in different states, but nowhere has the general power of the legislature to enact general laws on municipal affairs been seriously reduced. The state supreme courts have been highly consistent in upholding state legislative powers even over home-rule cities except on points where the state constitution makes it indubitably clear that legislative interference is constitutionally forbidden.

Another major difference is indicated by the number of cities to which the home-rule provision applies. In two states the power is limited in effect to a single city, Baltimore in Maryland, Philadelphia in Pennsylvania; in Louisiana to two cities, Baton Rouge and Shreveport; and so on up the scale to seven states whose provisions cover any city or village, or any municipality.

When I most recently analyzed the figures, 3,658 municipalities appeared to be legally entitled to frame their own charters—872 in Ohio, 764 in Minnesota, 520 in Wisconsin, 483 in Michigan, and so on down. Michigan's cities had made the most use of their home-rule powers: 180 municipalities in all. In Oregon, Texas, Minnesota, California, Oklahoma, and Ohio from 107 down to 33 cities had made use of their home-rule powers. In other states the numbers were much smaller. All told, 651 municipalities out of a total of 3,658 that were entitled to do so had utilized their home-rule powers. These are substantial numbers, especially in view of the fact that some of the nation's largest cities, New York, Los Angeles, Detroit, Cleveland, St. Louis, and others are included in the list.

It is still true, however, that in over thirty states the home-rule charter power is not even authorized, and that in the other states only a fraction of the eligible municipalities (a large fraction in Texas, Oklahoma, and California) have exercised their charter-making powers. In short, municipal home rule does not eliminate the necessity for extensive state legislative action on municipal matters. To the communities that use the privilege, especially the larger cities, home rule appears to have certain advantages and to give considerable local satisfaction. That satisfaction consists mainly in the power to change the form of the local government from time to time in accordance with local wishes and by local, autonomous action, and to establish certain local services that are locally important but not needed throughout the state. The same advantage can be given to some extent, but not completely, by general statutes that provide for optional forms of municipal organization and optional powers subject to local adoption. Optional charter laws are suitable primarily for places of small population that have rather uniform needs; the larger cities require fairly complex and individualized forms of local organization that cannot easily be provided by general laws. Optional laws on local powers and functions are useful to local governments generally.

In whatever way the constitutional home-rule powers for cities and counties are viewed, however, they do not put these local units into a relationship to the state that is comparable to that of the states to the nation. In other words there is no truly federal relationship between the local units and the state. Every state must make and, when necessary, alter its own constitution and laws without any express authorization by the federal constitution and without any legislative aid from Congress. Every state has the same range of powers reserved to it as every other state under the United States Constitution. While it is true, as I have said in Chapter 3, that Congress has enacted a number of laws to protect, to regulate, and in effect to limit state powers where they impinge upon the powers of Congress, it is still the United States Constitution that is the main source of state powers and not the acts of Congress.

By way of contrast no local unit of government in any state may make or alter its local charter without express authorization in the state constitution, the state laws, or both, and in most states no such power has been granted. Even in the states where home-rule charters are authorized, they are entirely optional and in practice exceptional. Because so relatively few cities and counties have availed themselves of the charter-making power, the state legislatures continue to be the chief source of the laws for local government. In enacting such laws, whether general or special, every legislature varies the provisions to suit its own ideas as to the varying needs of different local units. There is nothing like the uniformity of powers that the states enjoy under the United States Constitution. Even minor attempts by Congress to differentiate between the basic rights of one state and another have been rebuffed by the Supreme Court.

THE COURTS IN STATE-LOCAL RELATIONS

The national government has its own system of courts throughout the United States, and each state has a separate system for all state and local purposes. These court systems are constitutionally separate, as we have seen, and yet their responsibilities overlap at many points. State courts handle certain federal cases and decide questions of federal law, while federal courts in cases between citizens of different states decide many questions based upon state laws. As a result numerous cases that involve the powers and duties of local governments arise in federal courts or are removed to them from state courts, and where federal questions are involved, as in the Trenton and Tacoma cases, the United States Supreme Court may be called upon to render the final judicial decision. When federal law controls the determinative issue, the law of the state that created the local government, and whose creature and agent the local unit is, may nevertheless be rendered inapplicable to the case under the doctrine of federal supremacy and the decision may thus go against the state.

Local units of government do not, as a rule, have separate court systems of their own. What are called county courts and municipal courts in the several states are in law and in fact state courts and parts of the state court system. In Minnesota, for example, the justice of the peace courts, whose jurisdiction is countywide, the municipal courts, the probate and district courts, and the state supreme court constitute a single state judicial system, authorized by the state constitution and given organization and vitality by state laws. Each type of state court, from lowest to highest, exercises some part of the state's judicial power. The local state courts in the counties, cities, and villages handle the minor cases, both civil and criminal, and perform other judicial services subject to appeals to the state district and supreme courts.

These local courts have some connections with the local units of government within which their judges or justices are elected and located, and whose local ordinances they help to enforce. The local units of government provide them with courtrooms and facilities, while a portion of the fines and fees collected by these courts are assigned to the appropriate local government treasuries. Cases arising under city and village ordinances commonly originate in the municipal or justice of the peace courts in the community. Cities have also a limited power through their home-rule charters to impose certain additional judicial burdens upon the district courts that serve their counties. Aside from such formal legal connections of the state courts with the local governments, there is the continuing contact of the judges with the local people, but these contacts and relationships are properly with the people in their capacity as citizens and voters of the state and not of any particular local unit of government.

With possible minor exceptions in the case of home-rule charters, local governments may not create new courts or judicial offices, or abolish any existing courts, remove any judge, or change the terms of office, the salaries or other emoluments, or the powers or jurisdictions of local judges. In short, the judicial branch of the state government down through the local courts is in general well insulated against legal interference by the local governments. Furthermore, unless the legislature has provided otherwise, the decisions, judgments, decrees and orders, writs, and other documents of all local state courts are subject to review under proper procedures in the next higher levels of the state courts, up to the state supreme court.

By reason of this integration of local and state courts in a single system, there is no problem of the interrelations of the local and state courts that is truly comparable with that of the relations of the state to the federal courts as described for Minnesota by Forrest Talbott in the first monograph of this series. I write primarily of the situation as it appears in Minnesota, but I feel confident that substantially the same situation respecting the state and local courts prevails in all the other states.

To be sure, the local courts have relations with the local governing authorities—with county boards and school boards, with city and village councils, and with mayors, sheriffs, the local police, and other local officials. These relations are not essentially different from those that they have with such state law-enforcing agencies as the game wardens and the state highway patrol, with one principal exception. The exception is that the local police in any city or village have little choice as to the forum in which they will bring misdemeanor cases to trial. In some instances this has led to friction because the local justice of the peace or municipal judge does not always see eye to eye with the local police and prosecutors. In Minnesota the state game wardens and highway patrol officers, on the other hand, have some choice of forum. For bringing their cases they have been able to select in many a county that justice of the peace or municipal court that is most conveniently located or that is most inclined to "go along" with the arresting officer's charges and his ideas as to penalties. This is not illegal and it has the advantage of concentrating the litigation in a relatively small number of courts for better accounting control. It does raise some questions, however, about the rights of those arrested.

Numerous important legal problems have arisen in the state courts concerning state-local relations. Every known type of power claimed by local governments has been tested in the state courts, and the state supreme courts have throughout the history of the United States been the primary adjudicators of the states' relations to their local units. Various attempts to change those relations through state constitutional provisions have also been subjected to the processes of judicial interpretation with the result that they seem never to have achieved in practice what their proponents and draftsmen appear to have expected. Constitutional prohibitions against special legislation and provisions for municipal and county home rule, for example, have been changed in effect or given different meanings in their passage through the mill of judicial interpretation.

This is not the place to enter upon a detailed analysis of what the state courts have done in this field. It is clear that in one situation after another the judges have had to feel their way along for lack of any clear guiding principles in earlier decisions. In general the respect felt by the judges for the powers of the state over the local units—and that has meant in effect a respect for the powers of the state legislatures—has been such as to preclude any serious inroads upon the state's supremacy over local affairs. When the legislatures have been liberal toward the powers of the local units, the state supreme courts have usually concurred, but in cases where the legislature has not clearly spoken the courts have tended to apply the rule of strict construction to prevent local action until it has been clearly authorized by legislative act. Because the laws vary so much from one state to another, any further generalizations would be unwise at this point.

In this entire field of the judicial role in state-local relations I have a feeling that there has been less change over the years than in the legislative, administrative, and fiscal fields of activity, for example. I do believe that the judges and justices of the higher state courts since about 1900 have been more learned and competent in their handling of local government litigation, and that the judicial processes have been considerably improved. Municipal courts, too, have certainly advanced, and have generally justified the enlargement of their jurisdictions, but the justice of the peace system in Minnesota and in many other states still poses serious problems.

STATE-LOCAL ADMINISTRATIVE RELATIONS

Anyone who has not read widely in the administrative history of the several states might well be astounded at the almost revolutionary changes that have occurred. From the founding of the first state governments in 1776 down to about the Civil War the states had practically no state administrative departments outside of those under the constitutional officers—the secretary of state, the treasurer, the attorney general, the auditor—and these officers headed relatively small departments with more or less formal duties. The state itself offered practically no statewide services, in highways, in public health, in education, in social welfare, in agriculture, and very little in the way of regulatory services over railroads, banks, insurance, or other major services and industries. An observant and scholarly French visitor in the early 1830s, Alexis de Tocqueville, noticed that although the state laws were being carried out everywhere, there were no state officials in the ordinary European sense to perform this service. Instead practically every law enacted by the legislature was being enforced or administered, if at all, by locally elected and locally paid officials in the counties, towns, and other local units of government. Sheriffs, coroners, assessors, treasurers, tax collectors, and other local officials, all had various state duties to perform. Over these local officials acting as agents of the states there was practically no central state administrative supervision. Instead it fell to the state courts, acting in cases brought before them by indignant citizens or local prosecutors, to try to keep the officials within legal bounds and reasonably diligent in the performance of their duties.

Based upon towns in New England, counties in the southern states, and a combination of the two in the middle states, the systems of local administration tended to become more complicated through the separate organization within these frameworks of cities, boroughs, villages, parishes, school districts, road districts, and other local units and officers. From such a multilevel, changing, growing conglomeration of local authorities anything approaching a uniform statewide provision of essential public services was not realized and was hardly expected.

From the beginning the states provided for state capitols to house the state offices and the legislature, and state prisons for major offenders against state laws. A little later they began to establish other state institutions, like hospitals or asylums for the insane and state colleges and universities to provide higher education. In short, legislation, courts, public buildings, and institutions roughly defined the scope of the states' services.

Even before the Civil War, however, the states began to experiment with statewide services, especially of a regulatory nature, but their financial resources and their means of communication and transportation were insufficient, and the needs were not acutely enough felt, to permit the success of such ventures. It was mainly after the Civil War and toward the end of the century that the movements for state performance of statewide services began to be important and productive of results. In the initial phases of the centralizing trend the more industrial eastern states took the lead, but midwestern agrarianism and the widespread Progressive movement had their effect on developments. By the time of World War I the movement was making considerable headway, and the New Deal period of the 1930s, with its increases in federal aid as inducements, further quickened the tempo of change. Today practically all the states support a number of departments and agencies that provide public services directly to the people without recourse to the local units for administration.

The present state departments and agencies fall into several broad categories. The traditional constitutional officials—attorney general, secretary of state, treasurer, and auditor—call for no special discussion although some of them have been designated in certain states to administer statewide services like a state bureau of criminal apprehension and the licensing of automobiles.

A number of state departments have statewide services as their principal obligations—highway construction and maintenance, state police, public health, public welfare institutions, penal institutions, the conservation of natural resources, higher education through state universities and colleges, the regulation of commerce, utilities, banks, insurance companies, and the sale of securities, the provision and regulation of airports and air services, and the licensing and regulation of professions and occupations. The major departments in this category are not set up to supervise local governments and services, nor do they oust and replace the local units in the performance of services. They tend instead to complement the services of the local units by taking over the statewide, top-level, and more expensive types of service that many local units could not afford or could not provide on a statewide basis. Thus the state departments provide the main highways, the institutions of higher learning, the large and specialized welfare institutions, the statewide health services, while the local units provide the minor and secondary roads, elementary and secondary education, and so on. In a sense, then, the state service departments, as distinct from those that are regulatory, merely round out and complete the services of the local authorities.

This characteristic of these state agencies necessitates their keeping in fairly close and continuous touch with the local authorities. Many matters have to be adjusted continuously at the points where the state and local services in health, highways, law enforcement, and welfare, for example, come in contact with each other, and where frictions and differences in policy may develop. Frank discussion of differences, a harmonizing of points of view, and thereafter friendly cooperation and mutual assistance are the ideals toward which administrators in these fields seem to aspire, but which they do not always attain. Many problems concerning the human relations in this area are touched upon in the questionnaire replies that are summarized by Dr. Weidner in Monograph 9.

Another group of state departments have as a principal if not their sole function the improvement of the services of local authorities through stimulation, education, assistance, and information, and, finally, through the supervision if not correction of their work. Actually this is also in part the role of the service departments mentioned above. A state health department, for example, or a state welfare department, has a double function: to render certain services and to see to it that the local authorities in health or welfare carry out their duties effectively and well. Except in the states with the smallest areas, the major welfare and health functions cannot be well administered from the state capitol in all parts of the state's area. The counties, cities, villages, and towns where the people live are more suitable than the entire state as areas in which to administer old age assistance, aid to dependent children, to the blind, and to the totally disabled, and residual relief to all the needy, and to provide visiting nurse service, establish quarantines, conduct clinics, vaccinate and inoculate people, and register vital statistics. For such necessarily decentralized services the role of the state agencies is not to do the work but to see to it that the work is done by the local authorities according to law and as honestly and effectively as possible.

Besides these services the states today provide for the supervision and equalization of the property assessments made by local assesors; the supervision of primary and secondary education; the inspection of local water supplies and sanitary facilities; the inspection and approval of local plans for schools, water supplies, sewage systems, jails, hospitals, homes for the aged, and other local facilities and institutions; the examination and certification of teachers, social workers, engineers, lawyers, doctors, and other professional workers employed by local governments; the collection, analyzing, and publishing of local financial data, and the auditing of local accounts; the inspection of public buildings for fire safety; assistance in the consolidation and reorganization of school districts; the finding of personnel for local government appointments; and the supplying of information to local governments on a wide variety of subjects including their legal powers and procedures. This list could easily be enlarged—and, of course, the financial aids now extended to local governments by the states are important factors not only financially but as stimuli to better work.

How the states carry on these many activities in serving and supervising the local authorities is a sufficient subject matter for many monographs in many states, of which all too few have been written. In general the state legislatures have gone about the work of creating systems of state supervision over local governments reluctantly, slowly, and by piecemeal methods. No other way was really open to them, since the legislators were always fearful of enlarging unduly the powers of the state administration, a rival branch of the state government, over their own creatures, the local units of government.

A few states have experimented with the idea of a single state department to supervise the finances of local governments but this idea has not been adopted by the states generally. As a rule the legislators, before enacting state supervisory laws, have waited for specific proposals to come from the field concerned, such as education or public health, and have limited their legislation to provisions for single separate functions and departments. Thus it has developed that each one of a number of functional state departments deals directly with separate functional units or departments among the local governments, and practically not at all with other local authorities. The state department of education deals almost solely with the local school authorities, the state welfare department with the local welfare officials, and so on throughout the range of state and local service functions. The principal state agencies that cut across lines and deal with local governments generally are primarily those having to do with taxation and the audit of accounts.

There is, then, no state administrative agency outside of finance and accounting that deals with local government as a whole, and no agency at all at the local level that represents local government as a whole. The nearest approach to the latter is a consolidated city and county which operates as one unit and controls public education in addition to other local functions. Such situations are very few anywhere in the United States. Generally the local government structure is a cluster of many more or less separate units of government in the same area dividing up the powers and functions of local government among them. Consequently there is no official coordinating element in most local government situations.

This fact brings us back to the state legislature as the only available coordinating mechanism between state and local governments in the state as a whole, and to the local legislative delegations in the counties and the large cities to do the coordinating locally. It was this situation, coupled with the fact that the state and national governments were becoming more actively engaged in local services alongside the local authorities, without any effective coordination of activities, that led to the formation of the Councils on Intergovernmental Relations, one of which made the Blue Earth County experiment that is described in Monograph 7 in this series. The main objective of the experiments carried out under these councils was that of devising a local means of coordinating all the public services, national, state, and local, within the county. Dr. Ylvisaker's account of the Blue Earth County effort shows some of the reasons why this effort was not successful. It would have been marvelous indeed if at the local level, in any county, an administrative mechanism could have been devised and made operative to coordinate all the governmental programs and activities that impinge upon the people of the county. All intergovernmental relations, both vertical and horizontal, would have been affected.

State-local administrative relations are affected by various special factors. One is the somewhat suspicious watchfulness that state legislators generally, and the local delegations in particular, manifest toward any excessive zeal or exercise of power on the part of state administrators in supervising local governments in their districts. Legislators are especially sensitive in such matters, because they know that their constituents will hold them responsible. On the other hand, because of the possible adverse repercussions in the legislature from any excessive display of authority on their part, state administrative agencies are sometimes excessively cautious in their handling of local abuses and even violations of law by local authorities.

Another factor is the feeling on the part of the councils and administrative officers of the larger cities that the state departments have little to offer them in the way of financial assistance or superior knowledge or technical skill. In some cases it may happen, for example, that the big city's health officer or school superintendent is fully as competent and informed as the state health officer or school commissioner. Also, for financial reasons, including the prospect of federal aid, many big city administrations tend to look to the national government instead of to their states for help. For a variety of reasons, one of which seems to be the rural domination of state legislatures in most states even where the urban population greatly exceeds the rural, the big cities and their leaders claim that the state legislatures are not treating them with due consideration of their needs, and that it is necessary to by-pass the state legislature and go directly to Congress for a sympathetic hearing. The United States Conference of Mayors, a national organization of the larger cities, with headquarters in Washington, has taken a strong line against state legislative neglect of the needs of the cities, and has led the municipalities in the trend toward seeking aid from Washington. The American Municipal Association, a federation of the state leagues of municipalities, which represents small as well as large communities, has not been far behind in its appeals to Congress for help. In this connection also the National Institute of Municipal Law Officers and the Municipal Finance Officers Association should not be overlooked. The counties too have a national organization, as have the school superintendents, to look after their interests at the national capital.

In practically all the states, in addition, the different classes of local units—counties, municipalities, townships, school districts, and others—have statewide organizations of their governing bodies for presenting their needs and views to the state, including their desires for home rule. In addition the various classes of local officials, such as sheriffs, auditors, and clerks of the counties, mayors, attorneys, clerks, managers, police chiefs, fire chiefs, health officers of the cities, and welfare officials, school superintendents, and others from various local units, are organized for mutual aid in the promotion of their official interests in such matters as affect their functions, powers, emoluments, and retirement pay.

The best of these organizations, state as well as national, conduct research, publish periodicals and special reports, and have a considerable educational influence upon the officials who participate in their affairs. They are important in interlocal as well as in state-local and national-local relations.

The general impact of these organizations upon governmental finances, activities, standards, and relations cannot be measured with any degree of accuracy, but it would be hard to exaggerate their total long-run influence. The 1957 Census of Governments showed 514,000 elective local officials in the United States, while the total number of local government employees (including elective officers) was 4,249,358 (including both full and part time). Local governments accounted for over half of the nearly 8 million civilian public employees in the land. The elective officials in particular tend to be politically important. State legislators and administrators, members of Congress, and national administrative officers cannot afford to ignore them.

State officials, both those who are elected and the principal appointed ones in departments that deal with local finances and functions like health, highways, education, law enforcement, and welfare, are frequent participants in and speakers at the annual meetings of various organizations of local officials. It would be interesting to speculate, also, about the numbers of state-local official contacts through annual reports, visits for inspection, letters of inquiry, telephone calls, visits of local officials at state offices, and attendance at state legislative and administrative hearings. The sheer volume and variety of such contacts have prevented any compilation of the data. Most of the individual items may not be of any great importance but the mass aspects of these unnumbered state-local interactions are tremendously impressive. Widespread education and interest in governmental services, modern means of communication and transportation, the great increases in both state and local governmental activities, and the general tendency of Americans to create organizations and hold meetings for every type of interest or activity have combined with other factors to bring state and local officials into ever-increasing association. Even in the more remote mountain and desert regions, isolation of local government is impossible.

To return to the general theme of state-local relations, it is evident that things are far from being what they used to be, and that public thinking needs to catch up to the present situation. The basic controlling factors continue to be constitutional, statutory, financial, functional, professional, and "expediency" factors—the latter in the sense of the pull of local leaders for home rule against movements for state control or for consolidation of small local units into larger ones, and the desire of specialized and professional interest groups to control the services peculiar to them against movements to integrate their services with those of other agencies or units. Interacting with these factors and exerting considerable though variable force are the desires of large sections of the public for increased and improved public services, and the simultaneous counterforce of those elements in the population who resist any increase in taxation. In so complex and dynamic a situation there is material for many human-behavior studies in state-local relations. Such studies will not be easy, nor will significant results be assured in any case. Even between state and state the cultural and situational variables are considerable.

STATE-LOCAL FISCAL RELATIONS

In 1902, local governments in the United States were spending from all sources (taxes, borrowing, and miscellaneous revenues) $909 million annually as against a total of $655 million for the national and state governments combined. The local total was nearly twice the federal total of $476 million and over five times the state total of $179 million. In 1952 total government expenditures in the United States were $99.8 billion as contrasted with $1.6 billion in 1902, a sixty-fold increase. Of the 1952 total the national government accounted for 72 per cent, local governments for 15 per cent, and the states for 13 per cent. The 1902 percentages had been national 30 per cent, state 12 per cent, and local 58 per cent. These figures reveal the astounding changes that have taken place both in the totals and in the relative distribution of expenditures. When tax collections alone are compared, for the beginning and the end of the same fifty years the national government's share jumped from 37.5 per cent to over 75, the state rose from 11 per cent to over 13, and the local dropped from 51 to 12 per cent.

These figures point to a sort of double revolution in American public finance in 50 years—one the tremendous increase in the total amounts raised and spent, the other the changes in proportionate shares of the three levels of government. Local governments fell from an impressive first place in both taxes collected and expenditures made in 1902 to an undistinguished last place in tax collections and close to last in expenditures in 1952. Both the national and state governments gained upon or went well beyond the local governments. And yet the amounts of local revenues and expenditures were also increasing very substantially during this period.

When the period began the states depended largely (over 90 per cent) on the "general property tax" for their tax revenues. By 1952 the states were getting less than 4 per cent of their tax revenues from this source, while local units still received 88 per cent of their tax revenue from this one source. In short the states had practically abandoned the property tax as a source of revenue for state purposes, although Minnesota was something of an exception. In general the states had conceded that tax to the local units exclusively, expecting it to be their main financial support.

For many years even before this change, the property tax had been under strong condemnation as unjust, impossible to administer fairly, burdensome, hard to collect in periods of business recession, and defective in other ways. It was under constant attack from real estate interests, home and farm owners, and various business interests. State legislators made many attempts to restrict its use and to reduce its burden by tax-rate limitations, ceilings on the total tax, and exemptions for veterans, home owners, motor vehicle owners, railroads, and other classes of taxpayers. Nowhere were they willing to provide for statewide uniformity of assessments through a rigid and exclusive system of state valuations of property.

This was the tax that was in effect abandoned by the states and turned over to the local governments—battered, abused, unpopular, reduced in base, and administratively much neglected. Nevertheless it not only did not fail completely but survived all its mistreatment and continued year after year, except for a few years during the depression of the 1930s, to yield more revenue every year. In 1902 it produced for the local governments $624 millions, in 1913 $1.2 billions, in 1922 $3 billions, in 1932 $4.2 billions, in 1940 $4.2 billions, in 1946 $4.7 billions, in 1952 $8.3 billions, and in 1957 $12.6 billions. Thus in fifty years its yield in dollars for local governments increased more than twelvefold, and it is still growing. We need not stop to try to explain its remarkable vitality and resilience.

While the states progressively reduced their reliance on the property tax, they turned to other modes of taxation for needed revenues. This trend in fiscal policy produced a separation between state and local governments with respect to the "sources" or modes of taxation, a separation that had not previously existed. The states experimented with one new tax after another, and in time each one worked out its own combination of taxes for the support of the state services. These include today various types of corporation and business taxes, inheritance, estate, and gift taxes, selective sales taxes on motor fuels, liquor, tobacco, and other products, general sales taxes, income taxes, payroll taxes, and others.

This shift of the state governments to other methods of taxation for state purposes did not appreciably reduce the interest of the legislators in the property tax. Property taxpayers made up a large and influential part of the constituency of every member of the legislature, and these taxpayers looked to their state representatives for protection against increases in the local tax rates and levies.

However, the demand for increased local revenues continued to rise insistently in the growing urban centers where new and improved public services were constantly being proposed. City and village councils and urban county and school boards asked time and again for increased taxing powers to satisfy the demands upon them. On the other side the local legislative delegations of senators and representatives had to listen regularly to taxpayers' objections when they considered bills to enlarge the local taxing powers or to increase the maximum tax rates established by law. This explains in large part the importance attached by legislators to local legislation, and throws some light upon the tensions that developed in many places between the service-minded municipal authorities and the more taxpayer-minded local legislative delegations.

Noting the overrepresentation of rural areas in most state legislatures some persons have been inclined to hold rural legislators responsible for the failure of cities and villages to acquire what they consider to be necessary increases in taxing power from the state legislatures. In fact, however, this responsibility seems to rest largely with the more tax-conservative legislators elected by the urban people themselves.

Urban authorities have also asked for the right to share in the newer state-collected revenues. State legislatures have varied considerably in their response to this plea. A few states have been relatively generous in such tax-sharing, but the majority have not shared nearly enough to satisfy the urban authorities. Legislators have preferred instead to share such revenues, if they share at all, with the local units that cover the whole state, namely, the counties and the school districts. This enables the rural legislators, with their overrepresentation in the legislature, to put more of these shared revenues into the rural counties for expenditure. It is well known that the rural representatives have been able to drive some hard bargains at the expense of the underrepresented popular majorities in the urban places. The general reluctance of legislatures to share state-collected taxes at all may be partly explained by the fact that tax-sharing usually means putting the money into local treasuries for expenditure on the general services of the local units, according to the varying policies of local authorities, and this may result not only in local abuses but also in depriving the legislature to some extent of its control of local expenditure policies. Still, in the long run, local needs must be met. How can this be done?

The principal alternative, in order to meet legitimate local needs, is to resort to annual state-aid payments from general or specific state revenues to designated classes of local governmental units for strictly defined purposes such as primary and secondary education, secondary roads, and specific health and welfare services. State aid, which in 1902 amounted to very little in any state, had by 1952 become a major source of local revenue, next to the property tax in many states, and gaining on it. In 1952, out of a total of $19.4 billions in local revenue, $8.3 billions, or just under 43 per cent, came from the property tax and $5.3 billions, or nearly 28 per cent, from the state and national governments, mostly as state aid, a part as shared revenue. The rest, some $5.8 billions in all, or 29 per cent, came from utility and liquor store revenue, charges for services and miscellaneous, licenses, and insurance trust revenue, the latter largely for pension and retirement purposes. It was in 1946 that the property tax yield first dropped below 50 per cent of all local revenues. Since 1952 it has held steady at about 43 per cent of the total.

Various attempts to satisfy urban demands for more revenue through granting them the power to impose specified local taxes (on sales, payrolls, and other bases) have been made in Pennsylvania, New York, California, and other states. These have had some success, but in part they have been a means of "calling the bluff" of local leaders. Experience seems to show (1) that the municipality is in many cases too limited an area and base for the successful application of local taxes based on other factors than real estate and tangible personal property; (2) that central cities taxing businesses unduly find them at least threatening to move outside the city, and sometimes actually doing so; and (3) that taxes in any way burdensome to the local population, and unpopular in any case, are frequently defeated when put to a public vote. The general result seems to be that the urban places that most need the revenue have to get it mainly from the property tax, partly from various service charges and licenses, and for the rest have to fall back upon sharing in such state taxes as they can induce the legislatures to distribute.

State aids and shared taxes go largely into public education, highways and minor roads and streets, and payments to match federal aid for old age assistance and aid to dependent children, the blind, and the disabled. These are understandably distributed mainly to local units of statewide coverage, namely the counties and the school districts. Many of these local units get over half their revenue from state aids and shared revenues. Relatively little is turned over to the incorporated cities and villages. These units are forced to be financially more independent.

New York was the first state to recognize the needs of urban places for extra revenue for their general purposes. It makes annual per capita grants of modest amounts (from $6.75 down to $3.00 per capita) and in addition provides some loans and grants for such purposes as public housing. Other states have made some concessions to satisfy urban claims, but these cannot be summarized here.

By exercising their power of the purse, granting aids and sharing taxes with the local governments, the states have greatly increased their participation in local affairs and have put themselves in a position to exercise more control over them. They have been able to set standards for the qualifications of the local officers and employees who administer the funds, and to legislate statewide service standards higher than many local units would have been likely to establish, though presumably not as high as others might have instituted. Through inspections and audits the states are also able to do much to maintain an acceptable level of performance.

But a state-aid system is not an instrument for changing the basic relations between state and local governments. The aids that are granted provide some additional leverage for the exercise of state control, but not as much as might be expected. They are not long looked upon locally as grants made as a matter of grace by an all-powerful state to subordinate units of local government. Just as the taxes collected by the state are interpreted by the taxpayers as a concession they have made to the government, the grants-in-aid paid by the state are viewed by the local authorities as sums to which they have a legal right. For a state legislature ever to withdraw state aids that have once been begun without replacing them with equivalent funds from other sources would be considered almost a breach of contract.

Consequently, while state legislative control over local governments continues it is not greatly increased by the fact that state aids are paid. State administrative control over local units is also somewhat increased by legislative actions designed to ensure the proper expenditure of the state aids, but not beyond a certain point. Jealous to protect their own direct contact with and control over local governments, legislators do not confer on state administrative agencies drastic powers to withhold state aids from errant or delinquent local authorities. Besides, even when fairly strong powers are conferred on such state agencies, they are normally reluctant to act vigorously against local authorities. They tend to temporize and to try to obtain results by conciliation and education. As the personnel in local governments shows a constant turnover, year after year, the process of educating the local officials and employees in their duties is a continuing one.

Many details of state-local fiscal relations have been omitted from this summary. In conclusion I would like to condense the summary into a brief statement of the evident trends. The past fifty or sixty years span a series of interrelated movements that have brought about a number of veritable revolutions in American public finance and in the fiscal relations of national, state, and local governments. These may be listed under five headings:

1. Total amounts. The amounts of public revenues and of public expenditures have increased more than sixty-fold. These increases can be accounted for only in part by increased population and inflation. There has been and there continues to be an absolute increase in public services. The percentage of the national gross product being expended for public services is higher by a wide margin than at the turn of the century.

2. Amounts by levels of government. The revenues and expenditures of local governments once exceeded those of the national and state governments combined, but now national revenues exceed the combined state-local total by more than two to one and national expenditures exceed the combined state and local expenditures by nearly two to one.

3. Sources of revenue. Having found the tariff and such old low-rate excises as those on liquor and tobacco inadequate for its purposes, the national government has shifted to personal and corporate income taxes as its main source of revenues, while an expanded list of excises at generally higher rates provides considerable additional income. The states which, with the local governments, once depended almost entirely on the property tax abandoned that tax almost completely to the local governments, while at the same time keeping control over it, and themselves turned to various combinations of state income, sales, corporation, excise, payroll, inheritance, and other taxes for their revenue. This has meant a significant separation of sources between the state and local governments, but a corresponding overlapping of sources between the national

and state governments. Furthermore the states have become increasingly involved financially with the national government through federal grants-in-aid.

4. Limitations on property taxes. To placate the property-tax payers, prevent excessive or double taxation, and protect their own new sources of revenue, the states, while turning the property tax over to the local units, generally exempted various classes of property from taxation partly or entirely and put such limitations on tax rates, locally or statewide, that the local governments were unable to raise the revenues they felt they needed to meet the mounting demands for public services. They felt compelled to turn to the state legislatures for a share in the new state revenues and for state aid in supporting major statewide services like education, highways, and welfare, with results that I have already indicated.

5. From fiscal autonomy to fiscal interdependence. Local governments in particular have increasingly lost their fiscal autonomy in becoming so dependent upon the states. Indeed, state and local governments have become more and more tightly bound together in fiscal matters. The school districts throughout the nation are moving toward a situation where 50 per cent or more of their revenues will come to them as state aid or shared taxes. The counties are somewhat behind, but they are moving toward a 40 per cent dependence. Cities, in general, having been denied substantial state aid in most states, have retained a larger measure of fiscal autonomy, but to do so they have had to increase their revenues from local service charges, license fees, fines, and other sources, and to cut services below what many citizens and officials consider a desirable level. And even for so-called home-rule cities, those that are entitled to make and alter their own city charters, home rule in the sense of substantial power to shape their own fiscal powers has not been achieved and is not likely to be. Tax policy in particular is for the states, not the local governments, to make, and even the states are hemmed in to some extent by the national government's dominant position in the fiscal field.

CHAPTER 8

National-Local and Interlocal Relations, and Metropolitan Problems

As we move out of the more traditional though ever-changing field of state-local relations dealt with in Chapter 7 into the three topics proposed for discussion here, we enter fields in which changes have been even more pronounced and even greater changes can be expected. Although at first glance the three topics seem to be only distantly related, I hope that the discussion will reveal some close connections, both actual and potential.

The three groups of problems certainly have one thing in common. They were not foreseen, and the state constitutions contain practically nothing about any of them. They have come to be important only in fairly recent times, and that as a result of a combination of several factors: the increased demand for public services; the inadequacy of many units of local government for the functions assigned to them; rapid urbanization even beyond city limits; the rise of metropolitan areas; the beginning of a decline in parochial views about government; and the engaging of the national government's attention in local matters.

NATIONAL-LOCAL RELATIONS

In 1924 I published an article on the national government and the cities in which I pointed out the handicaps under which the sixty-eight cities of over 100,000 population labored at that time in trying to get legislation suited to their common needs out of the thirty state legislatures among whose jurisdictions they were divided; how poorly qualified most state governments were for dealing with the needs of large cities; and how much the national Congress and administration might be able to do for the large cities of the country. I was in no sense the originator of the ideas I expressed. They were rather widespread at the time. Rebuffed too often in the state legislatures, urban leaders were turning to Congress for the help they thought the cities needed. Seaport cities and their port authorities already had had favorable experience with federal cooperation through congressional appropriations and the work of the Corps of Army Engineers, and there were other examples.

At that time the national government was already doing a great deal to improve rural living conditions through the rural free delivery system, federal aid for highways in rural areas, county agricultural agents, and other projects. It took the depression of the 1930s with its great concentration of unemployment in urban places and the virtual bankruptcy of many cities (as well as other local governments), and the New Deal program under President Franklin D. Roosevelt, to shift the focus of national attention more fully to the cities, without any loss of attention to rural needs.

Though not limited to the relief of urban distress alone, the great New Deal antidepression measures were designed in large part to help urban people and their governments. I will only name some of the major agencies and laws I have in mind: Civil Works Administration, Federal Emergency Relief Administration, Works Progress and Works Projects administrations, Public Works Administration, National Planning Board, United States Housing Act, Municipal Bankruptcy Act, Home Owners Loan Corporation, Reconstruction Finance Corporation, Social Security Act and Social Security Administration. These acts and agencies, and others in the labor field, in public health, and in other areas, made provisions for specifically urban needs as well as those of statewide incidence.

Later came various acts for federal aid to major highways within cities, for grants to urban airports and even for direct national dealings with urban airport authorities, for grants and loans for urban planning and redevelopment, for urban facilities in areas of great federal activity, for civil defense aid, and so on. In short, since the early 1930s Congress has recognized that urban as well as rural problems are national in scope and equally entitled to national consideration and action. Now that urban people make up practically two thirds of the nation, any reversal of this position is almost unthinkable.

The new orientation toward urban needs has by no means meant a decline of national concern for rural problems. None of the major measures for social welfare, public housing, highways, health and hospitals, school lunches, and other projects make any serious distinctions between rural and urban. And Congress has in this same period enacted additional measures of special interest to rural populations, such as the acts for soil conservation districts, rural electrification authorities, rural secondary roads, and rural library services.

The nation's concern for the problems of local government, both rural and urban, is today at a high point; the number of contacts, direct and indirect, between national and local government agencies has never before been so great. As I tried to point out in discussing interstate relations, there are no governmental activities, state or local, in the United States, in which the national government does not have some interest, or in which its guiding or helping hand cannot be seen. One cannot survey local government in any of its important activities and fail to see the impact, contribution, or influence of the national government thereon.

In the fields of agriculture, labor, manufacturing, mining, commerce, transportation, power, communications, banking, finance, and even insurance, this has been obvious for some time. In the typical state and local functions of government such as courts, law enforcement, civil liberties, health, social welfare, highways, other public works, conservation, and even that holy of holies of the confirmed states'-righter, education, the hand of the national government is everywhere to be seen. Today even the retirement systems for state and local employees are being brought within the supporting influence of the national government through the system of Old Age and Survivors Insurance. Indeed the national system of social security is fast becoming the main support for state and local retirement systems. The inability or unwillingness of state and local taxing authorities to meet the expectations of state and local employees in this field, or the excessiveness of the demands of the employees (according to another interpretation), has created many state and local vacuums into which federal funds and powers have been drawn to meet the demands.

The states, particularly the state governors, have not been unaware of this increasing influence of the national government in state and local affairs. During the discouraging and hectic days of the Great Depression, national aid toward effecting economic recovery and assisting state and local governments regain their fiscal strength was accepted with little question, but once the recovery was on its way the mood changed. Many governors and other state leaders resented the direct dealings of national agencies with local governments as a trend that was undermining the control of the states over their local agents.

As a matter of history this wall of state sovereignty around the local governments had been breached many times before, and without any serious protest from the state governments. The Federal Power Act of 1920, which gave cities a sort of priority in applying directly to the national government for power rights on navigable streams, was a case in point, as the reader will have noticed in the Tacoma case discussed in Chapter 7 above. Congress, itself composed of senators and representatives from every state, had followed the practice of authorizing direct dealings with cities and other local governments by federal agencies, without their having to clear everything through the states. As a matter of fact most states were not equipped with agencies of their own empowered to approve or disapprove local dealings that were otherwise within the powers of the local governments.

The change of mood among the state governments in the late 1930s and the early 1940s came to a head when Congress was considering a new airport act for federal aid in stimulating the development of a nationwide system of airports. In the hearings a number of governors took a strong stand on having all federal grants for local airports channeled through the state governments. The states were not unanimous, however, and other witnesses opposed the plan. Apparently some states were not prepared to set up the necessary state agencies for this purpose, while local airport authorities, already accustomed to direct dealings, did not relish the idea of the change. In this as in other cases some governors learned that they could not speak for their state legislatures. The compromise enacted by Congress in 1946 left it up to each state to determine by law whether it wished state channeling or not. As of June 1951, when our field study was terminating, twenty-one states required channeling, the others did not.

The Commission on Intergovernmental Relations, reporting in 1955, recommended that the channeling provision of the 1946 act be retained. In fact it appears that the principle of the Airport Act on this point has become accepted. It is up to each state to decide as a matter of policy and legislation whether it wants channeling of federal funds to local governments through state agencies or not. Obviously, however, when a local government has made a valid agreement with the federal government under existing laws, a state may not undo the contract by a subsequent retroactive measure. That I believe to be the principle of the Tacoma decision, although the subject matter was different.

So much for the general law and policy of dealings between the national government and the local governments. The questions of tact, etiquette, and policy that face federal administrators present other problems. In most situations that we observed where federal grants were channeled through the state for expenditure by counties or other local units, the federal administrators were circumspect about notifying the state agencies, and even having a state official accompany them, before trying to inspect the local spending agencies. About one situation in Minnesota we heard serious criticisms, however. Under a Republican state administration that was trying to follow an economical course, it was alleged that field agents of the national administration, then Democratic, were trying to induce not only the state but the county officials to follow a more liberal spending policy with federal grants in old age assistance and other welfare cases under the Social Security Act. Similar complaints having been reported in other states, and not only in regard to welfare expenditures, we have reason to believe that the criticisms were valid. These cases were also among the few that we documented under federal grants-in-aid in which differences in party policy were important.

The impacts of national legislation, financial aid, and administration upon local governments have so many aspects that a complete catalogue is out of the question. The following are some of the more important points.

Financial aids by the national government to the local governments, whether paid through the states or directly to the local units, have been and are available to the local units for many functions and in a variety of ways. These include loans that have been available for certain capital projects at low interest at least since the days of the PWA. Grants appear to be even more numerous and varied, covering most of the major local services (highways, urban redevelopment, public housing, planning grants, welfare costs, health, hospitals, school lunches, and many more). The national government also makes payments in lieu of taxes (where it has taken tax-productive property into its own possession) and grants exemption from federal excise taxes for a wide variety of materials and equipment bought to be used by local governments.

National services to the local governments also cover a wide range. These include a regular census of local governments which provides a wealth of comparative information on local units, their organization, payrolls, services, and finances; special studies of many local problems in highways, public health, education, welfare, and other fields; informational services upon many local problems including standards for materials and the testing of materials; financial aid for and cooperation in the training of local government personnel for police work, public health, and the like; cooperation in law enforcement; the occasional loan of experts from the federal service.

There are some local returns of service, but these are in most cases paid for by the national government. The boarding of federal prisoners in local jails; the provision of urban water supply and fire protection for federal buildings; urban condemnation of land for federal use—these are a few examples.

The national government's entry into the field of local government is having definite effects upon the structure of the local government system as a whole. TVA has, of course, had a remarkable influence on local governments in its area. Other federal projects and installations, for land irrigation, for defense research and development work, for welfare purposes, have resulted in the establishment of special "government towns" and "greenbelt" villages of considerable interest that are but slightly related to the existing systems of local units in the states concerned.

Of more widespread concern, perhaps, are the apparently inconsistent federal policies of working through the existing local units for some functions, though perhaps insisting on some reorganization thereof, and of bringing about the creation of new units of local government, or pseudo-governments, for other functions.

Among existing units of local government the national authorities make most use of the counties, because these units cover practically the whole national area and are sufficiently large to be effective. The counties are the units that have been principally favored for administering federal programs in rural secondary roads, social welfare, agricultural extension work, agricultural action programs, and rural library work, for example. The larger cities come next in federal preference, for such functions as public housing, urban planning, slum clearance, urban renewal, and the construction and maintenance of port facilities, airports, and federal office buildings, as well as for aid in building the urban connections for the main state highways.

The towns and townships in the northern states from the Dakotas east have proved to be generally unacceptable for federal programs. They do not cover the entire state in most cases, and they are far from covering the whole nation. In addition they are too numerous to be effectively supervised, generally too small in population and resources to be service units, and inadequately equipped with trained personnel and public buildings. Also passed up by the federal authorities are the thousands of special districts for fire protection, lighting, water supply, drainage, irrigation, and other limited services.

As a result in part of these federal preferences, the financial and administrative importance nationally of the counties has increased greatly in recent years, and the same thing is happening to the cities. The smaller units continue to be useful for strictly local purposes, but they languish from a failure to find a larger usefulness on the national or even statewide scene.

In this context the position of the school districts is not easy to describe. The nation was never more conscious than it is today of the importance of its educational system. The public schools receive increasing aid from the states, but no substantial amounts from the national government, because of a national decision registered in the votes of Congress against federal aid for education. Except for informational aids offered mainly through the Office of Education, and a school lunch program, which is important to agriculture as well as to education, the national government provides very little nationwide aid for public education. Consequently the school districts have not attained status with the national government in the sense that the counties and larger cities have. School district consolidation is paving the way toward making the individual districts fewer and more important, but federal aid for schools, if and when it comes, will undoubtedly have to be channeled through the states and be state controlled more fully than most other federal aids are. It will be the states, not the school districts, that will control educational policy and the administration of the federal funds.

While the national government has thus, for some purposes, been building up the importance of the larger local units and not that of the smaller ones, it has for other purposes by-passed to some extent all the traditional local governments. With state consent through interdependent legislation, Congress and the national administration have encouraged the creation of new special districts or public authorities in the fields of public power development, public housing, soil conservation, rural electrification, watershed control, and hospital construction. These are not all strictly units of local government, but they are new types of public entities to serve local purposes in services that might have been assigned, in large part at least, directly to existing counties or cities.

As a result the map of local services in each state is complicated by the existence of these new districts and authorities, with their distinctive areas and boundaries overlying and crisscrossing the standard map of the traditional local governments. Some of the new units, also, are more dependent upon federal than upon state law, and are not subject to the usual state audits and supervision. In a sense they are local agents of the national government, like the former national farm loan associations, but the federal Census of Governments includes the soil conservation districts and the public housing authorities in the special districts category of the units of local government.

The possible long-run consequences of the creation of these new local units to local government as a whole, and to state control over local government, I shall not attempt to predict. Later in this chapter, however, I shall suggest possible federal action to encourage better organization of metropolitan areas.

INTERLOCAL RELATIONS

Interlocal relations is a comprehensive term to cover all the diverse relations between units of government, of every title and description, that operate below the level of the states. As creatures and agents of their states, all these units stand upon about the same legal plane, and for this reason interlocal relations fall primarily in the class of horizontal relations. In general, therefore, none of these units has supervisory relations over any of the others, and grants-in-aid are not made by one to another, although services rendered are paid for. Whatever minor exceptions there are to this statement need not be discussed here.

One the other hand there are many examples of what might be called "built-in" relations—built in, that is, by state laws that require one class of local governments, usually the counties, or certain officers thereof, to perform definite functions for other units within their areas. Counties in many states are required to assess property for themselves, for the state, and for all other units in their areas, or to supervise and equalize such assessments; to levy and collect certain taxes for them, and distribute the receipts among them; to conduct certain elections for them; to supervise the common schools; to give legal advice; and so on. In many instances these duties are actually imposed upon some officer of the county, like the assessor, the auditor or clerk, the county superintendent of schools, or the county attorney, but the county governing body is also so charged in some cases. Such relations being legally compulsory, they give little indication of what the counties might do voluntarily to assist or cooperate with other local governments if merely authorized to do so. The laws do reveal, however, that the state legislatures look upon the counties and their officials as agents of the state for a variety of state and local purposes.

Aside from these statutory requirements, the general theory of the laws has been that every local unit is a public corporation—a municipal corporation or a so-called quasi-corporation—that is legally separate from other governmental units and solely responsible for the exercise of the powers and duties conferred or imposed upon it. It is not supposed to delegate away its powers to any other unit of government, to take upon itself the responsibilities of others, or to get itself entangled with others so as to lose its freedom of action.

At one time the state courts were rather strict in enforcing this principle in cases brought by taxpayers to annul local actions. In many situations the courts would not imply that local units had the power to cooperate with each other on joint building projects or services. Specific legislative authorization was held to be necessary. This attitude was one phase of the general attitude that local governments should be held rather strictly within the powers conferred upon them by the legislature, a rule adopted by the judges to maintain state legislative supremacy and to protect the citizens and taxpayers against unauthorized local expenditures or other actions. The judges said in effect to the local authorities, If it is important that you be allowed to do this doubtful thing, get the legislature to authorize it.

Local citizens and officials who saw advantages leading to both efficiency and economy in having the local authorities cooperate with each other in providing joint local services, facilities, and buildings, where certain units were inadequate for the purpose, have induced the state legislators to enact one law after another to authorize such cooperation. The normal method of authorizing interlocal cooperation is by separate specific legislative acts for this and that service, and for this and that class of local units. The cumulative effects of this method are easy to see in the many separate and not always well-harmonized provisions of law scattered through the statute books, in many instances not well indexed. A recent New York State report discussed below lists 43 such laws of that state and gives the gist of each one. Minnesota has over 25 scattered bits of legislation providing for the interrelations of municipalities alone. These two states are probably fairly representative, as evidence from California, Pennsylvania, North Carolina, and other states indicates.

A development in legislation from the special to the general has begun in the past few decades in the authorization of interlocal cooperation and joint services. As we have seen, a trend in this direction began to be noticed in the decade of the Great Depression and the New Deal when a number of states authorized local governments to accept federal funds and to cooperate in federal relief and welfare programs without waiting for specific legislative authorization. Along with these laws or soon after came broad statutes to permit interlocal cooperation generally, over the whole range of local powers and services.

The Minnesota statute on this subject, passed in 1943, provides that any two or more local governmental units, acting by agreement of their governing bodies, "may jointly or cooperatively exercise any power common to the contracting parties or any similar powers, including those which are the same except for the territorial limits within which they may be exercised." The detailed specifications of the law make it clear that the local units may acquire property in common, waive their residence requirements for office holding, and disburse funds for the joint enterprise through any agency they agree upon. This law undoubtedly fills many gaps that existed in the older piecemeal legislation and makes it less necessary for the legislature to enact new piecemeal legislation.

This is a law of the general type that I mentioned above as contributing greatly to genuine local self-government and at the same time saving the legislature from the burden of enacting numerous laws of limited application. It recalls to mind the compact clause of the United States Constitution discussed above in Chapter 7. The two are similar in purpose and yet different. The compact clause, although a part of the United States Constitution and not subject to change by Congress alone, is actually somewhat restrictive on the states in that it calls for congressional approval of interstate compacts. The Minnesota law on the joint exercise of local powers is always subject to repeal or amendment by the legislature, but on the other hand it does not require legislative approval of interlocal contracts or agreements. The federal compact clause does not specify or in any way suggest the subjects on which the states may make compacts, nor has Congress enacted anything that either defines or limits the power. The Minnesota statute, however, extends the power to make interlocal contracts and agreements only to those subjects on which the legislature has by other laws authorized the local units to take action. Presumably this language is restrictive, and any extension of the power to other subjects would require new state legislation.

These differences are perhaps more formal than substantial but to mention them helps to remind us that the power conferred by the statute authorizes merely a form of procedure, namely by joint or cooperative action, and that the legislature has not given up its control over the substance of the actions of local governments. But in permitting all local governments in the state to join with each other in the cooperative exercise of any of their powers, without further approval by any state authority, the legislature has laid at rest, as fully as a legislative enabling act can do so, the old common-law principle of local government, that every local unit is a separate, exclusive, self-sufficient entity that is expected to act only by itself and for itself. Although this evidently never was an absolute principle, the emphasis both in law and in practice was clearly in that direction.

Today the emphasis has moved more toward intergovernmental collaboration. The old tendency was to place a high value on the formal and legalistic rules regulating the separate units of local government, while the new considers public needs for services, along with efficiency and economy, as the controlling criteria of desirability. It minimizes the importance of legalistic distinctions and formalism in action. The old view seems to have been suited to a condition of scarcity and the need for the strictest economy, while the new is appropriate for an economy of abundance, surpluses, and expanding activity. Just as the older attitude was associated with a suspicious and negative view toward government—the idea that the least government is the best and that every government should be held strictly within its stated powers—so the new is linked with the concept of government as a purveyor or provider of an extensive array of public services in order to elevate the standard of living. Because the maximizing of services without waste and inefficiency is the principal aim today, the instrumentalities for rendering the service have less value in and of themselves. They may be reorganized, combined, and even eliminated in order to find the best combination of productive factors to render the authorized services. Legal rules and formal entities that stand in the way may be brushed aside. In the language of Dr. Weidner in Monograph 9 in this series, such legislative acts for authorizing interlocal cooperation emphasize the "programmatic" or service-function values at the expense of the "expediency" or power values.

The state legislatures having opened the door more and more to interlocal cooperation, we may ask to what extent the local authorities have made actual use of the new powers. Some evidence that is briefly summarized below suggests a widespread exercise of these powers in the states that have been studied. But have the interlocal agreements come more under the many specific laws or under such general enabling acts as that of Minnesota? Since New York had no such general act at the time of the report to be summarized below, all the many examples of interlocal cooperation reported from that state must have come under rather limited specific acts. Lawyers advising local units prefer to rely on tested specific laws, if they are available and fit the circumstances. Although I have made no special study of this point in Minnesota, the evidence suggests that most of the interlocal cooperation in this state up to 1953 was brought about under various specific laws. Nevertheless the general Joint Powers Act has also been used, has been tested in court, upheld, and liberally construed by the state supreme court. It probably fills some important gaps in the older, piecemeal legislation.

Coming now to the actual data on the uses that have been made of these powers, I can say that the authors of those monographs in this series to whose fields the problem was pertinent made diligent separate inquiries, but that in the project as a whole we made no comprehensive survey of actual interlocal relations in Minnesota. In 1953 the League of Minnesota Municipalities put out a report on Inter-Municipal Cooperation in Minnesota, which presents valuable information for cities of over 10,000 population. The categories of airports, civil defense, civil service, fire protection, health, insect control, libraries, recreation, sewer and water service, streets and roads, and utility service are well covered. From California have come especially informative reports on the Los Angeles metropolitan area, and a University of Pennsylvania thesis of 1953 covers the city of Philadelphia thoroughly. A 1958 report on Interlocal Cooperation in New York State is the first fairly comprehensive statewide study that has come to my attention. Its data were derived primarily from the replies to a questionnaire sent to 1,600 multifunctional units of government in the state—counties, cities, villages, and towns. No questionnaires were sent to the school districts or other special districts in the state, and New York City was not covered.

Besides being somewhat limited in scope all these studies emphasize the final results and achievements in a positive sense. Cooperation is the keynote. Little attention is paid to controversies, noncooperation, or the bitter struggles that often precede and sometimes prevent genuine cooperation among governmental units. Controversies over annexation proposals, stream pollution, the location of workhouses and "pesthouses" by one municipality within another, tax exemption or taxation of outlying facilities, diversion of waters, flooding, and many other issues have arisen in countless cases to disturb the peace and good relations between governmental units. In general it appears to me, however, that such controversies are on the wane, and that local units now emphasize cooperation in order to achieve satisfactory services more than they do their points of difference. I mention the controversial side only to indicate that this aspect also needs to be explored if a well-rounded analysis of interlocal relations is to result.

The full extent of interlocal cooperative arrangements is not known, but such figures as are available seem rather impressive. In the New York State study over 1,100 cases were reported in ten selected categories (water supply, property assessment, recreation, health, fire protection, etc.). The Philadelphia study covers 756 cases among the eight Pennsylvania and New Jersey counties in the metropolitan area. The Los Angeles figures when added together also run high.

In New York it was found that, in general, the counties of largest population, which are also those of the densest and most urban settlement, tended to have many more cases than the counties of smallest population and least congestion. The counties in the metropolitan areas led all the rest. It was also evident that it was usually a unit of larger population and more urban characteristics that supplied a service, while the recipient or purchaser of the service tended to be a place of smaller and less urbanized population. Villages tended to have most of their cooperative arrangements with the towns in which they were located, and generally the village rendered and the town received the service. At the same time the towns in New York tended to have a few more service relations with units outside their own limits (with other towns, for example, on maintaining boundary roads and other activities) than with the local villages. In Los Angeles the county has become the great purveyor of services to the municipalities within its limits.

In general, interlocal cooperation seems to be easier to establish when separate units of government occupy, in whole or in part, the same land area and thus serve some or all of the same people. Next in order of ease come relations with immediately adjacent units. To reach beyond these is rare. Actual joint arrangements between two or more adjacent units to establish common institutions like sanatoriums are less common than contractual relations by which one unit provides the service and others pay for such service as they receive. The service contract appears to be, in fact, the most common method of cooperation. It is doubtful whether the units providing services for others do better, on the average, than break even on the payments they receive, but this possibility does not seem to deter them from undertaking the service. Cases involving fairly large joint efforts, like multiple county sanatoriums and hospitals, are greatly helped along by state or federal aid, just as federal aid has stimulated interstate cooperation on highways, bridges, and stream pollution control, for example.

It appears, then, that interlocal cooperation is most prevalent in metropolitan areas, where the need appears to be greatest, and that it commonly takes the form of contractual services by the larger to the smaller units. I would venture the guess, too, that it is the multifunctional units like villages, small cities, towns, and boroughs, that are most inclined to avail themselves of services from others, and other but larger multifunctional units that stand ready to render services. Unifunctional units like school districts are not generally in a position to render services except to adjacent units of the same type (school district to school district); and if such a service is to be anything but of an emergency, temporary nature, consolidation into one district makes more sense. A school district that cannot provide and conduct its own schools has little reason for corporate existence.

School districts do receive many services from the counties and from the multifunctional units (cities and villages) within and for which they function. There is, however, a strong tradition of independence among school districts, a feeling that does not seem to abate. It is based upon arguments concerning the uniqueness and high importance of the educational function and the necessity to keep it out of the ordinary politics of the community. This presents a problem in interlocal relations that I will not attempt to discuss here, other than to say that in fact the school districts get much help from their cities and counties in the assessment of property, conduct of elections, provision of office space, police and fire protection, health services, recreational facilities, libraries, and other things. Our Monograph 3 by Robert L. Morlan fully supports this generalization.

It is evident, therefore, that the pervasive social, economic, and ideological changes that have brought with them such great demands for more and better public services have affected state-local and interlocal relations as they have national-state and interstate relations. Even the differences between rural and urban attitudes, which still exist to some extent, have not prevented significant changes in attitudes toward local intergovernmental relations in rural areas. One reason is that the so-called rural areas are becoming urbanized in their thinking and in their demands for public services. To obtain such services they must follow substantially the same policies as the urban places do, and one of these policies calls for either larger units of government or more cooperation among governmental units.

To judge by the reports mentioned above and the evidence presented by current news sources in the field of local government, it appears that there has been a steady growth of interlocal cooperation in recent decades, but the rate at which the curve has been going up is not known. Local units still handle most of their own services. The laws that authorize interlocal cooperation are important stand-by measures, designed to enable local governments to cooperate with each other whenever the responsible officials deem it in the public interest to do so. The legislation simply enlarges their powers of self-government or home rule to include collaboration with others. They will not ordinarily use such powers as these until they are faced with some actual need that cannot be met as satisfactorily in any other way. When such a situation arises the governing bodies of the two or more local governments concerned must first study the problem and the need separately and then proceed to negotiate with each other. Even after they have negotiated they may not be able to agree, for example, on an acceptable division of the costs, and so decide not to go ahead cooperatively.

It is only when the legal bars to interlocal cooperation are all removed, and there is no inducement from outside like a grant-in-aid to overcome reluctance, that the true willingness of local units to collaborate with each other can be tested. Even then there may be good technical reasons for nonparticipation, or the legitimate demands and needs of other services for the required money in any one of the local governments concerned may be such as to make participation in a joint project unfeasible—and if only one of several participants in a proposed joint project is unable or unwilling to approve it, the project may fail.

All these considerations aside, there still remain human factors in the situation that may lead to a failure to go ahead. Old, traditional mistrust between units; the fears of the officials of small units about getting tied up with larger ones beyond their control; the fear of becoming committed to future expenditures and tax burdens beyond local needs or capacities; the desire to protect their local powers and independence—in short, a number of "expediency values" may well come to the fore and result in a refusal to enter upon a joint or cooperative project. These must be taken into account in almost every proposal to bring about interlocal cooperation, and to these must be added such factors as parochialism, clashes of personalities between leaders of the several units, and other highly subjective variables.

Potent as these factors may be in preventing formal and open cooperation through contracts and agreements on major matters, they do not seem to have the effect of preventing informal cooperation among units in countless small matters, many of which never get recorded. Our interviews with numerous local officials throughout Minnesota revealed a general spirit of neighborly cooperation between county, town, village, city, and school district authorities on joint programs, minor loans or rental of space and equipment, the timing of services to accommodate each other, and so on. Many of these were essentially private and personal acts, but others involved the exercise of official powers. Hardly any were evidently illegal, and all seemed to be reasonably justifiable in the circumstances.

The great masses of official actions on the part of local governments are, of course, strictly those of single local authorities, each one acting by itself. Interlocal relations are important but, as in the case of interstate relations, the activities and expenditures that they give rise to represent but a small part of all the activities and expenditures of the governments concerned. They mainly facilitate other actions and services, and are not independently important. These remarks seem to be necessary in order to keep these relations in proper perspective in our own thinking.

In situations where interlocal relations become much more important, and independently so, the need for them calls attention to the inadequacy of the local units that are involved in performing the functions for which they were established. Such is to some extent the situation in metropolitan areas which are to be discussed in the next section.

Conversely, when a former intergovernmental service for local units of government ceases to be important and can be abolished, this change may point to the fact that the units previously assisted by an interlocal service have either been abolished or been so consolidated and enlarged as to create units large enough to provide their own services. Such is the case with county supervision of schools in Minnesota and no doubt in other states. School consolidation in a number of counties has gone so far that it has been possible to abolish the office of county superintendent of schools. The school districts that remain are consolidated districts with their own professional superintendents who report directly to and are supervised by the state department of education.

In metropolitan areas where the central city renders contractual services to certain suburbs too small to provide them efficiently for themselves, or where several suburbs carry on joint services, the annexation of such suburbs to the central city, or the consolidation of a number of them into larger units, would put an end to the need for interlocal services by concentrating them in the enlarged unit.

METROPOLITAN PROBLEMS

Governmental systems and services must be adjusted to the needs of populations. Important movements of population and increases or decreases in numbers must be met by appropriate adjustments in governments.

Down to the adoption of the United States Constitution, immigration from Europe and the natural growth of the population were accompanied by a dispersion of population up and down the Atlantic seaboard and westward into the Appalachian Mountains. Cities there were, but they were small; not one had 50,000 people at the first census in 1790, even with its suburbs included. The next century was also one of population dispersion, throughout the Mississippi valley from north to south, and westward across the mountains to the Pacific Ocean. Land was being taken up everywhere in this vast area—for farming, grazing, lumbering, and mining, and for homes for the people.

Down to about 1890, therefore, the appropriate governmental response to this great movement of people, across the whole continent, was the laying out and organization, from north to south, and from coast to coast, of thousands of counties, cities and villages, townships, towns, and school districts, over 100,000 in all, to provide for the local needs of a widely dispersed population. While the cities kept on growing, the culture that was developed was essentially a rural one. The attention of the census takers was concentrated upon the population of the states and the counties, and emphasized population dispersion or spread. The growth of the cities was considerable by 1890, but the growth of population within city limits provided only a secondary theme for the census reports.

By 1890, however, a change was already in the making. The last great swarmings of people over the land after the Civil War were accompanied by impressive beginnings of industrialization on the eastern seaboard, in the Appalachians, and in the northern Mississippi valley. The concept of a new America began to take form, an industrial and urban America alongside the agricultural and extractive America with which men had become familiar. By the 1920s the Bureau of the Census was taking serious note of several new population phenomena in the United States—rural depopulation, the drift toward the cities, and the rise of metropolitan aggregations of population in and around the larger cities. It was this regrouping of the nation's population in a number of metropolitan areas, while a number of rural regions of large area declined in population, that gave rise to the need for realigning the system of local government to meet the new conditions.

The local government changes that are desirable and even necessary to meet the needs of a declining rural population are fairly easy to prescribe, but not so easy to achieve in practice. The abolition or consolidation of essentially unproductive and wasteful small local units like the petty school districts and even the towns or townships, and the establishment in their place of larger, more effective units, or, alternatively, the transfer of the most local functions up to the counties or even, in some cases, to the state governments, are the obvious remedies that have been proposed and in part already adopted.

Many persons continue to defend and justify the smallest of local units as "the last stronghold of democracy" because they do not realize how inadequate these little governments are even to give useful experience in the conduct of democratic government. Enamored of the institutions that had been devised for another era, they fail to understand how unsuitable these have become in the face of the great changes in the scale and character of public services that have taken place already and are still going forward.

While the defenders of the old system of local units were fighting their rearguard actions, even those who were moving into the metropolitan areas were in many cases unaware of what was happening. Both here and abroad, a large proportion of the new city dwellers sprang from essentially rural backgrounds. They were in the cities but hardly of them, and they did not at once realize what it meant to change to the new mode of living.

As I said above, however, the census authorities began early in the present century to appreciate the immensity and the significance of the decline of rural populations and the massing of great urban populations in the rising metropolitan areas. To define the metropolitan areas and to analyze their growth and structure became a subject of census study. In the past thirty years or more the data compiled by the Census Bureau on the areas, population, and governmental units and complications of these metropolitan areas have laid a substantial foundation for many scholarly studies.

From these compilations and studies it has become clear that the political and governmental life of the nation in the future is to be dominated largely by the people who dwell in the metropolitan areas and the activities that go on there. It is clear also that many of the most pressing problems of intergovernmental relations come sharply into focus in the 174 metropolitan areas defined by the Bureau of the Census. Because the thirteenth in population of these areas—Minneapolis, St. Paul, and their suburbs—is wholly within Minnesota, and another—the Duluth-Superior area—is predominantly so, the problems of the metropolises came within the field of our Minnesota studies. Had it not been for lack of time and resources to make a sufficiently thorough study, we might have published a separate monograph on the intergovernmental problems of the metropolitan areas in Minnesota. For such a publication this small section of our final report is clearly an inadequate substitute. The most that I can do is to state briefly the general problems of intergovernmental relations in metropolitan areas as I see them.

In 1950 over 85 million people, or more than 55 per cent of the nation's population, were concentrated in less than 8 per cent of the nation's area in 174 metropolitan areas as defined by the Census Bureau. Every such area has a central city of 50,000 or more people, but it includes also the suburban areas and counties. This agglomeration of so many people, with all their homes, businesses, traffic, and varied activities in these congested centers, presents some of the most complex and massive problems of human adjustment and public administration to be found in the historical experiences of mankind.

Some of the early studies of the metropolis were made by students of municipal government, who approached the phenomena as especially important from the point of view of local government and interlocal relations. That approach is still essential but it is no longer sufficient for dealing with the many issues involved. Today the national government is involved in metropolitan problems everywhere in the nation's area, because of its concern for civil and military defense, for commerce and industry, for railroads, highways, harbors, waterways, and airways, for the postal service, for public housing, slum clearance, and urban renewal, for an extensive array of welfare services, and because of its responsibility to maintain economic stability and high levels of employment. The states are concerned not only because of their almost equal interest in the functions listed above but also because of their constitutional responsibility for the system of local government, and for the general welfare of the people. All the local governments not only within but adjacent to the metropolitan areas are likewise deeply concerned, and most of them quite immediately.

As a result all classes of intergovernmental relations—national-state, state-local, interlocal, and even interstate—crop out in the discussion of metropolitan problems, the interstate because a number of the metropolises straddle the boundaries of two or three states. Along the eastern seaboard a giant string of metropolitan areas stretches from Boston, Massachusetts, down through Rhode Island, Connecticut, New York, New Jersey, Pennsylvania, Delaware, and Maryland to Washington, D.C., and into Virginia. The basic adjustments in government, administration, and public finance that must be made to meet the needs of these and other metropolitan populations cannot be accomplished without the joint efforts of all the levels and units of government that are concerned.

The main reason why the problems of metropolitan government are so permeated with questions of intergovernmental relations is that no metropolitan area has the single omnicompetent local government to provide its necessary services that some idealists have hoped for.

What has happened in the rise of so many metropolitan areas with their complicated problems is what could have been expected and was to some extent anticipated by intelligent observers here and there in the Western democracies. It has long been clear that in a dynamic free society where real estate developers, home builders and buyers, promoters of industry, and in fact practically all other classes are substantially free to make their own decisions in their own interests about what and where to build and where to live and work, the expansion of urban populations beyond city limits will be a series of uncoordinated, somewhat helter-skelter operations. When along with this condition the state laws for organizing local governments and for chartering new villages and cities are such as were never planned for the suburbs of large central cities but are a carry-over from simpler, more rural days, when villages were isolated and farm-encircled and had to be self-sufficient, it was almost certain that troubles of many kinds would develop, as they have.

There has been an obvious lack of foresighted physical planning for entire metropolitan areas even where the lines of outward growth have been fairly evident for years ahead. Similarly there has been very little planning of local governmental and administrative systems to match the ordinary needs of large populations packed into relatively small areas. Instead, in most states, the old familiar pattern has been followed of allowing the formation of one ring of suburbs after another around the central city, under old village incorporation laws, and on the basis of purely local and often parochial views, with little knowledge of how much area, population, and assessed valuation are needed for effective city or village government—and with even less knowledge of and regard for the needs of the metropolis as a whole, or even of the adjoining municipalities.

The governmental difficulties of most metropolitan areas are related to the fact that they lack a rational system of local authorities, and of fiscal and administrative powers and methods, that are suited to the many and varied local needs of the people. In practically no instance is the metropolis as a whole a unit of government. Within the 174 metropolitan areas studied by the Census Bureau in 1957 there were 15,658 units of local government, or an average of 90 for each metropolitan area; and in addition, of course, there are the national and state governments, which are present in every such area. The average number per metropolitan area, which is somewhat misleading, included 37 school districts, 20 municipalities, 19 special districts, 13 towns or townships, and 1 1/2 counties. The Chicago metropolitan area alone included 954 governmental units, New York-northeastern New Jersey 1,074, San Francisco-Oakland 414, and so on down the scale to considerably smaller numbers.

In Minnesota the Minneapolis-St. Paul metropolitan area, with a 1950 population of 1,116,509, included 4 counties in 1957 (Hennepin, Ramsey, Anoka, and Dakota), and 222 units of local government in all. In 1958 the Bureau of the Census added Washington County to the area, increasing the 1950 population count to 1,151,000, and the number of local units to over 250. The 1958 population estimate, including all five counties, is 1,458,000. The Duluth-Superior area includes the two counties of St. Louis, Minnesota, and Douglas, Wisconsin, with a total 1950 population of 252,777, of which 206,062 resided in Minnesota. The picture for this area is somewhat distorted because, by the Census Bureau's definition, the entire 6,500-square-mile area of St. Louis County is included.

There is no semblance of uniformity in the governmental structures of these many metropolitan areas, and I have found little evidence that these conglomerations of local units were ever planned with metropolitan responsibilities in mind.

In the central cities of these areas there may be two, three, four, or more "layers" of local government piled one on top of another—a county or two or more constitute the bottom layer, and on top of these are piled a city, a school district, one or more special districts. These do not occupy entirely conterminous areas; the central city may be crisscrossed by the boundaries of other units, or it may be smaller or greater in area than some of the overlying units. In the suburbs the conditions respecting "layers" of government vary tremendously, and are usually not identical with those in the central city or cities.

In short, present governmental conditions and structures in metropolitan areas are not the result of any comprehensive planning or action. The metropolitan area itself is not as a rule a unit of government at all, but a useful geographical and demographic concept worked out in the Bureau of the Census. It is not yet a commonly accepted term among legislators. I mention the varied and somewhat haphazard governmental systems that prevail in such areas not to blame any branch of government or any officials or individuals for them, past or present, but to give point to this discussion of them.

What are the difficulties that the unplanned metropolis with its many overlapping and conflicting governments is subject to? They are almost never catastrophic and seldom such as gravely inconvenience every resident at the same time. Those who live in outlying areas may be only slightly aware of them. Nevertheless the evils and the woes are many and they are endemic. They arise here and there, and it is sometimes one, sometimes another that is aggravated enough for serious public attention. Traffic and transportation congestion and the daily struggle to get to work, with all its waste of time and money and nervous energy, is one of the most obvious and most general. The widespread breakdown of urban mass transportation is obvious. Water supply and sewage disposal questions are constantly arising because there is so much uncoordinated pressure on the same sources and the same avenues of disposal. Other problems include nuisances created by one community for another; the failure to coordinate zoning laws, the location of industries and residence areas, and even the street layout; conflicting local policies on liquor control, on police and fire protection, on slum clearance and public housing; the common lack of any general system of parks and recreation facilities throughout the whole area; the inability or unwillingness of some of the local units to provide municipal services of even minimum standards and the resultant burden on neighboring units; the inequality of school facilities and lack of junior or other colleges because of inability to plan and work together. On top of these evident difficulties is the fear that the unplanned growth that is still going on at the outer edges of the metropolis will make things even worse.

To counterbalance these generally admitted difficulties those who oppose any metropolitan integration present various arguments of more or less validity about the advantages of home rule for their separate communities; the need for small units to preserve democratic control; the higher taxes that might result from integration; and the special values of the services being rendered in their own communities. Underlying all these considerations are more personal motives: a feeling for small units where one's personal influence can count and the fear of being caught up in a gigantic, impersonal government dominated by the politicians of the overshadowing central city of the metropolis.

To make up for or even to overcome some of the difficulties of metropolitan adjustment, many piecemeal measures are being carried forward in the larger metropolitan areas. The state itself does things about road planning and construction, about the health conditions resulting from poorly planned water supplies and sewage disposal systems, about educational planning and school district consolidation. The metropolitan counties, when authorized by law, are providing for zoning and platting control in new areas, lake level and stream control, county roads, and county welfare and health services at least beyond the central city. In some places a single county coincides well enough with the metropolitan area to become a fairly effective general metropolitan authority. As I indicated in the section above on interlocal relations, many difficulties that arise because there are so many small and weak local authorities in the area are overcome to some extent by interlocal contracts and agreements, one unit performing certain services for others. That unit may be the county, as in the striking case of Los Angeles County in California, or it may be the central city, or even some other unit in the area. When other arrangements fail to meet the requirements or at least to overcome local objections, the creation of a special metropolitan district under authority of state law, for sewage disposal, for airports, for water supply, for a metropolitan park system, or any other function, may be in order.

All these piecemeal measures amount to a recognition that there are grave defects in the pre-existing metropolitan organization, or a lack of such organization; and each one tends to complicate the local structure of government and hence to reduce the degree of direct popular control. The state legislature seems to be nearly always the court of last resort on metropolitan problems.

Today there is, understandably enough, great agitation over the problems of metropolitan planning and government. Piecemeal measures are not sufficing to meet the widespread demands for a more rational organization of at least the larger metropolitan areas. Many studies are being made, and many reforms proposed. How best to organize local government in metropolitan areas remains debatable. At the one extreme can be imagined a single omnibus unit of local government serving the entire metropolitan area and population for all local purposes. This is purely visionary at present, and necessarily so under democratic principles. At the other extreme one could imagine every city and village block in the whole area being set up as a separate municipal corporation to provide every local service in the block. This would result in a veritable anarchy instead of local government. Between these extremes there are many possible combinations and permutations of the existing local government structures. It is obvious that the various functions of local government that need to be performed in metropolitan areas vary greatly in the extent to which they need to be provided throughout the whole area, or only in some parts of it, and provided uniformly throughout the area. In many functions there are no criteria for determining the answers to such questions, and in all cases practical judgment is needed and no absolute standard can be applied indiscriminately.

The basic pattern of metropolitan organization that I visualize for the future involves a pseudo-federal structure based upon a division of powers and functions between a general area-wide authority for those functions and parts of functions that need to be dealt with on that basis, and a number of local authorities within the area, including the central city or cities and the various suburbs. These would be mainly of the multifunctional variety, but unifunctional units for schools and conceivably for other single functions would also fit into the general scheme. The general metropolitan board would need a certain priority of power, but it could well be composed of representatives from the other local units and possibly representatives from the state government also.

In devising such a scheme for any metropolitan area, and in subsequently amending and improving it, administrative efficiency and economy would certainly be important criteria but not the only ones. Local loyalties and traditions, the need for protecting local self-government and the democratic processes as fully as possible, and other moral and political criteria would have to be considered. Furthermore the arrangements that I visualize leave a considerable flexibility for local adaptation of means to ends, and for almost every kind of interlocal cooperation.

If anyone calls my attention to the similarities between this tentative outline for metropolitan organization and the federal system of the United States I shall not be surprised. I feel that the complexities of metropolitan life in their public aspects can be provided for governmentally only by an organization in which services that need to be supplied on an area-wide basis are separated to a considerable extent from those that call for or are capable of being provided for adequately on a more local basis. Such a division of powers and functions certainly has some federal aspects. The differences are also important, however. The general, area-wide metropolitan authorities may be one or several. They would not be based on any federal type of written constitution, nor would the local circumscriptions, "boroughs," or whatever they may be called, be component "states" within a federal union. As already stated, the area-wide authorities would need a certain priority of powers over the more local authorities, but nothing approaching "sovereignty" or any national supremacy over the states is implied. The legislature of the state rather than a supreme court would suffice as a tribunal for making local adjustments if the local authorities could not reach agreement among themselves.

I suggest in conclusion that the problem of metropolitan organization to meet the needs of the majority of the people in a rapidly changing society has become not only a nationwide but in fact a national problem. The state legislatures, entangled in their traditional ways of handling the problems of local government by special legislation, on the recommendations of county delegations and more or less only under pressure, have in effect abandoned the leadership that is constitutionally theirs in these matters, and the governors have not tried to assume it. Consequently legislation for metropolitan government is a field in which no one is taking leadership, and the needs of metropolitan areas have no spokesman at the state level.

My thought is that the power of the legislatures to control in this field should not be taken from them, but that new leadership toward decisive action is needed and it probably will have to come from the national level. Although we have throughout these studies tried to refrain from making recommendations on matters of public policy, in metropolitan government I am willing to recommend official studies on a national basis that may lead to national and state action in this field.

If a President of the United States could in the not too distant future find it feasible to urge at least a study of metropolitan problems, the steps to be followed to achieve a state-national program of action would not be impossible to work out. Some presidential talks on the subject leading up to a special message to Congress could pave the way for the studies. Then might follow the setting up of a special interdepartmental committee in Washington to consider how federal services and the expenditure of federal grants-in-aid in metropolitan areas are being affected by the multiplicity of local authorities in such areas, and what might be done locally to facilitate improvements. Especially important for consideration would be the question, if there were one general authority in each metropolitan area for the federal authorities to deal with, instead of a number of separate units, to what extent and in what ways the federal services might be improved and the local expenditure of federal grants be more productive of results.

If on the basis of its findings such a committee made any suggestions of importance for action by national, state, or local authorities, the next step might be to persuade Congress to establish a national commission on metropolitan problems to study metropolitan questions in a wider context, from the viewpoint of the general welfare of the people, as well as of local, state, and national governments. No single state is in a position to establish such a body, and no private foundation could lend it the support and prestige that the national government could. Such a commission should perhaps include as members five senators, five representatives, and fifteen citizens appointed by the President; it should be bipartisan in composition and be so constituted that there would be at least one member from each state with a major metropolitan area within its limits. This suggestion follows in general the structure of the Commission on Intergovernmental Relations. Such a commission should have its own research funds and staff, and should also bring together the results of the Census Bureau studies and the many metropolitan studies of recent years. The findings of such a commission should be laid before Congress and also transmitted to the state legislatures and governors for any action that might seem fitting.

My feeling is that such a national study would reveal the desirability of having in each of the larger metropolitan areas, at least, as well as in all those that straddle state lines, one metropolitan agency endowed with sufficient authority to make binding agreements, and with which the national and state governments could deal in all matters affecting civil defense, main highways, urban planning, public housing, slum clearance, urban renewal, stream pollution control, sewage disposal, water supply, port and harbor facilities, airports, rail and bus terminals, and perhaps other works.

Considering the great interest of the national government in all these functions, and the large amounts of money it puts into grants-in-aid and direct expenditures for the metropolitan areas, it should be in a position to induce the states to establish acceptable metropolitan authorities in all those areas where metropolitan planning and development should in the future take the place of the separate planning and development activities of a number of urban authorities. Federal aid to metropolitan communities might well be made conditional upon the proper metropolitan organization being established. This does not in any way assume the by-passing of the states in metropolitan affairs, but rather the implementing of their control through the establishment by them of suitable metropolitan authorities. Neither do I visualize any rigid uniformity of metropolitan organization on a nationwide scale. Every metropolitan area is in some respects unique, and every one calls for a somewhat different type of organization according to its own needs and local opinions and traditions. Most of the ordinary urban functions—ordinary streets and public works, parks and recreation, police and fire protection, regulatory measures, zoning, building regulations, public health, education, and others—could be left with whatever municipal authorities or school districts were provided for by state laws and city charters. The central city, the suburbs, the school districts, and other authorities could continue without much change. They might well, however, be represented in the general metropolitan authority.

CHAPTER 9

The Federal Equilibrium and the States

The great question in all studies of the federal system and of intergovernmental relations in the United States is undoubtedly that of the relations of the states to the national government, and of the role of the states in the system. Much of American history is wrapped up in this question, and many books, articles, and speeches have been written about it. This chapter is offered as another little contribution to the grand debate in the hope that it may provide some suggestions for new approaches to the problem.

To a considerable extent what follows in this chapter is a drawing together and restatement of facts and ideas that have already been put forward in the preceding chapters. The repetitions will, I hope, be justified by their contributions to a brief recapitulation of a complex situation wherein the very fact of repetition helps to indicate the factors I consider to be most important.

Scholars, statesmen, and publicists used to speak of the "federal equilibrium," a hypothetical or actual balance of powers and functions between the national and state governments. This balance was supposed to have been established by the people through the Constitution, and to be a desirable as well as a rather permanent and unchanging arrangement. It was the essence, so to speak, of the compact that was supposed to have been the consensual basis of both the Constitution and the federal system. In some ways the idea was rather vague, and I do not recall any publication in which it was fully worked out, not even anything by Calhoun or any other exponent of the states' rights position.

Little has been heard of this concept in recent years although some self-styled "conservative citizens" seem to have it in mind when they deplore certain recent changes in American government and make their pleas for "back to the Constitution" and back to "states' rights." Their utterance of these pleas indicates that they believe the states have been losing out to the national government in their competition with it for status and power, and that this is deplorable.

The alleged upsetting of the federal equilibrium calls for some analysis. If there was such an equilibrium at one time and if it has been upset, whether for better or for worse, to the disadvantage of state powers, this must be one of the most important consequences of the changes in American life and government that have taken place in recent times. The states are, in fact, the distinguishing element in a federal system. Every unitary government like Great Britain or France has a supreme central or national government and a number of subordinate local governments like counties and cities. Take out from any federal system the layer of states between the central and local governments and the system becomes a unitary one; and that is a change that is likely to have far-reaching consequences. Even a serious weakening of the states would have consequences of some importance.

THE CONSTITUTIONAL EQUILIBRIUM

There appears to be no disagreement over the fact that changes, important changes, in national-state relations have taken place. The historical record is to be found in the text of the written Constitution itself, especially in the amendments, in acts of Congress and Supreme Court decisions, and in many other places and forms. As to the supposed equilibrium there can well be disagreement. I for one do not agree that there was any compact to maintain a certain equilibrium between the national government and the states. There was no compact against change. The Constitution conferred upon the three branches of the national government certain powers to exercise if and when they so desired. Although few powers were exercised by the national government at the outset there was no promise not to exercise them later as need arose or policy dictated. Besides, the Constitution carried from the first a specific authorization for amendments or changes, and twenty-two such changes have been made. Some of them clearly altered the relations between the national government and the states, with the consent of the state legislatures or, in one case, of state conventions.

Not only was there no compact against change; there was no agreement either at the outset or at any later time as to the constitutional division of powers between the national and state governments. Nationalists like Alexander Hamilton and John Marshall disagreed with Thomas Jefferson and with others who took a states' rights view. Jefferson had no part in the framing of the Constitution, of course, but he developed strong theories about that document after it was adopted. Later political leaders and interpreters of the Constitution divided along similar lines. One side took the position that the Constitution properly construed gave the national government substantially all the powers necessary to meet the needs of the nation. The other held the view that the powers reserved to the states had a preferred position and stood as a limit to national action—the doctrine of dual federalism.

The controversy has been carried on not only by words but by deeds. State authorities have attempted to obstruct the work of the federal courts and of the post office, to tax federal instrumentalities, to nullify federal laws, to evade Supreme Court decisions, to establish interstate trade barriers, and even to have their states secede from the Union, by resolutions and by force of arms. In some states the provisions of the Fourteenth and Fifteenth amendments have never been carried out effectively to provide equal protection for the civil and political rights of Negroes. On nearly all major issues affecting the federal system some states have gone one way and some the other. Anything like an agreed equilibrium between national and state powers is an invention of the mind, and one man's equilibrium is not necessarily accepted by another.

To view the Constitution as a compact to establish a federal system with an agreed equilibrium of powers between the national government and the states it is necessary to go outside the words of the Constitution and even outside the events of the constitutional years and to create a theory not warranted by the plain terms of the Constitution. There is another way to look at the Constitution, and that is to take the words of the document and those of its drafters and proponents at their face value. On that basis the Constitution represents an attempt of the outstanding American leaders of the time, acting in the name of the people, to create a supreme national government, adequate for security, stability, and national growth at home, and for security against any enemies abroad, and to superimpose this supreme government on the existing states with the consent of the people.

On this basis there is no need to talk of a compact with or among the states, or of any equilibrium of powers between the nation and the states. What is needed is to follow the historical course of the national government—in which the peoples of all the states are trebly represented, in the President and in the two houses of Congress—to see how the official leaders of the nation have worked out the adjustments needed to make a central government adequate to the needs of the nation, while preserving as much autonomy for the states as has been consistent with the main national objectives. The story of the changes and adjustments that have been worked out right down into our own time, and which are still continuing, can be read in the constitutional, political, economic, and social histories of the United States. It is a story that has been told many times, and new chapters of it are unfolding all the time. To accept this record it is not necessary to approve of everything that has been done.

If then the interrelations between the national and state governments today do not conform to some theory of a constitutional equilibrium that one or another group or individual may have held, the answer probably is that they never did. Very few people have taken the trouble to investigate thoroughly even the major bodies of evidence bearing on the great issues that are involved; and any theory of equilibrium based on anything less than an exhaustive analysis of such evidence is hardly worthy of serious consideration. The evidence to be considered cannot be confined to the limited experiences and observations of the American people up to the time of the Constitution, but must take into account those of all the great nations, particularly in the West, from the days of the Greeks and Romans down to the present. The problem is to determine what are the powers that the central government of any great nation needs to ensure the nation's security and its economic and moral strength in a world of competing and rival nations, and to determine whether the words of the Constitution do not in fact confer those powers on the national government.

George Washington, Benjamin Franklin, Alexander Hamilton, James Madison, and other leaders in the movement for the Constitution did give most serious thought to the basic questions involved, and took a long, broad, and deep look at the problems of creating a strong national government. Their writings give no support to the idea of an equilibrium of national and state powers having been agreed upon and having been placed beyond the reach of future changes, although Madison changed his mind to some extent at a later date.

Washington, for example, did not like some features of the original document but favored its adoption because it had an amending clause to permit of future improvements. Hamilton in arguing for the unlimited taxing power conferred on Congress by the Constitution (The Federalist, Number 34) said that "we must bear in mind that we are not to confine our view to the present period, but to look forward to remote futurity. Constitutions of civil government are not to be framed upon a calculation of existing exigencies, but upon a combination of these with the probable exigencies of ages . . . There ought to be a capacity to provide for future contingencies as they may happen; and as these are illimitable in their nature, it is impossible safely to limit that capacity."

This line of reasoning he used also in connection with other powers granted in the Constitution to the national government. His conclusion was that the powers of the national government as stated in the Constitution were broad and general and that they should receive a liberal construction to achieve the purposes for which they were intended.

In his history-making decisions on the national powers Chief Justice John Marshall, backed usually by a unanimous court, followed Hamilton's reasoning and conclusions. The attempt of Maryland to tax the Baltimore branch of the United States Bank, and thus in effect to endanger or control a federal instrumentality chartered by Congress, raised several questions closely related to the equilibrium-of-powers theory and correspondingly to the dual-federalism theory. The Maryland argument was that (1) Congress had no power to charter a bank because such a power was not expressly granted to it in the Constitution; (2) the only power to charter banks rested in the "sovereign" power of the states, which had kept this power for themselves and had not delegated it to Congress as the states had delegated other powers; but (3) since this illegal bank existed de facto and had a branch within Maryland, it came within the sovereign power of that state to tax it as it taxed other property according to its own legislative discretion. In short, the powers of the state stood as a barrier to the expansion of federal activities, unless and until the states expressly gave them up to the nation; and the national government had only the powers expressly delegated to it by the states, and not any general sovereign powers.

The Supreme Court's decision in this case, as written by Marshall, rejected each one of the state's contentions. It was not the states as political entities but the people who ordained and established the Constitution of the United States and with it the national government. The government of the United States is, therefore, a people's government, and it acts for their benefit. Though limited in its powers, it is supreme or sovereign within its sphere of action. It is not confined to the powers expressly granted to it by the Constitution. Its legislative powers extend to the making of all laws necessary and proper to achieve the great ends for which the Constitution was established. The preamble was quoted by the Court as persuasive and the broad grants of power over foreign affairs, national defense, foreign and interstate commerce, and other subjects were cited as conclusive evidence of the vastness of the powers granted. For achieving these great ends the Congress can make its own choice of means. "Let the end be legitimate, let it be within the scope of the Constitution, and all the means which are appropriate, which are plainly adapted to that end, which are not prohibited, but consist with the letter and spirit of the Constitution, are constitutional."

Furthermore the choice of Congress as to what means to employ is final and conclusive on the states. The fact that Maryland had state banks which might have been used by Congress, the Court said, "can have no possible influence on the question. No trace is to be found in the Constitution of an intention to create a dependence of the government of the Union on those of the states, for the execution of the great powers assigned to it."

Despite some wobbling at times, and some fine hairsplitting at others, the Supreme Court has never departed far or for long from these views expressed in the Maryland bank tax decision. In Chapter 3, above, my discussion of constitutional developments shows how far the national government has advanced along the road toward a greatly enlarged legislative power. The scales in the field of constitutional power have definitely been tilted in favor of the national government. There is national supremacy, and state subordination.

This is not to say that the states have been relegated to a back seat by the Supreme Court. The point here is that the Court has in recent decades given up any ideas its members may once have entertained of raising laissez faire in government to the status of a constitutional principle. It has seen the wisdom or necessity of not trying to obstruct governmental intervention in economic and social affairs. Consequently, with the exception of the field of civil rights and liberties, it has tended more and more to uphold both national and state legislation in areas formerly left to private decision. In an increasing number of cases the test of the validity of state legislation has been not whether it is constitutional but whether the state has not intruded into a field already occupied by national legislation, in violation of the principle of national priority and supremacy. Clearly the latter is not a principle of equilibrium.

But an equilibrium of constitutional powers may not be the only one worth considering. For example, money is a potent "force" or "influence" in politics. What about the ability and willingness of the states to raise and spend money on public services as compared with that of the national government? Also, consider the closely related fields of party politics and of legislative or law-making politics. Is not this an area in which the fifty states may have some advantage in trying to redress the balance? These two topics call for some analysis and reflection.

THE FISCAL EQUILIBRIUM

When Congress, under the Sixteenth Amendment to the Constitution, began to make use of corporate and personal income taxes as principal sources of national revenue, a fiscal revolution had been accomplished. World War I, the depression of the 1930s, World War II, and several subsequent international crises saw national taxes and expenditures rise to unprecedented heights. Since early in 1942 federal taxes have generally exceeded the combined total of state and local taxes by a ratio of three to one and in some years even four to one. This is a complete reversal of the earlier ratios.

The Constitution still permits the states to exercise as wide a taxing power as ever, and the Supreme Court has been generous in its interpretation of this power. Furthermore the state and local governments have diversified and expanded their tax systems considerably, and have struggled against continuing taxpayer resistance to increase their tax revenues to meet their rising needs. What Hamilton argued in 1787 in The Federalist (Number 32), that the imposition of a tax by one government upon a thing or person does not preclude a concurrent power in another government to tax the same thing or person, is still true. But what Hamilton also clearly foresaw is equally true, that if the government with the greatest needs for revenue, and an unlimited power of taxation, makes heavy demands for revenue upon any source, other governments will find it inexpedient to use that source to the same extent. They will be forced to rely on perhaps less productive and less desirable modes of taxation.

This has actually come to pass. The national government, with its almost insatiable demand for defense funds, imposes such heavy corporate and personal income taxes and tobacco, liquor, and manufacturing excise taxes that the state and local governments, which always stand closest to the irate taxpayers, find it inexpedient to make great use of these sources. It is not lack of legal taxing power, but unwillingness to stand up against taxpayer resistance, plus a feeling that higher taxes will tend to dry up the tax sources, that prevents the states from making more substantial use of the same tax sources as the national government employs.

In short, the national government's priority in the collection of taxes is now so overwhelming that state and local governments have been pushed back into second and third places for a long time to come. Until cold war and potential hot war dangers have ceased to loom so large on the nation's horizon, state and local governments will in fact be financially weaker than the national government. And this would appear to be true even without taking into account those other weapons in the national government's fiscal arsenal: its predominant control in the field of banking, its almost exclusive controls over monetary policy, coinage, and credit policy, its tremendous borrowing power, and its ability and willingness to face unbalanced budgets—an advantage that is practically denied to the states.

THE POLITICAL EQUILIBRIUM

Turning to the essentially political factors in the national-state balance of advantages, I mention first the fact that the major political parties are organized along confederate lines, not federal and clearly not national. Since the state units appear to be the dominant elements in each national party, and since a national party convention or committee seldom attempts to discipline a state party organization, one might be led to believe that the states control national party policy and hence are in the saddle when it comes to making policies in Congress and the national administration. Except to a small degree, this happens not to be so. The state party delegations that go to the national conventions are primarily concerned with the nomination of party candidates for the national presidency and the vice-presidency. Control over these offices dwarfs all other considerations. Party platforms are secondary and are seldom very influential with Congress or the national administration. The candidates for United States senators and representatives in Congress are nominated separately, in each state, and more likely than not by a fairly open state primary not controlled by the party. Consequently the state party committees have little control over the members of Congress, and the national party committees practically none. The loose confederate type of organization of the major national parties is more a sign of party weakness than of strength. It seems to do almost nothing to add weight to the states in the struggle to keep them in equilibrium with the national government.

Neither major national party since the Civil War has taken a strong stand against measures like federal grants to the states, measures that tend to increase national influence in state affairs. Both have given lip service to the protection of states' rights, but they have generally avoided committing themselves on specific proposals to change the national-state balance of functions and powers. The major state parties have also usually avoided taking strong stands on such measures.

Within each major party, also, the leaders are divided approximately between those who seek office or control in state affairs and those who go into Congress and the national administration. Competition between senators and representatives in Congress on the one side and the governors and other state leaders on the other side is usually not proclaimed but it is frequently important. Those who seek national office are careful to retain their political followings in their home states, and they use their powers in Washington to see to it that their states are not neglected and that they, as senators and representatives in Congress, get credit for what they get out of the national government for their states. State governors and legislators, although relying primarily on what they can accomplish in their states, may also go to Washington to lobby for various national favors for the states. In this frequently friendly but occasionally bitter competition the goals are at least partly the continuance or increase of political power for the leaders who participate in it. Governors hope to go on to the United States Senate, representatives in Congress or state legislators to become governors or United States senators, and so on.

The permutations and combinations of measures that are espoused in this competition change with times, conditions, and personalities, and they are exceedingly varied. They do not always follow any party line, and we need to remember that sometimes the governor is of one party, and at least one of the United States senators of the other. In those states where per capita federal tax collections are high and the federal aids received are low, a Republican governor in one state and a Democratic governor in an adjoining one may stand shoulder to shoulder in denouncing federal aids as, in effect, robbing their taxpayers to grant funds to other states, and at the same time destroying the rights of the states and their capacity for self-government. Other governors with different conditions in their states may put out lists of new things the national government should do for the states. At the same time state legislatures may be adopting resolutions and memorials to Congress for other benefits and legislation to help their states. In general the United States senators and representatives from the less wealthy states, both Republican and Democratic, favor liberal federal aids to the states under distribution formulas that are especially beneficial to their own constituents.

One cannot say that these various positions taken by elective officials are designed only to enhance or assure their own political power. Their motives are undoubtedly mixed, and considerations of general welfare and a just distribution of benefits and burdens surely enter into their thoughts. Whatever the motives, however, this fact is clear: neither of the major parties, whether national or state, and no class of elective officers, state or national, stands strongly and unitedly against an expansion of national services and benefits to the states. There is no strong political barrier to prevent a continuance of national penetration into the financing of state governments, and this necessarily brings with it an increasing acceptance by the states of national standards for their legislation and their public services.

As I point out in Chapters 3 and 5 above, Presidents and the members of Congress have been aware of this to such an extent that they have taken measures to protect the powers of the states to govern themselves and to continue performing their accustomed functions. Certain justices of the Supreme Court have also taken a strong stand on this side, and while important Supreme Court decisions have gone against the states when they attempted to act in fields "occupied" by congressional laws, others have been generous in upholding state powers in fields not so occupied or not forbidden to the states.

THE LEGISLATIVE BALANCE

These gestures on the part of all three branches of the national government have not changed the general trend significantly. My discussion has emphasized developments in fields where federal grants-in-aid are employed and those in which there are other financial implications. But congressional legislation has been significant and expansive in regulatory fields also. The regulation of aliens, sedition and other internal security problems, labor relations, wages and hours, agricultural production, foods and drugs, shipping by land, sea, and air, the whole field of communications, the development of power from streams, other changes in waterways, ports, and harbors, fisheries, narcotics, firearms, banking, "interstate crimes" of various kinds—these and many more have become the subjects of important national legislation. Much of this legislation is definitely helpful to the states in enforcing their own laws, but the major effect is the occupation of the field by the national laws and a corresponding reduction of the field for state legislation.

Because the areas left for state legislation are not strictly comparable to those occupied by federal laws, one cannot strike a balance between state and national legislation on the basis of either quantity or importance. One fact is clear, however, and that is the direction of the trend, which is toward the expansion of national legislation and the constriction of the legislative areas left to the states. The federal laws, if within the constitutional powers of Congress, are, of course, supreme over state laws unless Congress otherwise provides.

THE STRENGTHS AND WEAKNESSES OF THE STATES

There are so many factors in the tendency toward national ascendancy over the states that I shall not attempt to mention even all the major ones. Consider the great streams of immigrants who came to "America," the people who knew not Massachusetts or Virginia or any other state save perhaps as geographical expressions. Consider also the great mobility of the people across state lines; the concentration of the media of publicity and communications upon national affairs; national dominance in the regulation of commerce, in agricultural policy, in labor legislation, in foreign affairs, in national defense, and in other fields; the great respect shown for federal administration and law enforcement; the national systems of social security and veterans' benefits; the post office. These and many more encourage a tendency to look to Washington, and not so much to the state capitals, for public policies and services.

But when all has been said that can truly be said about the superiority of the nation's government over those of the several states in constitutional power, in financial strength, in unity of action, in more effective administration, and in the attention accorded to it by the national media of publicity, something still remains to be said for the states. I do not contend that the factors I am about to mention fully counterbalance the factors of national supremacy, only that they are factors that cannot be ignored.

James Madison in The Federalist (Numbers 45 and 46) made one of the best statements ever put forth on this subject. It came out of his background of experience in both the Virginia state government and the Continental Congress under the Articles of

Confederation. It had behind it also his great logical powers at their best and his wide reading and deep thinking in the field of foreign government, both ancient and contemporary. Some of his arguments are no longer valid, because conditions have greatly changed. Others, especially those relating to "the predilection and probable support of the people" and to "the disposition and faculty of resisting and frustrating the measures of each other" still have considerable validity. I will not attempt to summarize his entire argument but will instead quote one of his paragraphs in order to give something of the flavor of his presentation. His second paragraph in Number 46 reads: "Many considerations, besides those suggested on a former occasion [in Number 45], seem to place it beyond doubt that the first and most natural attachment of the people will be to the governments of their respective States. Into the administration of these a greater number of individuals will expect to rise. From the gift of these a greater number of offices and emoluments will flow. By the superintending care of these, all the more domestic and personal interests of the people will be regulated and provided for. With the affairs of these, the people will be more familiarly and minutely conversant. And with the members of these, will a greater proportion of the people have the ties of personal acquaintance and friendship, and of family and party attachments; on the side of these, therefore, the popular bias may well be expected most strongly to incline."

Considerations such as these cannot be brushed aside, even though a more complete analysis and a more up-to-date statement of them might make the conclusions somewhat different. The relative valuations placed by people upon their political institutions have never been adequately analyzed. For example, the importance to many people of their local governments as compared with their national institutions is to me a cause of constant wonder. The people of the Greek city-states, after they had lost their national independence first to Philip of Macedon and then to the Romans, still clung to their local governments even though they had little more than municipal powers. The same appears to have been true in other parts of the Roman Empire, and centuries later, after the fall of the Empire and the Dark Ages had intervened, men of the Italian cities, the Hansa towns, and other urban places in the late Middle Ages, found great satisfaction in their local self-government when true national power was beyond their control. Indeed, I have heard it said by men and women in our own time that it makes little difference who is President if they have the right alderman. The students of high politics need to keep this disturbing and yet reassuring fact in mind.

Several other factors that are somewhat favorable to the states need also to be considered. All politics is based on choices, and the more mediums the people have through which to express their choices the more satisfaction they seem to gain. On most political issues there are those who wish to say "no" as well as those who wish to say "yes," those who stand for "less" as well as those who cry for "more," those who would go slower as well as those who wish to go faster. On many domestic issues that are within its constitutional powers each state can offer its people some compensatory choice of a policy different from that of the national government without actually obstructing the national decision. In such matters as taxation, welfare, and education, they can differ not only from each other but from the national policy as well. Although not as powerful in certain major respects as the national government, the states stand as continuing though limited competitors to the national authorities for the favor of the people.

In addition to this, the poeple in the states where a majority dissent from a national policy have it in their power to put a brake on the national authorities, to obstruct national activities, to drag their feet, so to speak, by getting their state and local governments to aid in their obstructive purposes. They can assert that the national policy is unconstitutional, as it may sometimes be, and utilize every device available to them in the courts, in their legislatures, in their administrative practices, in what amounts to a "sit-down strike," to attempt to frustrate or at least to delay the carrying out of the national decision. This capacity of the states is exemplified in our own day by the dogged resistance to racial integration in the public schools, in defiance of the Supreme Court decision of 1954, by the states that have long been practicing segregation. A similar resistance has been evident for over sixty years in the refusal of these states to accord full voting rights and equal participation to Negroes in the nomination and election not only of state and local officers but also of members of Congress and presidential electors—this too in defiance of Supreme Court decisions.

This obstructive and delaying power of the states is assisted by a number of important factors: a strong element of national opinion opposed to the use of force against any state; a corresponding and understandable reluctance of any national administration to employ force in local or state situations; a body of United States Senate rules and practices that make difficult the passage of suitable enforcement measures over a united and strong minority of senators; and a desire on the part of all national agencies, including the courts, to proceed only with due process of law and the utmost patience in spite of any resultant delays. In the short run these attitudes on the part of the national authorities may seem like weaknesses in the national government; in the long run they may prove to be important elements of its strength.

While the issues of race relations and the civil and political rights of minorities have engendered much political heat and widespread disappointment with the intransigence of the states involved, they have not noticeably changed the prevailing public opinion in favor of maintaining the federal system as it is. There appears to be no important body of public opinion that is in favor of even limiting the powers of the states, and certainly none in favor of abolishing them. The Commission on Intergovernmental Relations went even farther when it said in its 1955 report that "the enduring values of our federal system fully warrant every effort to preserve and strengthen its essence," and that "the strengthening of State and local governments would increase its effectiveness." At the same time, it went on to indicate the areas in which improvements in state government are needed and to emphasize the responsibility of the states themselves to undertake the reforms: "The strengthening of state and local governments is essentially a task for the States themselves. Thomas Jefferson observed that the only way in which the States can erect a barrier against the extension of National power into areas within their proper sphere is 'to strengthen the State governments, and as this cannot be done by any change in the Federal constitution . . . it must be done by the States themselves . . .' He explained: 'The only barrier in their power is a wise government. A weak one will lose ground in every contest.'"

It happens, however, that such a statement of a general rational principle has no strong appeal to those who exercise political control in the separate states. It is hard for those in power not to identify their own exercise of power with the welfare and good government of the state. To relinquish their power or to change their policies and their methods of government cannot produce better government from their point of view. A state whose government was reorganized so as to diminish their power and substitute other state policies for theirs would not be one whose "states' rights" they would care to preserve.

It is the judgment of many well-informed people with whom I am inclined to agree that the weakness of the states vis-à-vis the national government is due in part at least to the form of the state governments, and to the doings of those who rule the states, and that the seat of the difficulties is primarily in the state constitutions, and secondarily in the state legislatures. I do not use the term misgovernment of the states although I think that term would apply to many state practices that have come to be condemned by the informed public opinion of the nation.

The constitutional form of the state governments is in all cases based upon the separation of powers. This means that, the judiciary aside, there are two essentially political departments in each state, the executive and the legislative; or the governor, and other elective administrative officials, and the legislature, which is of two houses in all but one state. The governor or chief executive is not directly responsible to the legislative branch, and the latter has generally been so organized as to follow a course of its own, fairly independent of executive leadership. Furthermore, the legislature in most states insists upon having its own direct contact with the administrative departments and upon holding down the chief executive's powers.

In Canada and Australia, where the cabinet and parliamentary system of government prevails in the provinces or states as well as in the central government, and where the number of states is small, the prime ministers and cabinets of the several states are in a position to bargain with the prime minister and cabinet of the central government directly, responsibly, and with full power. They are in nearly all cases fairly sure that their legislatures will back them up, because they have the confidence and constitute the principal committee of their legislatures. This is unitary and responsible government. In their occasional conferences with the prime ministers of the central government, the state or provincial prime ministers have been able to speak with the full authority of their states and to drive hard bargains with the prime minister and cabinet of the central government. This has been particularly noticeable in matters involving the division of functions and of taxing powers between the central and state governments. In Australia it has also been important in state rejections of constitutional amendments proposed by the central government.

The situation in the United States is quite different. In the first place there are many more states, fifty today, as contrasted with six in Australia and ten in Canada. It would be more difficult to arrange a united front among the American states by reason of their numbers alone, if there were no other obstacle. A second and I believe more potent factor is the separation of powers in both the national and state governments. The President can meet with the Governors' Conference, and with them he can set up a committee to consider and recommend the transfer of certain functions and tax sources between the national and state governments and the elimination of certain grants-in-aid. This was done in 1957. The heads of several national agencies and a number of governors were on the committee. But the governors quickly learned what they should have known, and probably did know, before: the governors of a few states could not negotiate for the governors of all the states (some governors seem to have been opposed to the negotiation from the beginning), and the governors on the committee could not speak at all for the state legislatures, not even for those of their own states. Legislators have their own interests to serve and their own ways of dealing with questions of governmental functions and finances. They are, also, generally in no mood to give up federal grants-in-aid once established. The pressure groups that favor such grants are always quick to spring to their defense—and "legislatures cook by pressure." From the national side the situation was no better. Neither the President himself nor any officials designated by him can negotiate with power to give up any national tax, or any federal grant-in-aid, or any function of the national government. In such matters the President has the power of proposal, but Congress has the final power of disposal.

Then why should not Congress and the state legislatures get together to negotiate such transfers of funds and functions? There have been various suggestions to this end, but no one has found a way by which fifty state senates, forty-nine state houses of representatives, a United States Senate of one hundred independent-minded members, and four hundred and thirty-seven representatives in Congress could be fairly and responsibly represented in a negotiating body. I think a study commission of outsiders might be set up which would try to take into account the views of all the state legislators, the governors, the United States senators and representatives, and the national administration, as well as the functional and financial interests involved, but that would be a far cry from a responsible negotiating body.

The use of numerous specific federal grants-in-aid in the United States also complicates the problem of such negotiations, because each function that benefits from a grant-in-aid has its own organized support in the public, in Congress and the state legislatures, and in national, state, and even local administrative agencies. To threaten any one with abolition is to threaten all. The opposition to any change can be quickly mobilized.

The state constitutions contain other obstacles that hamper movements to modernize the state governments. There are constitutional restrictions on taxing powers, on spending and borrowing powers, on constitutional revision and amendment, on equality in legislative representation, on administrative reorganization. It is, indeed, generally recognized that the written constitutions of the states contain many provisions that no longer contribute to the general welfare, that give unwarranted protection to certain special interests, and that prevent or at least delay the modernization of the state governments.

While the written constitutions provide the basis for many archaic, undemocratic, and uselessly hampering practices in state government, long usage has developed others that are not required by the constitutions and some that are actually forbidden—but by provisions that cannot easily be enforced. It is widely believed—and the belief is well supported by evidence—that certain widespread abuses have led to a loss of public confidence in the state governments, and that the weakness of the states can be attributed in large part to these abuses.

While public opinion has, in general, become more democratic and more equalitarian for at least the past hundred years in the United States, the state governments continue to reveal certain definitely undemocratic traits. One does not like to use the word about anything American, but I would say that there is a definitely oligarchical quality about some features of state government, and that, far from diminishing, some of these features are becoming more pronounced. Oligarchy means, of course, rule by a minority under conditions that prevent the majority from overriding it except by actual revolt.

One obviously oligarchical feature of many state governments arises from systems of legislative apportionment that give representation to counties or towns without much if any regard to population, and that fail to give sufficient additional representation to the more populous districts to achieve equality by population. Some such schemes were written into the constitutions when population was more evenly distributed. Still others have resulted from deliberate gerrymanders, or from long-continued refusal of legislators to reapportion in accordance with population even where the state constitution clearly requires it. Members from the less populous districts simply refuse to go along with a redistribution of representation according to population, even though the inequalities are as much as ten to one. Re-elected time and again from their small and essentially one-party districts, these members look upon their districts as more or less their private domains. Collectively the members from the less populous districts stand together to resist reapportionments that might endanger their chances of re-election and diminish their present excessive voting strength in the legislature. To justify their position they raise the specter of urban domination, and argue for representation by "area" as well as by population; but area is a deceptive word since county areas themselves are distinctly unequal. The influence of the "federal analogy" is also evident in the arguments. Some try to raise the counties to the level of states and compare the state to a federal system composed of counties. The historical reasons for equal representation of the states in Congress are ignored, while a more important practical consideration is not mentioned. A candidate for the

United States Senate must win votes in all parts of the state, like the candidate for governor. He cannot be against agriculture or against the small cities and villages, or against urban interests, either, when he campaigns or when he sits as a senator. This would not be true in many hundreds of rural legislative districts throughout the country. Those who oppose representation according to population align themselves with the rural interest and tend to perpetuate the urban-rural conflict instead of trying to harmonize interests.

This failure of the state legislatures to reapportion in accordance with population and the related underrepresentation of urban populations in state legislatures have resulted in the situation we have already noted: urban distrust of those bodies and a tendency of mayors and city councils to turn to Washington for the sympathetic hearing that they feel they cannot get in the state legislatures as now constituted. State control over urban policies is thus being undermined.

The organization of power within the state legislatures also shows undemocratic tendencies. The state senates reveal most fully the principle of continuity in the state governments. Many members are elected time and time again, and under seniority rules they become chairmen of important committees. The most important of these are the committees on rules, on the judiciary, on finance or ways and means, and on appropriations. Under the ordinary senate rules the chairmen of these and other committees have great powers to advance the bills they favor and in effect to sidetrack others. Senators from the less populous districts receive committee chairmanships and other important committee assignments along with others who represent more people. Senators from the minority party (which is not necessarily the same as senators who represent a minority of the people) get fewer and less important assignments.

The inner circle of senior senators form a combination that is hard to defeat. Governors elected by large popular majorities often find themselves frustrated by it, even on measures for which they campaigned successfully throughout the state. Of course, governors come and go. Their average tenure is not long. The ruling group of senators goes on with only small changes from decade to decade. They can afford to delay and wait. They are not responsible to a statewide popular majority, but only to the local majorities in their own districts.

It appears that in most states the ruling powers in the senate have had a conservative, delaying influence. This is an important role in state government. The question is, however, whether it has not actually hastened the decline of the states in relative importance when compared with the national government in a period when more rapid progress on the part of the states might have offset to some extent the increasingly dominant position of the national government. Who can say? The inherent inequalities of the states and their marked divergencies in policy were present in any case to prevent united action among them.

I hope that nothing I have said is interpreted to mean that the states have made no progress toward improving their laws and administration or toward serving their people more effectively. While a considerable part of what they have done has been strongly influenced by federal grants-in-aid and federal standards, many states have also moved forward on their own toward more effective administration. State personnel standards, administrative practices, revenue and budget systems, social legislation, educational services, conservation practices, and many other things have been improved in recent decades. Although the record is a very spotty one when all the states are considered, the impression I have gained over a number of decades of observation is one of fairly general though uneven improvement. But it has not, I think, been enough to keep the states abreast of the national government in vital functions that are of increasing importance in an urban-industrial society.

In some fields the states are, of course, less affected by the expansion of national expenditures and activities than in others. I refer to their roles in legislation for a wide range of subjects such as property rights, business organization, family life, social relations, criminal and civil law; and provisions for law enforcement and courts, local government, elections, education, civil rights, conservation, and many more; as well as major aspects of the federally aided functions that are not directly affected by federal standards. There is certainly no lack of important services for the states to perform.

In view of such factors as these—the constitutional, the financial, the political and legislative, and others I have mentioned, it is hardly possible to think any longer of a federal equilibrium, if we mean by that an equal balance of opposing forces in the usual physical sense. I believe that we must try to think in somewhat different terms, of which two may be suggested. One is a sort of rock-bottom minimum theory, a thus-far-and-no-farther concept, for the protection of the states. The other is a more flexible concept that recognizes changes as not only necessary but also desirable if they can be worked out on the basis of a fair and appropriate allocation of functions, powers, and responsibilities between the states and the national government. These two suggestions call for some elucidation.

I have heard it said in state government circles that there are certain powers indispensable to the preservation of states as autonomous units in the federal system. If these can be assured exclusively to the states, and their relations with the national government stabilized on this basis, the states will continue to be important and the federal system will be preserved. There are differences among commentators on the scope of the minimum list, but the following powers of states have been mentioned: control over their own constitutions, control over their own revenues, autonomy in legislation and administration within their own powers, control over their own courts and law enforcement, control over their elections, control over local government, control over education. Presumably these powers and functions would be free from national interference and not dependent upon grants-in-aid from the federal treasury.

I will not argue about this particular list although I wish to point out that nothing in it is today completely and absolutely free from all national influence. The theory behind such a list is similar to one that several recent writers on federal government (Professors K. C. Wheare and Arthur Macmahon, for example) have discussed, namely that the member states must be truly independent of and coordinate with the national authorities; and the test of whether they are so is that they have exclusive control over some substantial and not merely trivial affairs. One writer (Professor Wheare) seems to think it sufficient if only one matter is thus vested exclusively in the states. He applies the same reasoning to the central government; if it has exclusive control over even one matter, the system will still be federal. In the latter respect he is in line with some writers on world federalism who have argued that the defense power, or power to preserve peace, would be all that a supra-national organization would need to be called federal. I do not think that such a division of powers is at all feasible.

I think also that the powers and functions of government affecting the same people cannot be divided into absolutely exclusive lists, and that if the governmental system as a whole is to be effective the central government must have the power to overrule the states on any matter that affects the national welfare, as determined by the national authorities. All the powers and functions of government are interdependent. To say that the states shall have exclusive authority over education, for example, sounds clear and simple, but is it? Education affects loyalty and patriotism, international relations, national defense, commerce, civil liberties, and many other things. In the matter of elections, if the states controlled only their own it would be one thing, but in fact national elections are involved with state elections, and as the Supreme Court has said it is practically a matter of self-preservation for the nation to control the purity of its own elections. Just suppose that some state were to go Fascist or Communist by election or otherwise—would there not be need for the nation to intervene in the interest of all the other states, and to preserve the "republican form of government"?

These are some of the reasons why I think that no list of state powers can be set aside exclusively for the states and that the states cannot safely be made independent of the nation or their governments be made coordinate with that of the nation. There needs to be an overruling power at the top.

There needs also to be a flexibility about any division of powers, and an opportunity for change in accordance with needs and circumstances. The idea of a fixed and unchangeable division of powers is not in keeping with the requirements of a dynamic society living under pressure in an insecure international situation. It is pleasant to dream about what might be done under the relatively secure and stable conditions of a new Victorian age, but in the present situation governments had better be adaptable to rapidly changing circumstances.

Furthermore, to tie any function as important as education so tightly to the state governments, and to deny it federal aid, which is implied in this allocation, is in effect to hold back education while functions like highways, public health, and social welfare are benefiting from national as well as state support. For while some states will provide liberally for education at all levels, others will be unable to do so or will be prevented from doing so by strong taxpayer resistance. The nation as a whole suffers from unduly low educational standards in any state.

I am, therefore, inclined to reject this idea of a minimum but exclusive list of state functions as unrealistic, just as I am minded to withhold support from an equilibrium theory if equilibrium means an equal balancing of opposing forces. Any equilibrium of national and state governments in the United States today would have to be an equilibrium without equality.

The alternative that I suggest is nothing new. It is in fact nothing more than a better understanding and a better utilization of the federal system as it is in the United States today. In over 170 years of experience under the Constitution a federal system has been worked out that is flexible enough to meet all demands upon it at all levels, and in all the crises that have yet come to the American people.

Under this system, although there is a certain amount of undeclared rivalry for public favor between the national and state governments, there is no real power struggle between them. All three branches of the national government have shown a restraint and a willingness to help in their dealings with the states that is but little realized by most people, and not appreciated by many state officials. In spite of proposals at various times to abolish all state control over banking, over insurance, over railroads, and other subjects of regulation, no President has proposed such measures and no Congress has given them more than passing attention. As I show in Chapter 5, above, Congress has enacted many laws designed to make more effective the states' powers of law enforcement, tax collection, and business regulation, and to aid states financially in supporting their public services. The very nature of the organization of the national government is such as to make the welfare of the states and their governments a chief concern of the national authorities.

In my opinion no state should ever be satisfied with a minimum list of functions such as I have suggested above. Instead they should continue to demand to be consulted and used as partners in every function that is important to the internal welfare of the nation and its people, and is one in which they can participate helpfully and appropriately. Such a partnership exists in a general sense today. I believe it can be made better and more effective. How can this be done?

Here again I present nothing original. The Commission on Intergovernmental Relations covered the ground very well in Chapter 2 of its 1955 report. My own book of the same year, The Nation and the States, Rivals or Partners? outlines a similar program in Parts III and IV. In essence these publications call upon the states to rise more fully to their responsibilities for better government and better service, lest the national government be forced to step in to do things that the states neglect.

One thing more is needed, I believe. More public officials and more lay citizens need to be brought to a realization of the advantages they derive from a federal system of government and the requirements that must be met to keep such a system strong and viable. One item among these requirements is the ability at times to put political values, such as the long-run advantages of a sound democratic form of government, ahead of desires for immediate economic advantage or some new public service. The American people have come to take their federal system of government too much for granted. In my judgment, this is not safe for any people to do.

CHAPTER 10

Finished and Unfinished Business

I come to the final chapter of our unduly prolonged study with mixed feelings about what to say in conclusion. There is either so much to say, or so little new, that I wonder if I should say anything.

Before me are the first nine monographs in our series of studies. They represent the finished business of our project, a category in which they will soon be joined by this one. Obviously I cannot summarize them although I will try to characterize each one briefly. Near at hand are many files of notes and other materials gathered in the course of our work. Clearly I cannot go over all those materials again. And then there are the uncounted books and monographic reports in my libraries at home and at the university. Surely I cannot read them all over again. There is a time to stop and it is almost here.

I recall that early in our work we took to referring to intergovernmental relations by the letters IGR. Perhaps I could summarize by saying that we tried to pursue the elusive IGR to his lair but found he had no lair, or wasn't there, because he was everywhere.

To one who starts work on a subject with as many ramifications as intergovernmental relations, and remains alert to the possibilities, there is hardly a newspaper or a magazine that does not yield items that ought to be clipped and filed. I have found them in the New York *Times* and the Forest Lake (Minnesota) *Times*, in the Washington *Evening Star* and the Minneapolis *Star*. Their numbers are legion, their variations in detail are practically infinite. There are items in federal and state supreme court reports, in national and state laws, in government documents and reports, in publications of all kinds—and in the memories of tens of thousands of public officials and interested citizens. Soon the body of potential materials becomes overwhelming and practically unclassifiable. This is just the difficulty I face right now.

The studies that we have produced clearly do not constitute a complete, well-rounded, and systematic study of the entire federal system of government. It was never my thought or intention that they would. It seems to me that the term *federal system* is a sort of collective name for a vast mass of different and yet interconnected phenomena that are too numerous and too continuously interacting with each other, too fluid and too changing, ever to be reduced to a written record or description at any one time. One slight evidence of this generalization is the continuance of disagreements among well-informed persons as to what the system is. In its immensity, its complexity, its ever-changingness, it seems to me the federal system is comparable to such widespread institutions as private property, marriage, religion, and civil liberties. Who can understand all the ramifications of any of these ubiquitous institutions? I, for one, claim to have considerable knowledge of the federal system of government, but I often feel appalled at what I do not know.

In all that I have said, and in what I am about to say, then, I hope the reader will understand that I call the balls and strikes, the outs and runs, as I see them, but that I do not pretend to have any superhuman knowledge or insight, or to be infallible.

THE SCOPE OF OUR STUDIES

As can be seen from their titles, our monographs obviously cover only a few of the major topics that are important in the federal system. In what may be called the functional fields we deal with highways, education, public health, social welfare, and employment security. To these we added the courts (a whole separate branch of government) and fiscal relations (which concern all functions). Clearly, the fields we chose for exploration are those domestic functions in which there are substantial federal grants-in-aid, broadly defined, or in which grants-in-aid, though relatively small, present important issues of public policy. With the exception of employment security, these functions also involve the relations of national, state, and local governments, so that all three levels needed to be taken into account. Furthermore, all but highways and some educational functions represented rather recent developments in intergovernmental relations; and in all there were current problems of a fairly urgent nature. All could be studied to advantage in Minnesota, and all were somewhat comparable domestic functions.

This does not mean that we thought all this out in advance, or that we deliberately chose only these functions for our study. Quite the contrary is true. We desired to make studies also in the fields of conservation, general law enforcement, government regulation of commerce and utilities, and agriculture. We had to back away from the fields of conservation and law enforcement because we found conditions of tension in those areas that warned us it would be difficult to conduct fruitful interviews or to expect objective results. Less controversial fields seemed more likely to produce reliable findings. In agriculture we made a substantial start, but our staff member found himself unable to carry out his assignment, and then it was too late to employ another worker. Regulation of commerce and utilities, we concluded, would have been too vast and varied a field for one staff member to explore, and the same was true of labor relations. It was for such reasons that we stayed out of these areas. And in any case we did not have the staff or resources to cover all the fields.

As it turned out, then, our main studies were fairly well bunched and interrelated, and our coverage of the field was far less comprehensive and diversified than might have been desirable.

What we left out I will indicate only briefly. In so doing I in effect list some major subjects for further intergovernmental relations studies, although some of them have already been written about in various works. We left out, among others, international relations and foreign affairs; national defense, including the National Guard, and civil defense; government promotion and regulation of commerce and business, power, transportation, communications, labor, and agriculture; conservation of natural resources; direct federal welfare programs for veterans, aged and retired persons, farmers, and other classes; general law enforcement; civil liberties, civil rights, and race relations; public housing, housing finance programs, urban planning, urban redevelopment; atomic energy; regulation of political parties, elections, and suffrage.

Within the functional fields that we studied we feel that our coverage was reasonably thorough, and that our findings were fairly well supported by evidence. These findings were partly corroboratory of other studies and partly new. While I recognize that studies of the same functions in other states or of different functions in Minnesota, or replicated studies of the same functions at a later time in Minnesota, would probably produce somewhat different findings, a brief characterization of each of our studies, limited as they are, may be worthwhile at this point. The reader will bear in mind that, while the studies published in Monographs 1 through 6 were being carried on, Dr. Weidner and I were making our own more general studies, and that the findings in his Monograph 9 and in this one include these to some extent.

SOME OBSERVATIONS ON THE MONOGRAPHS

The following comments are necessarily brief and cannot cover all of even the major points made in the individual studies. They are intended to provide a general framework and to point up certain findings.

Before going into the strictly functional monographs I should like to point to the first monograph in our series, written by Forrest Talbott, Intergovernmental Relations and the Courts. It is a rather detailed study of the organization of the national and state courts in Minnesota, the division of work between them, and the limited relations that they have with each other. It reveals the jumble of jurisdictions that exist, with federal district courts deciding cases under state laws where diversity of citizenship of the parties is alleged; state courts deciding cases under federal laws; and even municipal courts being designated and required by Congress to handle rent control cases under national wartime legislation.

Mr. Talbott's study does not go into the effects of Supreme Court decisions in guiding the development of national-state relations under the Constitution. I have discussed that subject in Chapter 3 and elsewhere at considerable length. He does point out, however, the very interesting contrast there is between the courts and the administrative agencies, national, state and local, in the way they handle their work. The primary task of the judges is to decide individual cases in adversary proceedings. Each judge decides the case before him, issues the appropriate court order, and when that is done he is done unless the lawyers bring the case back for some reason, when the process may be repeated and another decision made. In most cases it is not up to the judge to follow through to see that the court's order is carried out, or to study the effect of it. Although receptive and even cooperative, the court sits aloof, on the sidelines, while lawyers and their clients and public administrators struggle with the steps that follow the decision.

Unlike the state administrative agencies that work on national-state programs in highway construction, public health, public welfare, or education, the state courts receive no grants-in-aid and no significant federal payments for handling cases under federal law, are subject to no national supervision or audits, and do not need to keep in close touch either with the federal courts or with federal administrative agencies, through national conferences or otherwise. These are some of the elementary differences between judicial organization and the administrative services in national-state relations.

To be sure, some state court decisions that raise federal questions do get to the United States Supreme Court for review, and a number of them get overruled, but this also occurs in an impersonal process, one that operates by a sort of remote control.

Intergovernmental Relations in Highways, as observed in Minnesota, are discussed by R. A. Gomez in the second study published in the series. His monograph deals with national, state, and local relations in a function that had begun to receive substantial federal aid over thirty years earlier. The original federal aid in Minnesota was dedicated to the state trunk highways, a limited mileage that ran throughout the state in the rural districts and through the villages, but left the larger cities burdened with the expense of improving the connections through their areas, and made no provision for secondary or county roads. Soon began two separate lines of attack upon these arrangements, one by the large cities to get a share of state and federal road funds.

the other by the counties for the same purpose. Two rival local interests thus demanded consideration, in competition with the interests of the state highways. Congress yielded by granting federal aid for both city streets and county roads, but in yielding it also reached down through the states to satisfy a local demand. A few years after Mr. Gomez's study was published the state of Minnesota also yielded to these local pressures. The state constitution was amended so as to allocate 29 per cent of the gas tax and motor vehicle license fees to the counties and 9 per cent to the cities. Congress had in the meantime made the state's reduction in revenues from these sources more palatable by guaranteeing to pay 90 per cent of the cost of the new federal interstate highway construction costs without eliminating grants for state, urban, and county roads. State and local governments throughout the nation had thus executed a "squeeze play" on the national treasury to get more money from it for both state and local highways.

In the administration of federal highway grants in Minnesota, Mr. Gomez found that professional engineers were generally in charge of operations at national, state, and local levels, that they were in constant contact with each other and worked together in the greatest harmony. State and county relations were especially close, informal, and cooperative. Engineers moved from county to state and state to county payrolls with ease. Partisan considerations were practically lacking in these relations. Remember that in Minnesota, county officials and state legislators are all elected without party designation. This fact does not remove partisanship from state politics, but it seems to help to reduce its area of operation and to some extent to discipline it.

At the most local level, that of the township and village road administrations, while township roads were declining in importance and in the relative level of their financial support (without state aid), county and town cooperation and inter-town cooperation were widely prevalent, and mainly informal. The counties were assuming the responsibility for more mileages of town roads and granting a small amount of aid for other stretches of town roads. Thus the responsibility for support of the road system was moving upward from the towns and villages to the counties, to the state, and to the national government.

Intergovernmental Relations in Education as observed in Minnesota was the subject of Monograph 3 by Robert L. Morlan. His study covered not only public elementary and secondary education but also higher education and various special programs in agricultural extension, vocational rehabilitation, apprentice training, education for veterans, and other projects. By covering the state-local and interlocal relations of the public schools with care, he showed that the "independence" claimed by the leaders in many school systems was very qualified. Nevertheless the ideal of independence had remained strong among public school leaders, even to the advocacy by some of a national school board in Washington, free from presidential and congressional control, to carry on the educational activities of the national government and to serve the state and local school systems.

Aside from constitutional and legislative obstacles to independence for the public schools there is the question of finance. Congress controls the federal revenues and expenditures and the state legislature those of the state. State aids in Minnesota were providing over 30 per cent of all public school funds in the late 1940s when Mr. Morlan was making his study. In other states the percentage varied from less that 5 in Iowa, New Hampshire, and Kansas, to over 85 in Delaware and New Mexico. Mr. Morlan found no consistent relationship between the percentages of state aid and the degree of state control over the schools. In Minnesota, where the legislature had dedicated the revenues of the state income tax to the schools, the local educators had learned to live with state control and were not unhappy about it.

The question of federal aid being before Congress at the time, Mr. Morlan inquired by interview and questionnaire about Minnesota attitudes toward it. He found no great fear of federal control among local educational officials, and over a fifth seemed to welcome the idea of a nationally controlled system. Some disliked the idea of such control for the reason that they would probably have to keep more records and make out more reports under a federal-aid system, but more recognized this as necessary to good school administration. Mr. Morlan noted that in the limited federal-aid programs he had studied (for vocational education, agricultural experiment stations, etc.), while the federal requirements were rather strict at first, they tended to become less so over the years. Furthermore these federal requirements seemed to be less strict than the state controls over state aids to the school districts.

In general he found a harmony of views and close cooperation among educational officials, national, state, and local, in striving for the independence of education from outside controls. This was attributable in part, no doubt, to their having a common goal of promoting education and a common professional background and interest. This attitude appeared clearly, for example, among the higher educational officials in the state in a common opposition to controls by the state budget office over their appropriations and over their policies in expending the funds appropriated. They did not wish to have to justify their requests for funds or their expenditures twice, or to anyone but the legislators.

Intergovernmental Relations in Public Health is the title of Laurence Wyatt's study, Number 4 in the series. It is a detailed study of public health organization, functions, problems, and interrelations from the national level down to the local units. The picture presented is one of various national health authorities (the United States Public Health Service, the Children's Bureau, the Food and Drug Administration, the Bureau of Animal Industry, and others) scattered through various departments and agencies, a strong Minnesota state health department flanked by a state livestock sanitary board, and a state department of agriculture, dairy, and food, and a spotty local situation in which only Minneapolis, St. Paul, Duluth, St. Louis County, and a Rochester-Olmsted County "health unit" provide full-time organized health services. In other local areas there are nurse services in most counties that cooperate with the local schools, and part-time health officers in many cities, villages, and organized townships; physicians designated as health officers by the smaller units and townships are in many cases nonresidents. By law the local health functions belong mainly to some 2,600 towns, villages, and cities, most of which spend little on health services.

In both the national and state governments there are problems of interagency as well as intergovernmental relations. In the national government this problem is simplified by the fact that the Public Health Service, the Children's Bureau, and the Food and Drug Administration are now all within the Department of Health, Education, and Welfare. Neither in the national nor in the state government has there been serious lack of interagency cooperation, but there is frequent need for consultation.

Steady and substantial increases in national and state public health services and expenditures have characterized recent decades, along with remarkable increases in medical knowledge and the discovery of new treatments and even cures for disease. Under these circumstances Mr. Wyatt found a buoyant spirit of progress, good-will, and excellent cooperation among national, state, and local health officials. The emphasis was on continuous consultation between agencies, the joint formulation of health programs before they were undertaken, and the use of educational methods: short courses for health personnel, clinics, mobile health and diagnostic units, and a variety of other devices. The 1946 Hospital Survey and Construction Act which authorized considerable federal aid for the building of new hospitals brought all levels of government into cooperation. The methods of cooperation were many and varied—demonstrations, loans of skilled personnel, surveys, and others.

The state of Minnesota instead of creating large, effective local health units, which in many areas would have necessitated the joining of two or more counties into one health organization, authorized the state department of health to set up health districts of its own to bring the public health message to the communities, a measure that has satisfied the public sufficiently so that there has been no real movement for strong local health units. State grants to assist local health units have not been significant, but Mr. Wyatt found that national grants have been increasing and reaching not only the states but local units.

State supervision over local health services in Minnesota has been limited largely to sanitary measures affecting water supplies, sewage disposal systems, milk-pasteurizing plants, and the like.

Intergovernmental Relations in Social Welfare, the fifth monograph, was written by our only woman contributor, Ruth Raup. She not only studied laws, reports, regulations, and other printed or duplicated documents from all three levels of government, but also conducted over a hundred interviews and used three rather detailed questionnaires. She formulated hypotheses on many points in advance and was able to check them to a conclusion in many cases.

To understand some of her findings, for example on the subject of state official attitudes toward cooperating with national agencies in the welfare field, and county agencies' attitudes toward the state agency, several points must be kept in mind. The national administration was in Democratic hands and was in general pressing for larger grants to recipients of various forms of relief, while the state administration was in Republican hands, and it was more economy minded, as was the state legislature. The counties were only slowly being brought over from a nonprofessional type of service in welfare work to a more professional level, wherein trained social workers were essential, but the county board members were in many cases not yet convinced. The national authorities administering the large new federal grants for social welfare were in general anxious to see the level of service raised. In these circumstances Miss Raup found evidences of a real power struggle—some state resistance to advice and standards from the national government, and a great deal of county resistance to the new welfare standards, traceable to a strong local desire to keep power over welfare personnel and services in the elected county board.

In short her detailed findings on a number of such points reveal the great differences between the public health field, where trained physicians controlled standards and programs at both state and national levels, and where the public had come to accept new health measures rather eagerly, and the social welfare field, where much was still under heated debate and the new trained workers and their ideas and the new national policies were not yet fully accepted.

Miss Raup's findings cover both supervisory and nonsupervisory relationships (national, state, and local), the allocation and the proposed integration of grants, local administrative areas, and interstate and intercounty problems arising out of the laws of settlement for relief recipients.

Intergovernmental Relations in Employment Security by Francis E. Rourke (Monograph 6) deals with a unique program in the public services of the United States. It involves the national and state governments in a close and unusual relationship, but concerns the local governments hardly at all. (The program is described in Chapter 3 above.) With only one program and the top two levels of government to deal with, Mr. Rourke was able to probe deeply into the attendant national-state relations. He interviewed national officials in Washington and Chicago, and state officials in Minnesota, and then, with the evidence obtained by this method and from the published materials in the field, he formulated a questionnaire that was submitted to those national officials of the Bureau of Employment Security who might be expected to know conditions in more than one state.

Mr. Rourke's questionnaire listed twenty-six hypotheses as to why the plan was working as it was. His concluding chapter discusses each one and shows the percentage distribution of "yes," "no," and "undecided" replies. These hypotheses touch upon such questions as whether the separation (if not complete divorce) between financial responsibility (national) and policy control (largely state) is not an inherent source of trouble; whether professionalization of the state services and lapse of time were not improving national-state relations; whether the state agencies were not more "employer minded" and the national bureau more "employee minded"; and whether "experience rating" in the state schemes of taxing employers on their payrolls had not led to pressures on the state agencies antagonistic to "good relations" between the national bureau and the states.

Intergovernmental Relations at the Grass Roots (Monograph 7) was supplied by Paul N. Ylvisaker on my request, in 1954-55, when it became evident that our projected monograph on intergovernmental relations in agriculture was not going to be completed. I was in touch with Mr. Ylvisaker in the years 1943-45 when the spade work for this monograph was being done by him for the Council on Intergovernmental Relations in Blue Earth County, Minnesota. Later he amplified and reinterpreted the material for our series in a way that would bring out more clearly the intergovernmental relations in his home county.

Instead of dealing with a single governmental function or group of closely related functions, this study analyzes for a single county area and population the impact on it of all the levels, units, and functions of government in the early and middle 1940s. A number of threads are woven together in the book: the growth of the population and of the local governmental structure of the county; the impact on the people and their local governments of the coming in of new federal programs during the depression; the resultant confusions and misunderstandings when authorities from both national and state levels began to elbow their several ways into the local scene; the search through the Blue Earth County Council on Intergovernmental Relations for effective means and methods of coordinating the services of the three levels of government in the area; the influence of local political traditions, ideas, and personalities upon the efforts to coordinate; the substantial victories of the local forces of resistance to change, the actual strengthening of local government, and the ultimate failure of the efforts at coordination. There are separate chapters on intergovernmental relations in agriculture, health, highways, and finance; a concluding chapter that brings out some of the inconsistencies and the ambivalence in the local attitudes that permit the people to fight "centralization" while actually accepting substantial benefits from it; and an appendix entitled "Government Locally" that lists the major state and federal agencies that were at work in the county when the study was made.

I wrote Intergovernmental Fiscal Relations, Monograph 8, when unforeseen circumstances prevented the originally scheduled author from doing so. This study deals primarily with the broader problems of national-state-local relations in adjusting revenues to the needs of the several levels. These adjustments take place through the selection of revenue sources suitable to each level, and through partial transfers of revenues received at the national level to the state and local governments, and at the state level to the local units.

I made no attempt to go into the details of intergovernmental administrative cooperation in the collection of taxes or in the making of transfer payments from one unit to another. These subjects offer a sufficient wealth of interesting details to make up a separate study even for a single state like Minnesota. How the states help each other collect the gasoline tax, how the national government helps the states collect their income and cigarette taxes, how the counties serve the state and local governments in administering the property tax—these are examples of problems in which tax officials have shown a great deal of ingenuity.

Of the material that is included perhaps the following may be considered the most important: (1) a statement of the basic financial problems of all federal systems (Chapter 1); (2) a survey of Minnesota's general economic and fiscal rank among the states of the Union (Chapter 2); (3) a historical demonstration of Minnesota's substantial financial dependence on the national government since before the state was formed (Chapters 3 and 4); (4) a survey of the interrelations of the taxing powers and the tax systems of the national government and Minnesota; (5) a consideration of the actual fiscal balance between the national government and the state of Minnesota, and between the state and its local units (Chapters 7 through 10).

The extent of national financial dominance over the state and local governments, since the federal income tax became important about the time of World War I, is a fact that needs no demonstration. The consequences of this dominance reach into every relationship between the three levels of government. How this dominant power has been employed is dealt with to some extent in every monograph we have put out, except the one on the courts, and Monograph 8 adds something to round out the general picture.

Intergovernmental Relations as Seen by Public Officials, Monograph 9, is the work of Dr. Edward W. Weidner, assistant director of the entire research project. It represents an attempt to get at some of the characteristics of public officials who are concerned with intergovernmental relations that may influence their thinking and their actions in such relations. Most of the data for this study were obtained from the replies of officials to a series of questionnaires sent to them to elicit their views and their knowledge of the field. Additional information was obtained from a large percentage of the respondents to the first questionnaire who filled out a separate personality inventory questionnaire that was currently being used at the university to analyze the factors of political participation, awareness, and responsibility of voters generally.

Unlike the majority of the monographs, therefore, this one is not a functional study but a general behavioral study that cuts across all the others. It probes into the attitudes of officials toward the increase or decrease of the functions and powers of their own units of government and those of others; from their own answers it reveals their attitudes toward cooperation with the officials of other units, and to what extent those who had less frequent contact with the officials of other units are more distrustful of such outside officials than those who have had more frequent contacts; it appraises their respective attitudes toward "expediency values" (the protection and even increase of their own powers and importance), and their concern for the functions they are performing (programmatic values) as against the protection of the powers of the unit of government they serve. Since the questionnaire responses revealed a great deal also about the respondents, such as their education, professional status, the level and units of government they served, the types of offices they held, and so on, it was possible to bring out many distinctions between the official attitudes of different groups of officials.

In its appendixes this monograph also presents the basic questionnaires that were used, and a critical résumé of the research methods employed in the project as a whole.

HYPOTHESES AND TENTATIVE CONCLUSIONS

The nine studies that have now been reviewed are, in general, partly historical and partly analytical, detailed and factual, and as objective as can well be expected. At the same time they are limited in scope, geographically, functionally, and temporally, to such an extent that, taken all together, they do not warrant many broad generalizations about intergovernmental relations generally in the United States, perhaps none. Extrapolation can easily be carried too far. Broad and many-faceted though it was, ours was essentially a case study, or a group of related case studies, covering a short time period among a particular people.

By taking these studies as a basis, however, and adding to them the results of a considerable amount of reading, observing, and thinking, I am willing to present a series of hypotheses and tentative conclusions such as I think I owe to those who have supported and followed the research project that is now being brought to a close. What generalizations I make must not be taken, however, as proved scientific truths. They are my personal and rather subjective formulations. They are put forth for the use of others who may wish to carry on the study of intergovernmental relations in the United States. If any of them are propositions that can be tested by evidence, logic, and reason, I hope that they will be so tested, even if the result is to prove them to be utterly wrong. They represent the unfinished business of the project, or perhaps some ideas for points of departure from which other studies of intergovernmental relations might take off.

Why Comparisons Are Difficult. One handicap under which anyone labors in trying to generalize about developments in the American governmental system results from the lack of strictly comparable systems abroad. The Canadian and Australian federal systems probably come closer than any others to being comparable entities. In basic political philosophy, legal system, language, history, culture, and geographical extent, these countries are fairly similar to the United States. In certain other respects they are distinctly different. I refer, among other things, to these facts: their populations are much smaller than that of the United States, as are their wealth and resources; their international responsibilities and defense needs are much less; even though they are now constitutionally independent, their development up to about 1930 was within the British Empire, and they have kept their connections with the British Commonwealth; and their political institutions are based upon the principle of parliamentary supremacy instead of upon the separation of powers that prevails in the United States. These differences are paralleled if not actually reinforced by others, such as the relatively greater importance of local government in the United States as compared with state government; the greater use of federal grants-in-aid in the United States; national ownership of the public domain in the United States as against state ownership in the other two; the apparently smaller role given to interstate relations in Canada and Australia; the almost complete lack of written state constitutions to hamper the states and provinces in those countries; their much smaller use of the referendum in their states; the different divisions of powers between the central government and the states in the three; the differences in the positions of the senates in the central governments, and the general absence of second chambers in the Canadian provinces.

I feel, therefore, that there is no system of government outside the United States that is nearly enough like the American system either in its constitutional form or in the conditions under which it operates to support broad comparative generalizations. This conclusion, if sound, seriously limits any use of the comparative method, but will not preclude me from making a few comparisons that may have some explanatory value. In general, however, one seems limited to identifying and describing those factors within the United States that may conceivably have been causes or at least conditioning factors in the reshaping of the American federal system, and trying to explain the changes in the light of the conditions and ideas that have prevailed or developed here while the governmental trends or changes were taking place.

The Concept of Change. Within the memories of men now living, great changes have taken place in the United States federal system and in the intergovernmental relations that arise within it. In Chapter 2, above, I sketched out some of the background factors for these changes, and in Chapters 3 to 8, I discussed a number of the changes in the various classes of intergovernmental relations. Briefly summarized, the changes have been as follows: tremendous increases in governmental functions and activities; more legislation, more public administration, more raising and spending of public funds; closer and more numerous links and more cooperation between national, state, and local governments; the penetration of the national government into more and more phases of state and even local government and into the interrelations between them; the determination of minimum standards in many phases of state and local government by national authorities, legislative, executive, and judicial.

At the same time, the state governments, stimulated in part by national leadership and financial aid, have entered more fully into local government activities, with state aids, state standards for local performance, and state supervision of what the local units do. At the local level the smallest and least capable units of government, the common rural school districts and the rural towns and townships, have been and are being eliminated or reduced in numbers through consolidation and otherwise, while in the metropolitan areas, where population is rapidly increasing, new local units are being created and with them new networks of interlocal and state-local relations.

In general the trends of change have been and still are toward what is called centralization of functions; closer integration of activities; the increase of governmental functions; the upward movement of functions toward larger and larger units; a similar upward movement of tax-collecting activities, modified by some countervailing transfer of centrally collected funds downward through federal and state aid for expenditure more locally, so that for certain major nondefense functions money-raising moves to higher levels, money-spending partly to lower levels of government. With all these changes there is a general tightening of the bonds between governments, both vertically and horizontally.

The evident results are a closer integration of all units of government, and a constant raising of the level, improvement of the quality, and increase in the expenditures of public services up and down the line. The old days of relative isolation of governments from each other, low-level amateur performance of services by small units, and tightfisted economy in public expenditures, are passing though by no means entirely gone.

And these great transformations in the public services and in intergovernmental relations are by no means at an end. During the years since we began our studies, in 1946, we have seen an almost steady continuance of such changes and reorganizations.

Considering the various changes as having been established as facts by the historical record, I would state as my first hypothesis that these changes in intergovernmental relations and in the federal system have not been absolutely determined by other "forces" and tendencies in American society but that they have been closely correlated with and influenced by such forces and tendencies; that they probably have in turn influenced the other forces of or tendencies to change; and that if the two lists are placed alongside each other some historical and rational if not deterministic relations between them can be found. I state the hypothesis in this rather flexible way in order to leave such an area of fairly free choice to the people and their governments as I think they have.

What, then, are the economic, social, cultural, and attitudinal changes and the major events that have taken place pari passu with, and that probably influenced, the changes in government and in intergovernmental relations outlined above? I list herewith a number of such changes and events that seem to be well established by the historical records. The list is by no means exhaustive, and the items listed are certainly not of equal value or importance.

1. Education and literacy have spread to almost the entire population, and the levels to which people have been educated have gone up and up—through high school, through college, through professional and graduate schools, for increasing proportions of the people.

2. The facilities for transportation and communication have increased in number and variety, have become more and more mechanized and almost automatic, have tended to become nationwide. Communications media have become informative about all sorts of public questions, breaking down many old barriers that left people isolated and unaware of public affairs. Newspapers, the radio, television, postal services, and advertising practically blanket the whole nation.

3. Specialization, professionalization, and research have invaded almost every field of human endeavor, raising the possibility of improved service standards in both public and private affairs. This trend has among other things deepened and improved the people's general knowledge about government, public issues, public administration, and public finance, as well as about science, technology, industry, and other aspects of modern life.

4. These developments have been accompanied or followed by the rather general acceptance of new ideas about public finance and fiscal policy, the use of public expenditures, borrowing, and unbalanced budgets to maintain high levels of employment and to promote an advancing standard of living.

5. A national ideal or goal of a constantly rising standard of living has come to be generally accepted in industrial, commercial, financial, and governmental circles. To satisfy this general yearning, industries have rationalized and mechanized production, have engaged in research to improve and multiply their products, have striven for growth and increased productivity, and have used advertising both local and nationwide to induce people to take the increased volume of goods off their hands so that production can continue at high levels. The assembly line is being supplemented if not superseded by automation in production.

6. The standard of living and the per capita and total production of consumer goods and capital goods have in fact been rising, though not at an even rate, for many years, along with the increase in population.

7. Labor organizations, growing in numbers, have in general fallen in line with this trend and have insisted on constantly rising levels of wages and increased employment so as to enable their members to get higher real wages and thus benefit from the increases in the production of goods.

8. Agriculture, although employing numerically a declining sector of the national population, has also been an area of increased productivity, as have other segments of the national economy. Surpluses have become a chronic problem.

9. The location and growth of industries, communications, financial and commercial facilities, education institutions, amusements, and other means of human livelihood and satisfaction have been accompanied by the growth of hundreds of congested population centers, 174 of them classified as metropolitan, in which an increasing majority of the people live. This process is usually called urbanization, but recently "metropolitanization" would seem to be a more fitting term.

10. The two major political parties have come to dominate national and state elections more fully than before, while the minor parties have sunk to virtual insignificance. Furthermore the major parties seem actually to have come closer to each other in acceptance of the essential rightness of the American mixed economic-political

system, based on "private enterprise" but with public regulation, certain public services, and even a little public productive enterprise acting as "yardsticks" or controls over the private sector of the economy. Both parties have also accepted the idea that government has a responsibility to step in to meet public "needs" and demands for more and better public services, and both have had parts in developing the system of national-state-local relations, including grants-in-aid and tax-sharing. The differences between the parties on these matters are essentially matters of degree and emphasis, not of principle. Neither party has come out strongly for any basic change in the federal system, and both assert the importance of preserving the states. A minority in each party is, however, greatly disturbed about the tremendous power and the great activity of the national government and urges a return to "states' rights."

11. The educational, religious, cultural, and moral leaders and institutions of the land have taken very little stand one way or another on the general issues of intergovernmental relations, with a few exceptions relating to federal aid for education and before that to federal aid for infancy and maternity care.

12. Two major wars and a severe and prolonged depression created conditions that were met during the period under consideration by leadership, financial support, and action coming from the national government as never before in United States history.

13. In the aftermath of World War II, international problems and tensions brought new pressures on American institutions and a program of international activities and defense expenditures by the national government never before approached in size, cost, and intensity.

14. Also during and after World War II a demand has arisen and grown stronger for the equalization in fact of all the rights of the people without regard to race, color, religion, or national origins. The emphasis has been on equalizing the rights of colored people with those of whites in political participation; in public employment, both civil and military; in access to and use of public facilities like schools, parks, and public housing, and in private services like those of hotels and restaurants; and in the acquisition of private housing by rent or purchase. But latent opposition has become active, organized, and even violent. These issues have thrown increased burdens on governments at all levels, and brought new tensions in national-state relations.

I make no defense of this particular list of potentially influential factors in American society during the time when intergovernmental relations were undergoing such marked changes. I submit the list, incomplete as it is, only for purposes of illustration and inquiry. I have not thought it necessary to emphasize the general background of American history, the constitutional system, and popular control over government through elections and public opinion.

The questions I raise are simple and elementary questions of method and logic. Can we take any factor in this list, education, for example, and say "the more education the more centralization in government"? Alexis de Tocqueville practically asserted this over a century ago in his Democracy in America. Is it necessarily and always true that increases in the spread and depth of education are accompanied by increased centralization? If it is true, then the next question is whether one is the cause and the other the effect, or whether both are not effects of the same cause or combination of causes? If one is the cause, the other the effect, which is which? But if both phenomena are effects of some other cause or group of causes, how do we go about finding those causes?

The same questions may be asked about any of the other changes that I have mentioned. Do great wars always bring about great centralization in government? Or is centralization in government a cause of great wars? Is urbanization a cause of increased centralization in national and state governments? Or is the reverse true? Or is neither the cause of the other?

In this way we could go through the list of possible causes of centralization of government. But centralization is a very broad issue. If it were broken up into various more specific problems, like centralization in legislation, in public administration, in taxation, in public expenditure, and so on, it would be necessary to take different approaches, such as are suitable to each field, in analyzing the data and finding the correlations. Something might even be tried by way of gauging the relative rates of speed at which different changes were taking place, and the time lags between one trend and another.

But this is not all. Centralization is an important trend, but there are others to be considered. The total growth, the multiplication of types, and the diversification in methods of carrying on intergovernmental relations need to be studied separately since they appear to be, to some extent at least, means of putting off centralization, whether only briefly, for a long time, or indefinitely. The development of intergovernmental relations results in part at least from deliberate decisions against centralization. If this is so, and if educational advance has been to some extent a cause of or contributing influence toward centralization, then it may also have contributed to the increase of cooperative intergovernmental devices that delay centralization. Such seemingly contrary results from one factor, the increase and spread of education, would be hard to explain except in the light of some theory, political, economic, or philosophical, perhaps, that can harmonize the two apparently conflicting trends.

It may be, also, that increases and changes in governmental centralization and in intergovernmental relations have been as helpful to education as the spread of education has been to them. Federal aids for land-grant colleges, agricultural experiment stations, vocational education, agricultural and home economics extension work, and school lunches, not to forget the land grants for public schools, are important cases in point. They represent both a certain amount of centralization and a development of intergovernmental relations calculated to prevent further centralization; and they also serve as aids to education. Similar interactions between governmental changes and various social, economic, and cultural changes could be traced out from the historical record in a number of instances. They suggest not a straight-line cause and effect relationship but a more circular pattern of action and reaction, or interaction among variables. More than that they make me think that there may be more general and more potent social "forces" at work that are responsible for the whole pattern and network of interconnected changes in American society that are partly outlined in the foregoing lists. Before I get into that subject, however, I would like to say a word on other possible methods of finding interrelations among the changes that have been listed.

I have thought it might be possible to use some method of multiple correlation or factorial analysis on the available historical data about the many changes in American society during the past sixty to a hundred years with a view to finding close relations between some series of data and less close relations between others. I have little reason to doubt that something of this kind would be possible, and to some extent valuable. Recent developments in computing devices give much ground for hope, but I know too little about such methods of research to speak with any confidence. The main difficulties I foresee in this direction lie in the relative vagueness or inexplicitness of the data. It is hard to put the growth of governmental centralization and of intergovernmental relations in fifty states and the nation on cards in the form of figures and dates. In other words, the statistical units that could be developed for such a quantitative study would leave much to be desired. The time period may also be too short for producing significant and reliable results.

It would be possible, of course, to formulate a lengthy questionnaire on the major questions involved and to get the opinions of a sample of some thousands or tens of thousands of Americans thereon, and put their answers on cards for tabulating and computing. For example, questions could be asked about the relations between the growth of federal grants-in-aid, or state supervision over local governments, and the general increase of education, or the rise in the standard of living, or urbanization, and so on. Cause and effect relations and other types of relations could be well distributed throughout the questions in such a list. But the results of such a questionnaire could not rise much above the data. In other words the results would be almost entirely in the realm of opinion, and many of the opinions would be those of people not well informed and of people who had given but little thought to the questions. Many questions would, indeed, be very puzzling even to people who are in general well informed about public affairs.

Intergovernmental Relations and Political Power. According to one theory of politics all political activity is either motivated by or resolves itself into or can be explained only in terms of a struggle for political power. I had this theory in mind when we made our studies of intergovernmental relations but we did not take it as our central theory or hypothesis. I thought that to do so might color or bias our efforts and our conclusions. My aim was to get the members of the staff to concentrate on identifying, describing, and analyzing the activities that arise in connection with the interrelations of the different governments and the dealings with each other of national, state, and local officials. Then if the power motive or the power struggle came insistently into the record, through the documents, interviews, and questionnaires it would be available to us for purposes of explaining the activities. The emphasis was more upon how things were being done intergovernmentally than upon why or with what motives. Furthermore, to the extent that I was interested in motivations I thought it not unlikely that other motives than the getting and holding of political power might be at work—such as, for example, the desire to promote public services, to raise their standards, and to achieve results in the direction of the general welfare in the various functional fields. The selection we made of fields to study and the emphasis that this selection placed upon public administrators as distinct from the more policy-oriented elected officials like chief executives and legislators no doubt helped to emphasize in our minds these other motivations. This actually may have given our studies a bias away from political power.

Of course the power orientation of many recent political analysts is in part a result of their concentration upon international politics in an era of great wars and international tensions. No one can deny the existence of power struggles among nations, although in this field, also, power is not necessarily an end in itself but may be in large part viewed as a means to protect or to bring about other ends. However, power as a means is necessary to some extent in politics both within and between nations. Officials, governments, and peoples are not ruled by reason alone, or by the desire to do good to others. Is it not likely, then, that the relations of the national government to the states and of the state to the local governments will yield important examples of a power struggle? I will speak briefly of this problem a little later.

There is another possible concept of political power that needs first to be examined. In a deterministic sense political power might be looked upon as a natural, self-operating, and self-realizing force that pulls always in any population toward a sort of center of gravity, that is, toward the central capital of the nation, no matter what the political leaders and groups may or may not do. In the United States the recent drift has been generally toward Washington with halfway stopping points at the state capitals en route. This offers an interesting theoretical speculation but one that I think is not sufficiently supported by evidence over a long stretch of time and in enough countries to warrant its acceptance as a history-long and planet-wide proposition. Aside from the fact that it allows no room for the individual, group, or national choices that have been made and that are fairly well documented by historical evidence, it postulates a sort of "universal" centralizing trend that is belied by the many historical examples of nations and empires that have broken up with a resultant decentralization and disintegration if not complete atomization of political power. I think we cannot leave out of the study of politics the people and the choices they make; from time to time people reverse their decisions and change their political direction.

Let me ask next, is there evidence of a continuing struggle for power between the national government and the states? In a very general sense the answer is yes, but to reach even this loose a conclusion one has to generalize somewhat superficially about numerous historical events, each one of which is a case of mixed evidence and somewhat uncertain result, and at the same time it is necessary to ignore much countervailing evidence. The whole record is much confused. To picture the national government as a strongly united organization struggling continuously and successfully to take power from the states is almost to discover a mare's nest. To visualize the states as standing up unitedly to protect themselves from national encroachment is almost equally a figment of the imagination. Congress, the President, and the Supreme Court seldom see eye to eye on relations with the states. State governors and legislatures are even more frequently at outs on the issue of national-state relations. Congress has been most reluctant to legislate against the powers of the states in any field, as witness recent congressional acts to protect state control in the insurance field and in employment security. I have covered much of this ground in my chapter on national-state relations. From the state side some governors have been vocal if not vociferous in defense of states' rights against the national government, but the state legislatures and some governors have gone right along demanding more action by the national government and accepting federal aid on almost any terms.

What many people do not see is the unadvertised and seldom even mentioned competition for public favor and support that goes on continuously between the national elective officials and those of the states. While campaigning for office and when in office, United States senators and representatives seek ways to win support from their state constituents, and that usually means offering to try to get national benefits for agriculture, for the unemployed, for rivers and harbors improvements, for hospital construction, and many other things. In this they are frequently backed up by the President and by presidential candidates. At the same time the state governors and legislators, and candidates for these offices, are offering their own promises for action and services from the state. Often the competition becomes confusing to the citizen, as when a state official outlines things the national government should do for the state, and even proceeds to Washington to lobby for his proposals.

Partly as a result of these promises and demands, and partly because of its superior financial resources and nationwide appeal, the national government appears to be gaining relatively more nationwide popular support all the time, and to some extent at the expense of the states. And while it is true that many increases in the nation's expenditures and services for the people are in the form of grants-in-aid that clear through the states and help them too, the long-run effect is to put the national government, little by little, into the lead over the states in what were once considered state functions. Here is no power assault upon the states by the national government, but instead the actions of numerous individual candidates for Congress and members of Congress trying to meet the demands of their constituents in the only way they can, by promising to work for national action and national aid—for they obviously cannot promise action by the state governments.

There are other evidences, also, of continuing power struggles in national-state relations, but they seem to have little effect on the total distribution of powers between these two levels. One interesting example arises from the attempts of many governors to preserve or to increase their budgetary control powers and to extend them over the funds derived by the states from federal grants-in-aid. In this situation the national officials who supervise the expenditure of the grants seem to be relatively neutral. Some have expressed a willingness to accept proper state budgetary controls and Congress has not legislated against them. The real conflict seems to be a triangular one within each state, between the governor and his budget office (if any), the heads of the state departments who direct the expenditure of the federal funds, and the legislators and their committees. The heads of the spending departments naturally want more freedom than they might have if everything they did were subject to control and even veto by the state's central budget office; and the legislators are not in many states anxious to increase the control powers of the governor. It is easy enough in any state to list the expected federal grants in the budget document for the coming year or biennium, but for the governor to get control of the expenditure of these funds requires legislative approval.

Here again the issue of who shall have the power is not the only one. Governors can cite good evidence and authority to show that the state's financial affairs are better handled under proper central controls than without them. The desire to improve the state's administration cannot be ignored. It should be mentioned, too, that the desire of one official or group to gain increased power over any part of the governmental system is usually confronted by the desire for more freedom in the exercise of power on the part of those who are to be controlled. The resistance of state administrative agencies to central state administrative controls represents, no doubt, a desire to keep power in their own hands, but it too can be justified or at least rationalized to some extent by the argument that their services will be better if they have freedom of action. When a department represents not only a function of government but also a profession, as public health represents the medical profession and highways the engineering profession, the professional desire for freedom and power in the field, free from control by "political" considerations, arises to reinforce the departmental demand.

The issue of power in state-local relations needs but brief consideration. One of my early hypotheses was that the "vertical relations" between governments, namely, national-state and state-local relations, would reveal many of the same characteristics despite the fact that the constitutional power of the states over their local units is more direct and more complete than the national powers over the states. I still think that there is some merit in the hypothesis.

Vertical relations do show considerable differences, however. The state-local relationship is far more a matter of direct legislative control over the local units than national-state relations are of congressional control over the states. The state-local division of powers is less clear-cut than the national-state division; at least, there is more mixing of functions. State aid is less needed to buy local consent and cooperation than federal aid is to get state cooperation. The local units are legally creatures and agents of the states in all they do, whether it be in education, public health, highways, law enforcement, or any other function. Local governments are geographically nearer to and much more under the thumb of the state legislature and state administrators than the states are in comparison with the national authorities.

In these and other respects there are clear differences, but changing circumstances have brought a diminution of the differences and an increase in the similarities on every point mentioned. Indeed the image that many state and county people have of their states is that the counties should play the role of states in the Union, even to the point of having equal representation in the legislature without regard to population. In the national-state relationship, as I have pointed out, the legislative powers of the states are more and more being regulated by acts of Congress, the division of powers and functions is far less clear-cut than it used to seem to be, and the time may not be far distant when the Supreme Court will have to say that the states are agents of the nation, and that the powers reserved to them by the Constitution are not optional with them, but in effect impose duties upon them to perform services such as public education that are necessary to the national welfare—in short, that powers are reserved by the Constitution to the states in order that the appropriate functions shall be performed and not that they shall be neglected.

The "horizontal relations" between state and state, city and city, and so on, raise practically no issues of power relations. There is here no question of supremacy and subordination, although some state and local officials are suspicious even of such relations.

In Monograph 9 Dr. Weidner contributes significantly to the discussion of political power in intergovernmental relations in his treatment of "programmatic" and "expediency" values as revealed in the views of public officials. I will not attempt to restate here his findings, but it is evident that many elective officials in particular are very conscious of a threat to their positions and powers from certain intergovernmental developments.

The Prime "Force" in Governmental Integration. Is there any one factor in the American social and political situation of recent decades that can be singled out as being more influential than any other in bringing about the ever-closer integration of the political system through the centralization of some functions and the great increase of cooperative ntergovernmental relations in order to provide others? If there is one I would venture to suggest it is the strong desire that seems to permeate, motivate, and energize practically all the people to raise and improve the standard of living for themselves, their families, and others, in every department of life. I do not say that this is a cause that stands by itself. Most of the other factors listed above in this chapter and many more have been interacting and contributing factors. Some of these probably have stemmed from the same or similar urges within the individual, and all probably have contributed something toward making possible the governmental changes with which our studies have dealt. The conditioning factors in political and social freedom, the constitutional system, and popular control of government have also had their effects.

In the total process of the interaction of many forces, political values have undergone some changes. The federal system as a whole has not been scrapped, but it has undergone significant changes and the people have not been greatly disturbed. Indeed, it is a question as to how widely the people ever entertained and how deeply they felt the old fears of certain pre-Civil War leaders about the dangers of national dominance over the states. When the states failed to render the services that people seemed to think they wanted and needed, they did not hesitate to turn to the national government for help. Leaders in Congress and in the state legislatures, in governorships and in administrative posts, in fact men from a number of walks in life, found ways within the federal system to achieve those advances in governmental services that were deemed necessary in order to enable the governmental system to contribute to that rising standard of living with full employment that men so generally desired. Clearly the government could not remain backward when the economy as a whole was advancing toward higher levels of production. Even the old interpretations of the Constitution that placed severe restrictions on the power of the national government to act for the general welfare had to give way before the rising public demands for governmental regulations and services.

In general this attitude toward the existing governmental system on the part of an informed people who have control over their government through elections and the media of public opinion is a practical and instrumental one. In this view the system of government is not something to be merely revered or worshipped and kept unchanged through the ages, but an instrument or set of instruments to be used for the general welfare of the people. If it is not providing the people with the services that an educated public opinion demands, then it must either change its policies and methods so as to achieve these results without change of structure, or the structure of government must itself be so altered that it can and will. Political conservatism demands that structural change in the system be a matter for last resort. It is held to be far better if those in authority find ways and means within the existing structure to achieve the desired results. The latter is, in fact, what has been happening in the United States in recent years in connection with the increased centralization of functions, the rise and spread of the system of grants-in-aid, and the development of all the many kinds of intergovernmental relations that are at one and the same time increasing the integration of the governmental system and facilitating the performance of the many new services that the people have demanded. Thus the "living" or "working" constitution of the country is being changed continuously practically without any changes in the formal structure of government or in the words of the constitutional document.

The Question of Political Morality. Our studies were not directed toward the end of passing a moral judgment on the governmental changes and practices that we were studying, and the evidences that we have presented, as is usually the case, offer very little foundation for a simple moral judgment upon so complex and widespread a set of phenomena. Nevertheless, many able and vocal critics of the modern trend do present the problem as being largely a moral one, and their insistence upon it calls for a little analysis even though anything like a final or scientific answer to their charges will not be forthcoming. They are right at least in calling attention to the moral issues that are involved, because I think that most thoughtful men would agree that some of the most important issues of politics are moral ones.

Their basic contention, often put in Biblical language, is simply this: that in accepting centralization of government and the increased integration of national, state, and local governments that goes with the new and enlarged public services, and especially in asking for and accepting federal aid to finance state and local functions, the people have "sold their birthright for a mess of pottage" and have broken the ancient covenant of government under which the founding fathers established so admirable a system of governance. They see a nation in decline and headed toward the degradation of totalitarian absolutism. Personal responsibility, local self-government, and other ancient virtues are on the way to oblivion. The road to redemption lies through the admission of these sins, a reaffirmation of the states' rights covenant, and a restoration of the pristine condition of the Constitution. This language is no more figurative and is rather milder than some of popular critics of recent governmental trends have actually used.

The first question is whether the usual instrumentalist attitude toward the Constitution and the federal system is a wholesome one. Since I can find no absolute moral principle that applies to this issue, I find myself saying that the answer to this question will depend on what a person thinks the Constitution is in essence, what it was in the beginning, and what the system of government was. If a person thinks that the Constitution is and was a solemn and unchangeable compact, like a covenant with the Deity, that the parties to the compact are still the same as they were, and that the meaning of the compact is indubitable, he will properly condemn an instrumentalist attitude. If, on the other hand, he looks upon the Constitution as an instrument of human government, drawn up and adopted by fallible men, recognized as being imperfect even by its stanchest supporters, uncertain in meaning even in the beginning, but provided with clauses under which not only its text but its interpretation could be developed and even changed by those responsible to the people as new light came to them from new conditions and new experiences, he may reasonably take a different and a more approving attitude toward the changes that have taken place. As between the two broadly contrasting views, I think that the second view not only has more history, tradition, and authority from the "founding fathers" to support it, but also conforms better to the essentially moral principle that the welfare of the people is the highest law.

But as this reasoning is rather too general, one needs to face the more specific question whether the changes in the federal system and in the system of intergovernmental relations have themselves been generally good or bad. Critics of these changes, and they are a respectable minority group, tend to condemn all the centralizing and integrating changes that have taken place in the governmental system. They set as their standard of value the federal system as they understand it to have been in the beginning, and indeed until very recent times, and they set the preservation of this value or the return to it against all that may have been achieved through governmental integration and centralization in social, economic, and other fields of values, as a superior value. This is simply their way of expressing their political values and of setting them up as better than others. There are others who hold that not enough is being done even now by the national and state governments for the welfare of the people, and who would be willing to see even more centralization and integration of the governmental system in order to have these results achieved. I find myself unable to compare two such sets of values, and equally unable to compare the respective moral and other values of different governmental programs in education, health, welfare, law enforcement, highways, and so on.

One possible basis for passing moral judgments upon the governmental changes and policies of recent times lies in the differences in the relative emphasis placed upon material as distinct from cultural, moral, and spiritual objectives in governmental policy. National security expenditures aside, have the increases in public services and in governmental centralization and integration in recent decades been accompanied by more or less emphasis upon promoting material things like highways, airports, and power developments? How have services of a more cultural and moral value such as education, libraries, youth conservation measures, the promotion of morality, the protection of civil liberties and the dignity and equality of men fared under all these changes? And what about major programs like stabilizing agriculture and promoting full employment where both moral and material objectives are involved? Any such analysis would have to depend to a considerable extent upon popular and expert opinions, along with more objective data, but an intelligent and thorough analysis from this point of view might help to tell something of interest if not of great scientific value about the alleged "materialism of our age."

Even while suggesting the possibility of some good coming from such a study I must confess to a deep skepticism about the whole idea. I doubt that the results could tell us much about the consequences of recent trends in the federal system and in intergovernmental relations for several reasons. First, most of the religious and spiritual realm is, by the national policy of separating church from state, excluded from the field of governmental action and control. Second and similarly, most of the production, advertising, sale, and consumption of material goods is left to private corporate and individual enterprise. Even when this results in permitting the crudest sorts of advertising appeals to sensuousness, ostentation, and the love of luxury instead of to ideals of moral living, public policy is generally opposed to official interference except in extreme cases. This policy, like that concerning religion, has little or nothing to do with the problems of governmental centralization and intergovernmental relations. Third, the idea that public expenditure on physical or material things is somehow harmful to, or that it diminishes the resources available for, the promotion of educational, cultural, and moral purposes runs counter to certain rather widely held opinions. For one thing, as has been said before, it is generally believed that a high standard of living, including a substantial command of money income and material goods, is a necessary prerequisite for promoting human dignity and security and for general advances toward cultural, moral, and spiritual goals. Consequently, good housing, adequate sanitary and medical services, public works, school buildings, highways and streets, parks, and many other material things contribute greatly to more nonmaterial ends. Furthermore, it is believed that these things do contribute something, and in some cases a great deal, toward increasing the productivity of the people, so that more and more people can, by their own efforts, earn that minimum of income or more that is necessary for decent living. That those who are unable to support themselves should also be provided with at least a minimum of goods and income for decent living at the public expense there are few who will question. In short, material, cultural, moral, and spiritual goals and values cannot be clearly separated from each other. They all contribute something to the total life and living of each person.

In all this weighing of the moral and other values of the public services and of the means that make them possible, there is one thing of which I am personally fairly certain. The moral value of any public service is the same whether it is performed by the national government, by the states, by the local units, or by some combination thereof working together. The implication that there is a greater moral value in having a function performed by a smaller instead of by a larger governmental unit is hard to justify. When it is realized how markedly unequal various local units and even states are in their capacity to provide a service adequately or even to provide it at all, how poor a stewardship it is to assign functions that are necessary to the public welfare to units that are incapable of performing them properly, and how unequal the tax burden would be if they all had to perform services up to the same standard of effectiveness, the entry of the national and state governments upon the scene with both advice and material aid may well be accounted a highly moral act, an act of justice. For a higher level of government, representing a larger public, to show consideration for the governments of the smaller units below and to try to ease their burdens and improve their services may be accounted in many ways a truly moral act. There is, of course, another side to this: the combining of states that should be able to do more for themselves than they are doing to put pressure on Congress to give them aid that they do not all need, and the similar pressures put upon the states by various classes of local governments that are not making adequate efforts to help themselves. But to follow that line of thought would open another long chapter.

Of course, none of these considerations are really decisive of the questions concerning the moral aspects of recent changes in national, state, and local relations. The changes that have come about have been in part conditioned by factors that prevailed before and during the changes, but the timing, the extent, and the nature of the changes have been largely a matter of political choice by the various participants in the decisions. There will always be differences of opinion about the initial wisdom and the moral rightness of the changes that were made—and the same will be true about all future changes.

Within the amplitude of the United States system of government as a whole there is room for many more changes such as I have been discussing: transfers of functions up and down, grants-in-aid and the abolition of certain grants, interstate and interlocal arrangements of many kinds. I can safely predict that such will take place, and that they will not mark the end of the federal system. If the United States remains free from foreign domination and also continues to practice freedom internally, as I hope and expect it will, the people's attachment to the federal system is likely to hold firm. In addition to all the other advantages that have been claimed for it, and they are many, there is one that I should like to add. The American people generally have a deep dislike of monopoly, although there are many who try to practice it. The great majority of people, I believe, want no monopoly to control their lives, in business, in education, in religion, in communications, in the arts. In the field of government a federal system offers as near an approach to the ideal of competition as can reasonably and safely be constructed. The states are still to a considerable extent competitive with the national government, and the local governments with the states. They are able to cooperate with each other in many things while still competing in others. I see no reason why, under conditions of general democratic control, this competitive-cooperative situation should not continue to prevail.

This is certainly a comforting thought, but the scholar cannot afford to be satisfied with a hope. He is, as Emerson said, "man thinking." One seriously engaged in the study of public affairs finds almost unlimited numbers of questions and hypotheses to arouse his thoughts as he surveys the trends of his time. Some of the trends are truly disturbing to many. All call for analysis in relation to others, because no trend in public affairs seems to operate in isolation from others. In our limited studies we have made some explorations in the fields of intergovernmental relations within the United States federal system. We have presented some hypotheses and conclusions about that system, and have offered considerable evidence in support of them. Other scholars in other states have been doing the same, while governmental commissions and committees have also begun to pay attention to the problems of intergovernmental relations. The field is immense and the sod has only begun to be turned; the spade work is only partly done. There is almost no limit to the possibilities of developing significant hypotheses as to what lies beneath the surface, and of testing them by empirical evidence. There is much unfinished business. Let the good work go on!

Notes and Bibliographies

The reader will observe that there are no footnotes in the main body of this study. The reasons for this are several. The present volume is, in the first place, the final general review of a long study. It is not itself a detailed and factual consideration of a limited area or subject like the earlier monographs in the series, each of which provides its own footnote references. In the second place, the materials for this volume come not only from the earlier studies in the series, but also from a large amount of reading carried on over many years and covering many of the works cited in Graves' Bibliography, mentioned below. But that is not all. The ideas in the work, whatever they may be worth, have been turning over for so long in my mind that I would have great difficulty in referring them back to any particular printed source, letter, interview, or group discussion that could be documented. It has been my good fortune to have had numerous contacts and discussion with men in the fields of federal, state, and local government and intergovernmental relations, as I try to show in the Preface. From many of them I am sure that I have learned much, and yet I cannot trace back to any particular individual or printed source most of the statements I have made. In general those statements will have to stand without any visible means of support.

For most of the chapters I have, however, provided in the following pages some brief notes on sources. The few unpublished reports produced in the course of our studies to which reference is made in the text, along with the notes and other materials gathered in our studies, have been deposited in the library of the Public Administration Center of the University of Minnesota, where the more useful items will probably be retained.

GENERAL BIBLIOGRAPHY

The most comprehensive and authoritative bibliography on intergovernmental relations in the United States in recent years is Intergovernmental Relations in the United States: A Selected Bibliography, Prepared by the Legislative Reference Service, Library of Congress, at the Request of the Intergovernmental Relations Subcommittee of the Committee on Government Operations, House of Representatives; Committee Print, 84th Congress, 2nd Session, November 1956 (Washington, D.C.: United States Government Printing Office, 1956; viii + 119 pp.).

As this publication indicates (p. vii), Dr. W. Brooke Graves, chief of the Government Division, Legislative Reference Service, was chiefly responsible for the preparation of this bibliography. He had prepared an earlier bibliography for the Commission on Intergovernmental Relations and had also, at that time, for over twenty years been a principal contributor to the study of the subject.

This general bibliography has the advantage of being arranged by topics that conform closely to the chapter headings in the present volume. It will be referred to hereafter simply as Graves' Bibliography. In connection with it the reader will find the following more recent work by Dr. Graves especially valuable: Intergovernmental Relations in the United States: An Annotated Chronology of Significant Events, Developments, and Publications with Particular Reference to the Period of the Last Fifty Years (mimeographed; Chicago: The Council of State Governments, December 1958; ix + 110 pp.).

CHAPTER 1. DEFINITIONS AND OBJECTIVES

Federalism and federal government are related but not identical concepts. On federalism see Max Hildebert Boehm in Encyclopaedia of the Social Sciences, vol. 6 (1931), pp. 169-72. On federal government see William Anderson, Federalism and Intergovernmental Relations (Chicago: Public Administration Service, 1946); Arthur Macmahon in Encyclopaedia of the Social Sciences, vol. 6, pp. 172-78; Macmahon, ed., Federalism Mature and Emergent (Garden City, N.Y.: Doubleday, 1955), pp. 3-27; K. C. Wheare, Federal Government, 3rd ed. (New York: Oxford University Press, 1953), pp. 1-96, 222-67. For a rigorous analysis of Wheare's "federal principle" see Rufus Davis, "The 'Federal Principle' Reconsidered," in the Australian Journal of Politics and History, 1:59-85, 223-44 (1956).

For a "world federalist" view see The New Federalist (New York: Harper and Brothers, 1950), by Publius II (Justice Owen J. Roberts, John F. Schmidt, and Clarence K. Streit).

The nature and principles of federal government in the United States are dealt with in almost innumerable works, of which Graves' Bibliography lists a selection of the best. See especially his pp. 1-15. A few works that may prove to be especially helpful are William Anderson, The Nation and the States, Rivals or Partners? (Minneapolis: University of Minnesota Press, 1955); Commission on Intergovernmental

Relations, A Report to the President (Washington, D.C., 1955), especially pp. 1-149; Carl Brent Swisher, American Constitutional Development, 2nd ed. (Boston: Houghton, Mifflin, 1954), especially pp. 769-1085. But there are many more.

CHAPTER 2. THE CHANGING SCENE AND THE AMERICAN FEDERAL SYSTEM

Anyone who studies developments in the federal system and intergovernmental relations needs to know in some detail the history of one or more of the states as well as that of the United States as a whole. Although it comes down only into the mid-1920s, William Watts Folwell's A History of Minnesota (St. Paul: Minnesota Historical Society, 1921-30), in four volumes, still provides the best background for that state's history. The great economic, social, and political changes in Minnesota in the past third of a century are not adequately recorded in any single work. For these years and their developments I had to use many scattered sources.

The developments in the United States as a whole since, let us say, World War I, are, on the other hand, set forth in such a wealth of books that it is impossible to select one or even a few books that will meet all requirements. (This great difference between the amount of published historical material for the United States as a whole and that for any single state is itself an interesting evidence of scholarly and public concentration of attention upon national as distinguished from state affairs, as well as of the potentially greater rewards to successful authors who write on national affairs and history.)

As background reading for the more recent period of American history, the volume entitled America in Midpassage by Charles A. Beard and Mary R. Beard (New York: Macmillan, 1939), which is Volume III of their The Rise of American Civilization, is excellent factually and in style of writing. For more recent developments one ought to read many works of biography, history, economics, politics, and on general social, cultural, and ideological developments. Among the more compendious general works on recent American history, down to the middle 1950s, I can recommend John D. Hicks, The American Nation 1865 to the Present, 3rd ed. (Boston: Houghton, Mifflin, 1955); and Arthur S. Link, American Epoch: A History of the United States since the 1890s (New York: Knopf, 1958).

CHAPTER 3. THE CONSTITUTIONAL LAW OF NATIONAL-STATE RELATIONS

This note lists the principal Supreme Court decisions discussed in Chapter 3 in substantially the order in which they are mentioned in the text.

The decisions of 1819 and 1833 written by Chief Justice John Marshall in which he discusses the source and the nature of the Constitution are McCulloch v. Maryland, 4 Wheat. 316 (1819) and Barron v. Baltimore, 7 Pet. 243 (1833). The Taney decision involving the fugitive from justice is Kentucky v. Dennison, 24 How. 66 (1861). The famous phrase about the "indestructible union, composed of indestructible states" comes from Texas v. White, 7 Wall. 700 (1869).

The dictum of 1872 about the dualistic nature of the Union appears in Tarble's Case, 13 Wall. 397 (1872). Like Tarble's Case, the suit of Kansas v. Colorado, 206 U.S. 46 (1907), over water rights had no great significance in itself, but it led to some judicial philosophizing that was revealing of current judicial ideas about the Constitution.

It was in 1923 that the Supreme Court decided the two cases involving the constitutionality of the Sheppard-Towner maternal and child health act of 1921. The citations are Massachusetts v. Mellon, and Frothingham v. Mellon, 262 U.S. 480 (1923). These decisions did not declare the act to be constitutional but simply held that the appropriation to carry out the act was beyond the power of the plaintiffs to challenge.

Thirteen years later the Agricultural Adjustment Act of 1933 was held invalid for the reasons given in the text in the decision of United States v. Butler, 297 U.S. 1 (1936). The next year, 1937, brought a series of decisions that in effect reversed the position taken by the court majority in the AAA case (without overruling that decision) by upholding the national-state arrangements for unemployment compensation, Steward Machine Co. v. Davis, 301 U.S. 548 (1937), and Carmichael v. Southern Coal and Coke Co., 301 U.S. 495 (1937); and also upholding the scheme enacted by Congress for old age insurance (social security) directly under national control, Helvering v. Davis, 301 U.S. 619 (1937).

Four years later the Court upheld under the commerce power the act of Congress to establish fair labor standards (as to wages, hours, child labor, and other points) as applied to a lumber manufacturing concern that produced lumber for commerce, in United States v. Darby, 312 U.S. 100 (1941). This was but one of a number of decisions in that period that in effect opened to Congress the power to regulate labor conditions, industrial relations, and other aspects of industry, agriculture, and other fields of production. These fields had been in large measure beyond the power of Congress to regulate under earlier decisions that distinguished rather sharply between production and commerce, and held that the Constitution delegated to Congress no power to regulate production. See United States v. E. C. Knight Co., 156 U.S. 1 (1895) and the famous child labor case, Hammer v. Dagenhart, 247 U.S. 251 (1918). The Darby decision and several others of about the same time effectively overruled this limitation on Congress, and put down the Tenth Amendment, which reserves powers to the states, as a mere truism that does not limit the powers granted to Congress as liberally construed.

The 1936 decision concerning the "external powers" of the United States is United States v. Curtiss-Wright Export Corporation, 299 U.S. 304 (1936).

Two important decisions that uphold executive agreements as legally binding on all persons and as supreme over state laws are United States v. Belmont, 301 U.S. 324 (1937), and United States v. Pink, 315 U.S. 203 (1942).

The old restrictions on national powers referred to under "internal powers" are those previously mentioned as arising out of the "sugar trust" decision, United States v. E. C. Knight Co., and the child labor decision in Hammer v. Dagenhart, cited above. The overruling decisions are perhaps best exemplified by United States v. Darby, cited above, and, in the matter of congressional control over agriculture, Wickard v. Filburn, 317 U.S. 111 (1942).

The decisions upholding the unemployment compensation plan and other parts of the Social Security Act of 1935 have already been cited above, the Steward Machine Co. case and Helvering v. Davis, for example.

The decisions of 1954 outlawing segregation in the public schools as being in violation of the equal protection clause of the Fourteenth Amendment and, for the District of Columbia, in violation of the due process clause of the Fifth Amendment, are as follows: Brown *et al.* v. Board of Education of Topeka; Briggs *et al.* v. Elliott *et al.*; Davis *et al.* v. County School Board of Prince Edward County, Va., *et al.*; and Gebhart *et al.* v. Belton *et al.*, 347 U.S. 483 (1954).

Graves' *Bibliography*, pp. 1-5 and 10-15, lists a number of excellent books and articles pertinent to the subject matter of this chapter. I would suggest that special attention be paid to Carl B. Swisher, *American Constitutional Development*, rev. ed. (Boston: Houghton, Mifflin, 1954), and Edward S. Corwin, ed., *The Constitution of the United States, Annotated* (Washington, D.C.: Government Printing Office, 1953). My own work, *The Nation and the States, Rivals or Partners?*, pp. 53-136, is also directly pertinent.

CHAPTER 4. THE NATIONAL GOVERNMENT IN MINNESOTA

The note on sources for Chapter 2 mentions Folwell's *A History of Minnesota*, in four volumes, as the best available history of the state, and cites two works on recent American history, namely John D. Hicks' *The American Nation 1865 to the Present*, and Arthur S. Link's *American Epoch*, which goes from 1890 to 1958. These works are useful for general background for the present chapter also, but are not exactly replete with specific information on the questions discussed herein. A great deal of information can be derived from the other monographs in the present series. A number of other publications that I found to be especially useful are cited directly in the text of the chapter.

The quotation from Ignatius Donnelly is given by Martin Ridge in *Minnesota History*, March 1959, from the *Congressional Globe*, 38th Congress, 1st Session, p. 2037.

CHAPTER 5. NATIONAL-STATE RELATIONS

The sources of information for this chapter include Monographs 1 through 9; the bibliographies contained in the first seven of them; and the works listed in Graves' *Bibliography*, pp. 10-15 and 87-119, *passim*.

CHAPTER 6. INTERSTATE RELATIONS

Graves' *Bibliography*, pp. 50-66, provides an extensive and excellent list of works on interstate relations in general, many of which I have used. On interstate compacts specifically, see Frederick L. Zimmerman and Mitchell Wendell, *The Interstate Compact since 1925* (Chicago: The Council of State Governments, 1951). The research assistant who supplied me with excellent notes on Minnesota's relations with other states was Robert W. Powers, while the graduate student who wrote independently a long paper for me on the same subject was Arthur L. Peterson. There has been no comprehensive official study of Minnesota's interstate relations, but there has been a notable series of such studies for New York by committees of that state's legislature.

CHAPTER 7. STATE-LOCAL RELATIONS

My original enumeration of governments was entitled *The Units of Government in the United States* (Chicago: Public Administration Service, 1934). The last edition was published in 1949 by the same organization. Publication of the Bureau of the Census enumerations of local units began in 1942, and the most recent one came out in 1957 as a part of the comprehensive 1957 Census of Governments, under the title *Governments in the United States*.

The legal position of local governments in the states under the United States Constitution has not been made the subject of any major study that is known to me. The reader will find various references to the subject in Graves' *Bibliography*, pp. 27-31. Their legal position under the several state constitutions varies from state to state. The law reviews published in the various states in many instances contain good articles on the local legal situation. The basic sources are, of course, the printed state constitutions, the state statutes, and the state supreme court decisions. For Minnesota my two articles on "Special Legislation" and "Municipal Home Rule in Minnesota," published in the Minnesota Law Review for 1923 (7:133-51, 187-207, 306-31), are still useful for interpreting the old constitutional provisions on the subject. However, no writings on the old provisions have much value any longer, since a drastic change was made in the local government provisions of the constitution by an amendment to Article XI of the constitution adopted in November 1958.

Practically all aspects of state-local relationships are covered by the publications listed in Graves' Bibliography, pp. 67-86.

On the courts in state-local relations in Minnesota, see Monograph 1, Intergovernmental Relations and the Courts, by Forrest Talbott. On the financial relations of Minnesota state and local governments, see my Monograph 8, and also the publications listed in Graves' Bibliography, pp. 74-86.

CHAPTER 8. NATIONAL-LOCAL AND INTERLOCAL RELATIONS, AND METROPOLITAN PROBLEMS

My article on "The Federal Government and the Cities" appeared in the National Municipal Review, 13:288-93 (May 1924).

On the issue of channeling all federal aid for airports through the states, see A Staff Report on Federal Aid to Airports submitted to the Commission on Intergovernmental Relations (Washington, D.C., June 1955), especially pp. 91-92, and the Commission's Report, pp. 167-75.

For references on national-local relations generally, see Graves' Bibliography, pp. 27-31.

On the subject of interlocal relations Graves' Bibliography includes no separate list, but many of the entries under "Metropolitan Regionalism," pp. 37-49, are pertinent. For interlocal relations in Minnesota, see the following monographs in our series: Number 2 (highways), pp. 97-110; Number 3 (education), pp. 40-69; Number 4 (public health), pp. 181-90; and Number 5 (social welfare), under the index headings "county system" and "township system." Monograph 7 by Paul N. Ylvisaker, on the single county of Blue Earth, is replete with data and comments on interlocal relations.

To these references should be added these: Inter-Municipal Cooperation in Minnesota, a mimeographed digest of some twenty-five laws, put out in February 1953, by the Municipal Reference Bureau and the League of Minnesota Municipalities at the University of Minnesota, Minneapolis; J. J. Carrell, "Inter-Jurisdictional Agreements as an Integrating Device in Metropolitan Philadelphia" (Unpublished Ph.D. thesis, University of Pennsylvania, 1953); and Interlocal Cooperation in New York State, a study prepared under the direction of Dr. Guthrie S. Birkhead of Syracuse University with the assistance of the state department of audit and control, for the Governor's Committee on Home Rule (Albany, N.Y.: State Department of Audit and Control, 1958).

Many important studies on metropolitan government and on intergovernmental relations in metropolitan areas up to 1956 are listed in Graves' Bibliography, pp. 37-49. Since this list was compiled a number of major studies of metropolitan government have been initiated, and additional publications of considerable significance have been issued. Among recent studies special mention should be made of those sponsored by the Haynes Foundation of Los Angeles and carried out by the late Professor Edwin A. Cottrell, Professor Winston W. Crouch, and others in the Los Angeles area, where some rather unusual developments in intergovernmental relations have been taking place.

A Bureau of the Census report of 1957 on Local Government in Standard Metropolitan Areas provides the basic data on the units of government in the then 174 such areas in the nation.

CHAPTER 9. THE FEDERAL EQUILIBRIUM AND THE STATES

The literature on the so-called federal balance or equilibrium theory is neither extensive nor systematic. Alexander Hamilton and James Madison expressed some ideas on the subject in The Federalist, as did others during the time when the Constitution was in the process of formulation and adoption. The opponents of the Constitution, the so-called Anti-Federalists, had their own ideas on what the balance between the state and national governments should be, as did Thomas Jefferson and other leaders after the Constitution went into effect. John C. Calhoun later expounded a theory of "concurrent majorities" which, if it had ever been put fully into practice, would have given every substantial minority, whether of states, or of a section, or of some other grouping of people, a veto on the national majority, with the possible result of complete stalemate or paralysis of governmental action at the national level. Indeed, the usual equilibrium idea is a conservative if not a reactionary one, and opposed to effective governmental action. Some of those who have held such ideas in the United States have looked upon the Constitution as a rigid compact among the states and one that was intended to preserve states' rights. The theory was that the national government was to be only an agent of the states, and that the latter were to retain a sort of veto power upon the national government, or the power to "interpose" their "sovereignty" when national actions displeased them or seemed to violate the compact. Thus the balance was to be preserved between the nation and the states through the device and right of state obstruction to national action. This theory of the Constitution was emphatically rejected by the Supreme Court under Chief Justice Marshall, and has never had the Court's approval. All appeals for a "return to states' rights" appear to be based upon some such theory of a balance or equilibrium of national and state powers, in apparent disregard of the national supremacy clause in Article VI of the Constitution. The theory is a static and mechanical one as distinct from an organic or developmental one—a theory of separate "spheres" of powers, and of a fixed, built-in balance of forces. It is not a theory that recognizes the ebb and flow and the constant transformations of ideological, social, economic, and political forces in an ever-changing human society.

Aside from the usual states' rights appeals, a few recent writings that discuss some aspects or variations of the so-called federal balance or equilibrium are worthy of mention. Professor K. C. Wheare's work, Federal Government, in its several editions, does not mention either "balance" or "equilibrium" in its index, and yet much of his discussion of federal theory turns on questions of how to ensure that the national and regional governments, within their respective "spheres," can be kept "coordinate and independent." The word "coordinate" I take to mean equal and in some sort of balance. Professor Arthur W. Macmahon in his work Federalism Mature and Emergent indexes several brief passages under "balance of power" and also includes an article on "Prerequisites of Balance" by John Fischer, pp. 58-67.

As to a fiscal or financial balance between the national and state governments, which is a somewhat different concept, see my Monograph 8, Intergovernmental Fiscal Relations, especially Chapters 5 through 8.

Index

This being the final volume in the series on Intergovernmental Relations in the United States as Observed in the State of Minnesota, the index includes one see or see also reference to each of the nine earlier monographs under its appropriate subject-matter heading.

INDEX

STAFF MEMBERS OF THE INTERGOVERNMENTAL RELATIONS PROJECT

William Anderson, Director

Edward W. Weidner, Assistant Director

Research Assistants

Charles R. Adrian	Robert W. Powers
Gary P. Brazier	Ruth Raup
Waite D. Durfee, Jr.	Francis E. Rourke
Rosendo A. Gomez	Forrest Talbott
Robert Macdonald	Lloyd W. Woodruff
Robert L. Morlan	Laurence Wyatt

Secretaries

Muriel Wyatt (Mrs. Laurence Wyatt)

June Ethel Peterson

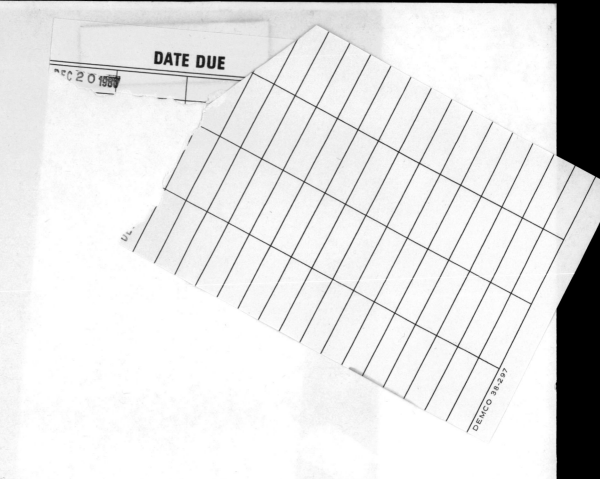